answered by experts

How can I interpret my dreams? Erich Fromm explains why your waking personality is the indispensable clue to understanding your dreaming mind.

Are my dreams normal or unusual? Dr. Ann Faraday discusses common dream themes—and why recurring dreams may be danger signals.

How can I remember my dreams more often? Dr. Patricia Garfield shows how keeping a dream diary can increase your self-awareness—and even change your life!

Plus much, much more, from the top thirteen experts in the field. Each chapter is a vital key to unlocking your dreams . . . and using your unconscious potential.

Thirteen Authorities Tell You
WHAT YOUR DREAMS MEAN

Also includes . . .

What dreams of flying and falling *really* mean . . . How men's and women's dreams differ—in ways that may surprise you . . . Why the most sexually explicit dreams are often not about sex at all . . . And more!

THIRTEEN AUTHORITIES TELL YOU WHAT YOUR DREAMS MEAN

POLLY STRONG

BERKLEY BOOKS, NEW YORK

This Berkley Book contains the complete text of the original edition.
It has been completely reset in a typeface
designed for easy reading
and was printed from new film.

THIRTEEN AUTHORITIES TELL YOU
WHAT YOUR DREAMS MEAN

A Berkley Book / published by arrangement with
William Mulvey Inc.

PRINTING HISTORY
Bull's-eye edition published 1988
Berkley edition/April 1990

ISBN: 0-425-12049-X

A BERKLEY BOOK® TM 757,375
Berkley Books are published by The Berkley Publishing Group,
200 Madison Avenue, New York, New York 10016.
The name "BERKLEY" and the "B" logo
are trademarks belonging to Berkley Publishing Corporation.
PRINTED IN THE UNITED STATES OF AMERICA
10 9 8 7 6 5 4 3 2 1

ACKNOWLEDGMENTS

The editors wish to thank the authors and publishers of the following books for permission to excerpt copyrighted material:

Sleep, Our Unknown Life, copyright © 1972 by Richard Deming, is reprinted by permission of the author and the author's agents, Scott Meredith Literary Agency, Inc., 845 Third Avenue, New York, NY 10022.

Sleep, copyright © 1966 by Gay Gaer Luce and Julius Segel, is reprinted by permission of the authors.

Creative Dreaming, copyright © 1974 by Patricia L. Garfield, is reprinted by permission of Simon & Schuster, Inc.

The Forgotten Language, copyright © 1951, renewed © 1979 by Erich Fromm, is reprinted by permission of Henry Holt and Company, Inc.

The Dream Game by Ann Faraday, copyright © 1974 by AFAR Publishers, is reprinted by permission of Harper & Row, Publishers, Inc.

The Complete Book of Dream Interpretation, copyright © 1983 by Robert Wayne Pelton, is reprinted by permission of Arco Publishing, Inc.

Dream Work, copyright © 1983 by Jeremy Taylor, is reprinted by permission of Paulist Press.

Dream Power, copyright © 1972 by Ann Faraday, is reprinted by permission of The Putnam Publishing Group and The Julian Bach Literary Agency, Inc.

Is the Cat Dreaming Your Dream? copyright © 1980 by Margaret O. Hyde, is reprinted by permission of the author.

ESP in Life and Lab, copyright © 1967 by Louisa E. Rhine, is reprinted by permission of Macmillan Publishing Company.

Living Your Dreams, copyright © 1979 by Gayle M. V. Delaney, is reprinted by permission of Harper & Row, Publishers, Inc.

Lucid Dreaming, copyright © 1985 by Stephen LaBerge, Ph.D., is reprinted by permission of Jeremy P. Tarcher, Inc.

Dreams: God's Forgotten Language, copyright © 1968 by John Sanford, is reprinted by permission of Harper & Row, Publishers, Inc.

Every effort has been made to locate the copyright holder to the Canadian edition of *Dream Power* by Ann Faraday.

Now I do not know whether I was then a man dreaming I was a butterfly, or whether I am now a butterfly dreaming I am a man.

CHWANG-TSE

Contents

Foreword

OF ALL THE mysteries of life, none are as fascinating as those that arise within us. The first love, the first pain, the first dream. They and all their ilk bring a special poignancy to our secret memory bank of treasured thoughts. And what sparks these thoughts? What brings the past to our minds again? And again? Why do they spring into vivid being, unbeckoned, unwanted, feared and forgotten? What is this mental dance? A grim rigadoon or a gay fandango?

"To sleep, perchance to dream," quoth the Bard of Avon in his immortal but scientifically faulty lines. For we dream during every sleep regardless of our wishes, and wake to wonder what those phantom thoughts signify. Death or wealth or love or sin. Falling, flying, fear and helplessness. Any and all emotions come beating their way through the cerebral tangles, forcing us to consider ourselves in ways that we cannot bear to accept, and yet undeniably children of our own conception. Thus we face ourselves in every dream, reject or accept ourselves in every dream, know ourselves better or fail to learn.

"I see, said the blind man" is an old anecdote but much like our therapeutic gain from the study of our mental functions. Dreaming is our window, a path. It is a blind man's vision of himself in ways his eyes could never reveal.

"Dream on, little dreamer, dream on" croons the music. Is dreaming the music of the spheres, God himself, or replays from the past, jumbled and uncontrolled without the passion or the pattern of reality? Is dreaming the music or is it the chemicals of the brain? The electricity of the brain? The recharging of the cellular batteries? Or the highway to the unconscious?

Here we have some of the most brilliant thinkers of the age and their most entrancing concepts of dreaming. Can they answer or can they challenge the eternal questions of dreaming and of the meaning of life itself? What inspiring ideas will you find in these pages? And which concepts will lead you to weigh and interpret the shifting images of your own dreams? Can you even recall your dreams— much less understand them? Well, read on, dream researcher, and choose from the scientific approach of Deming or the extrasensory conceits of Rhine. Learn how to recall and notate your sleeping fantasies through the skilled advice of Garfield, and plan your life by your own inner revelations as counseled by Luce and Segel. Erich Fromm will lead you into multihued worlds of Freudian brilliance as he guides you to dream understanding that surpasses the master himself.

Through the inspired writings of Faraday and Pelton, relive your dream life with eyes open to the truth that you yourself were blind to see when you were awake. Rules of dreams by Delaney give you a solid foundation upon which to build your practical utilization of night memories. Fantasies and phantoms come readily to mind as you peruse LaBerge and Hyde and their erudite insights into the world of sleep thoughts. Further exotic and exciting sexual insights are revealed by Taylor as he dissects our deepest emotions and their hormonal bases. But some of the deepest religious theories are presented by Sanford, and his vibes will touch your cerebral connections in a sweat-bringing flash that will lead you to reread again and again as the allure of the unknown is dispelled by truth.

Oh yes, and again will you savor these pages. For what is more delectable than a look into yourself? Dreams and their meanings lead us to a new vision, a better vision, a revelation. As the poet said:

A thousand dreams that men have never known
Spread mighty wings and fold me when alone.
I lie upon my couch in haunted sleep,
Yet, waking, still a throb of phantom drums
Comes echoing across the mystic deep.

So I advise you to follow my guidance. As a psychiatrist of twenty-eight years in practice I can personally speak of the value in self-insight and self-evaluation. Dreams are valuable tools in developing these skills. Use them and find yourself in ways you never dreamed of until you dreamed and then awoke to evaluate your dreams.

Dreams may be religious visions, or just the electro-chemical rumblings of a recharging biologic system. Dreams may be the way to comprehend the unconscious, or the playback of a day's thoughts and feelings. Dreams may be sexual, or childishly innocent and helpless.

So read these thoughts and search yourself to sense the mysteries and revelations in your dreaming. Be your own psychiatrist. Follow these leaders in the field of dream research, dream history, dream meaning and dream prediction. Enjoy and revel as you enlarge your perspective of your own self and your own mind.

Especially, enjoy.

William H. Hampton, M.D.

1.   The Dream Doctors

Richard Deming

IT CAN BE said that the era of modern sleep research began at the University of Chicago in 1953, when Dr. Nathaniel Kleitman and his graduate assistant, Eugene Aserinsky, discovered REM sleep.

While observing sleeping subjects, Aserinsky noticed that the eyes behind the eyelids moved rapidly during regular periods throughout the night, a phenomenon common to all of their sleep subjects.

Convinced that this rapid eye movement (REM) was an indication that the subject was in the midst of a dream, Kleitman and Aserinsky introduced an EEG machine into the laboratory to monitor brain activity during sleep. To their amazement, they discovered four distinct stages of sleep that are repeated in cycles throughout the period of sleep.

Stage one is not usually even recognized as sleep by those entering it. You are still aware of your surroundings, and if someone suddenly asked you whether you were awake, you would probably answer yes and believe it.

However, the EEG graph would show that you are definitely asleep. Your respiration, pulse, blood pressure, and temperature will all have lowered. Your brain waves will have suddenly changed from the smooth regularity of alpha rhythm to a small, crabbed pattern that is constantly changing.

In this stage you may have conscious thoughts, such as pleasurably dwelling on the memory of some happy event of the day, but you will have no *directed* thoughts. That is, you will not be able to bring your mind to bear on any problems that have to be worked out. Your mind will be too relaxed to entertain any thoughts other than those that form more or less of their own volition. Your mental images will not quite be the thoughts of a wakeful mind and not quite dreams, but somewhere in between, a mixture of the two.

You can be quite easily awakened from stage-one sleep, merely by having someone say your name in a conversational tone. You probably would deny having been asleep at all.

Stage-one sleep usually lasts about ten minutes. As you sink into stage two, you become functionally blind. Although it is not usual, there are people who sleep with their eyes open. When an object is held before such a person's eyes just before he enters stage two and he is then awakened, he will not remember seeing the object.

Researchers believe that the eyes themselves continue to receive images in this state, but that the nerve system simply ceases to transmit proper messages to the brain. Experiments have been conducted where subjects had their eyelids taped open. Then, as they entered stage-two sleep, someone held an object, such as a key which was illuminated by a flashlight, in front of their eyes. Awakened immediately thereafter, they had no recollection of seeing the object, but frequently reported dreams indicating that they had been aware of the light. Sometimes they dreamed of gazing at a lighted neon sign, a fireworks display, or some similar brightly illuminated scene.

In stage two your eyes, whether open or closed, will slowly move from side to side, as if you were watching a tennis game in slow motion. The EEG graph pens controlled by the electrodes fixed to your eyelids will move up and down in rhythm with these eye movements.

Oddly, the EEG will also show that your brain has become more active than it was in stage one, even though, technically, you are more deeply asleep. Both the amplitude and frequency of your brain waves will increase, and there will be periodic fusillades of nerve impulses fired from the brain's outer layer.

You may do some vague dreaming in the second stage of sleep, but your mental images will be disjointed and would be difficult to describe if you were suddenly awakened and asked to tell what you were dreaming. They will tend to be fleeting, unconnected scenes, lacking even the vaguest sort of continuity.

You can easily be awakened from this stage of sleep, and again you might not believe that you had fallen asleep, although that is not as likely to happen as when you are awakened from stage-one sleep. If undisturbed, however, you will remain in stage two for anywhere from twenty minutes to half an hour, after which you will sink into stage three.

As you pass into stage three, the EEG graph will show that your muscles are now totally relaxed, and your pulse, temperature, and blood pressure have fallen even lower. The voltage of your brain waves will increase, but the frequency will drop. The pen depicting your brain waves will trace long, slow rises and falls spaced at regular intervals. The frequency may drop as low as three impulses per second.

You may or may not lie still in this stage. If you are the type of sleeper who periodically changes position during the night, you probably will do most of your rolling over in this stage. You may also mutter in your sleep.

Until relatively recently, researchers thought that no dreaming took place in either stage-three or stage-four sleep. But recent studies have led to the conclusion that dreams occur at both levels. Apparently the misconception resulted from subjects' difficulty in recalling dreams occurring in these deep stages of sleep, even when they were awakened in the middle of a dream. It seems that just climbing up through the layers of sleep to an awakened state takes enough time to allow memory to fade. On the other hand, people awaken instantly from stage-two sleep, and therefore are able to retain vivid memories of dreams.

Numerous experiments have been conducted in which subjects were awakened from dreams and asked to describe them immediately. The next time their dreams were interrupted, three to five minutes were allowed to elapse before they were asked to tell what they had been dreaming. It was found that in most cases people could describe their dreams in considerable detail immediately upon awakening, but that memory often completely failed them after a period of time. The dreams you remember seem to be those from which you momentarily awaken and consciously think about before you go back to sleep, thus fixing them in your memory.

Because of this quick fading of dream memories, with the subsequent difficulty of recalling anything at all dreamed in the deeper stages of sleep, scientists long thought that all dreaming occurred in certain lighter stages. In recent experiments, however, memories of deep-sleep dreams have sometimes been revived by hypnosis, so it is now believed that dreaming takes place in all levels of sleep.

Ordinary movements or noises, such as someone walking through the bedroom, will usually not awaken you from stage-three sleep, although a phone ringing in the next room might do so.

After ten to twenty minutes in stage three, you will pass into stage four, also called *delta sleep,* because it is the deepest abyss of unconsciousness. In stage four the pulse, blood pressure, and body temperature drop to the lowest levels they will reach all night. Again the amplitude of brain waves increases, but frequency slows down even more, often to only one impulse per second. The graph will show a jagged line that slowly climbs to towering peaks, then tumbles into deep chasms. The pattern is called *delta wave.*

Once you attain the deep sleep of stage four you do not remain that way for the rest of the night. Most people stay there for only about twenty minutes, then begin drifting back upward.

You come back up through stage three to stage two. But this time stage two is different. On descending into stage two you could easily be awakened if someone merely spoke your name in an ordinary tone. But when rising back into it from a lower stage, you approach nowhere near such wakefulness. It would now take a loud noise to awaken you.

The pens of the EEG machine do not behave in the same way as they did during the descending stage-two sleep either. They show brain waves that are very close to those emitted when you are awake. Your pulse, blood pressure, and respiration increase, sometimes to a level that usually occurs during wakefulness only when you are engaged in violent exercise or are experiencing intense emotion. Your fingers and toes twitch.

But your body is totally slack. Your chin droops and your mouth may gape open.

When you passed into stage two on the way down, your eyes moved back and forth slowly. Now they begin to move again, but this time at greatly increased speed, as though the slow-motion tennis game you watched on the way down had greatly speeded up.

Because of this phenomenon, this stage is called rapid-eye-movement sleep, commonly abbreviated to REM sleep.

It is during REM sleep that all dreaming was once thought to occur. It is still the stage in which most *remembered* dreaming occurs. Laboratory subjects awakened from REM sleep can describe dreams in some detail about 85 percent of the time if questioned as soon as awakened. If you recall a dream when you awaken in the morning, you can be sure it took place during REM sleep. You can also be sure that it took place shortly before you awakened, or, if it occurred in the middle of the night, that you woke up long enough to think about it and fix it in your memory. During every period of sleep you will have many dreams that you will have no recollection of whatever when you wake up.

Initially it was thought that the rapid movement of the eyes during this stage of sleep indicated that the dreamer was following dream images with his eyes. But regardless of the dream, the eyes always move back and forth. Subjects awakened from REM sleep have described dreams in which, logically, their eyes should have moved in an up-and-down direction, or not moved at all, if they were watching what occurred in the dream. But their eyes had been moving back and forth all the time they were dreaming.

The differences between REM sleep and stage-two sleep when descending are distinct enough for many researchers to feel they should be classed as separate stages. Most of the other researchers carefully avoid referring to REM sleep as rising stage-two sleep, even if they recognize it as the same stage, apparently because they are uneasy about the differences. Yet both are at the same level, and descent from REM sleep takes you back into the same stage three that you were in before.

REM sleep usually lasts about twenty minutes; then you descend back into stage three, and finally again into stage four. This cycle keeps repeating itself all night.

The time it takes from the onset of stage-one sleep, down into delta sleep, and back up to REM sleep is generally about seventy minutes. Since the REM period lasts about twenty minutes, a complete cycle takes about an hour and a half. Although these figures represent a rough average, it is generally conceded that five cycles occur during a normal seven-and-a-half to eight-hour sleep.

There is no doubt that Kleitman and Aserinsky set off the stampede of dream research that is now going on all over the world, but it should be kept in mind that what they did was bring advanced technology to bear on the subject that has been under scrutiny for thousands of years.

Since man first began to wonder about the nature of things, he has been puzzled over the mystery of dreaming. Probably dream lore goes back into prehistoric times, but the earliest written evidence still in existence of man's interest in the subject is roughly four thousand years old. It is an Egyptian book of papyrus, now in the British Museum, that explains the meaning of dreams.

Over the centuries, theories to explain both the causes and meanings of dreams have been countless. Probably the earliest widespread belief was that dreams were revelations from the gods. At least that is the explanation offered in the Egyptian dream book, and the same explanation appears in the literature of ancient Babylonia, Assyria, Chaldea, and Greece, and in the Old Testament.

Ancient clay tablets tell the story of the goddess Ishtar assuring King Ashurbanipal of Assyria in a dream that he would win if he went to war against the Elamites. He did, and indeed won, proving, at least to the storyteller's satisfaction, that the dream actually had been a divine vision.

In Homer, Achilles says: "For dreams too are sent by Zeus." In Numbers 12:6 of the Old Testament, the Lord says: "If there be a prophet among you, I the Lord will make myself known unto him in a vision, and will speak unto him in a dream."

Usually dreams came to the ancients with their divine messages in code form, which had to be deciphered by seers. Thus, in Chapter 41 of Genesis, Pharaoh dreamed that seven fat cattle came out of the river and grazed in a meadow. Then seven lean, ill-favored cattle came out of the river and ate the fat ones. In a second dream he saw seven fat ears of corn grow on one stalk. Then seven thin ears grew on the same stalk and devoured the fat ears.

When Pharaoh's seers were unable to interpret these dreams, he called on Joseph, who was repining in a dungeon at the time. Joseph told him the dreams were a message from God, and meant that Egypt would enjoy seven years of plenty, followed by seven years of famine. He advised Pharaoh to appoint a general overseer of all the land to collect and store part of the harvest of the good years against the needs of the lean years to follow.

Pharaoh's choice of an overseer, of course, was Joseph.

The belief in dreams as omens of what is to come persists to some extent even to this day, although belief that the forecasts come directly from God has considerably declined. Books explaining the meaning of dreams in fortune-telling terms are still routinely published, but now the explanation of what causes prophetic dreams is usually either pseudoscientific and vaguely mystical, with more stress on magic than on religion, or entirely missing.

Another early belief was that during sleep the soul leaves the body to roam abroad, and that dreams are the experiences the soul is having during these periods of free flight. This belief still persists in some modern primitive societies. In the Fiji Islands it is unquestioningly accepted by the natives that it is taboo to awaken a sleeping person. The islanders are convinced that unless the sleeper is allowed to awaken naturally, the wandering soul may not have time to reenter the body, and will forevermore be trapped outside in a kind of limbo.

Dreams have always had immense importance in primitive societies. In some they are regarded as so important that they literally rule all behavior.

The Senoi tribe of Indonesia exemplifies such a society. Among its people the first order of the day is for each family member to describe his dreams to the rest of the family. After a group analysis of their meanings, they jointly decide what each dreamer has to do to dispel any evil forces indicated by his dreams, or how he can take advantage of any good forces.

If a child dreams that he hit a friend, he will be told he must go and apologize to the friend and do something nice for him, such as give him a gift. If, on the other hand, he dreams his friend hit him, he must find out what he did to offend the friend and get the matter straightened out. If the father dreams that a neighbor got a new canoe, it may mean that the father should build one and give it to the neighbor.

Because the actions indicated by their dreams are so often friendly ones involving doing something nice for other individuals or for the whole community, the Senoi are a happy people. Mental illness is almost unknown, and violent crime is rare among them.

In 1900 Sigmund Freud published a book entitled *The Interpretation of Dreams*. In it he advanced the theory that dreams represented repressed drives and emotional conflicts in the dreamer's subconscious that surfaced during sleep as certain recognizable symbols. Because of inhibitions and social taboos instilled in everyone while growing up, these symbols, according to Freud, were disguised so that the dreamer was unaware of their true meaning. The reason for it was that the rules of morality drilled into a person as a member of a conforming society made it impossible for him to admit to himself, even while asleep, that he could be possessed by emotions and desires unacceptable to society's rigid moral code.

Thus a Victorian maiden, to whom even the thought of sexual relations was taboo, might disguise her subconscious desires by dreaming of being bayoneted by a soldier. The upright church deacon, who feared the thought of adultery, might dream with equanimity of passing through an ellipsoidal opening in a wall into a beautiful garden.

Freud said that every suppressed desire had its own secret symbol. A snake, he said, was a sex symbol. Dreaming of falling meant emotional insecurity. The symbols thoroughly disguised the hidden emotions producing them but could be recognized by a trained psychoanalyst and be quite useful in treating neuroses (a disorder of the mind) and psychoses (a deep, serious, and prolonged mental disturbance that might lead to criminal acts).

Freud's theory is still accepted by many psychologists and psychiatrists, but few of them now accept it in its entirety. Even the earliest and most ardent of Freud's disciples soon became aware that much dreaming was too prosaic to have any deep emotional significance. What hidden drives are disguised, for instance, in a dream of walking along a sunny street where nothing at all happens?

Obviously much dreaming also had its basis in the events of the day. When a man dreamed of being chased by a vampire immediately after viewing a stage production of *Dracula,* it seemed a little ridiculous to probe for symbolism in the dream.

The basic premise of Freud's theory seemed to have validity, though. During the mid-1950s two unique experiments in sleep laboratories seemed to substantiate his teaching that in at least some of our dreams we create symbols to hide from ourselves secret thoughts and desires that our moral precepts reject.

The first experiment established that no such symbols are employed by very young children whose minds have not yet been pressured into accepting the rigid taboos of society. A number of children of five and under took afternoon naps in the sleep lab. Each time they went into an active dream stage, they were awakened and asked to describe their dreams.

Most of the dreams were undisguised wish fulfillment. Dreams of eating candy and ice cream abounded. One little girl described a birthday party where all the child guests could have all the candy, ice cream, and cake they wanted, and "nobody got sick."

Some rather startling revelations of childish hostility also emerged. One little boy reported matter-of-factly that he had dreamed his baby sister died and his parents bought a puppy to replace her. Questioning revealed he was jealous of the new baby and that the dream was simple, unvarnished wish fulfillment.

The investigators pointed out in their report that this

type of open wish fulfillment expressing hostility toward someone whom society decreed you were supposed to love never occurs in the dreams of people old enough to have learned society's taboos. A teen-aged boy who secretly hated a younger sister would wrap the dream desire for her death in some kind of obscure symbolism. He might, for instance, dream of having a car that required many frustrating repairs and of trading it for a motorcycle that ran perfectly. Even asleep, his moral conditioning would refuse to permit the open thought that he wished his sister were dead.

Very small children have no such inhibitions, however, and therefore are able to fantasize their desires without disguise. The seventeenth-century French author Jean de La Fontaine once referred to early childhood as the "conscienceless age."

In the second experiment a number of patients in psychoanalysis whose dreams seemed to be rich in symbols were the subjects. Although many of the symbols were obvious to the analyst, no explanations of them were given to the subjects. Instead the researchers placed the patients under hypnosis and asked them to interpret their own dreams. In a surprising number of cases the dreamers were able to reveal the hidden wishes that had been disguised by the symbols.

Another thing tending to support Freud's theory is the excellent record of psychoanalysis in relieving patients of recurrent nightmares by exposing their underlying causes and getting the patients to face and accept them. However, you can get a lot of argument from psychiatrists who reject Freud's theories about the effectiveness of psychoanalysis. One of them made the flat statement to me that he knew of no case of a psychosis ever being cured by psychoanalysis, although he did concede that the method might be of minor value in treating neuroses. In fact, it is generally agreed even by those who reject Freud that the technique is effective in at least this one area.

The principle of psychoanalysis is that, when the hidden causes of neuroses or psychoses are brought to the surface by the analyst, so that they may be understood and faced by the patient, the mental stress caused by them will disappear. This probing has to be done gently, of course, and with considerable moral support by the analyst, or the revelations may do more harm than good. For instance, abruptly facing the knowledge, without any previous preparation, that he wished his younger sister dead might drive a neurotic to suicide.

Freudian psychologists originally postulated a theory to explain the seemingly meaningless dreams that are interspersed with those that seem to have symbolism. They speculated that possibly the harmless dreams were red herrings deliberately planted by the subconscious so that the dreamer wouldn't suspect the symbolism of those dreams that disguised upsetting secret cravings.

The more common-sense view of most modern psychoanalysts is that dreaming may occur for a number of reasons, and that only in some dreams are inhibitions obscured by symbols. In this view Freud's theory of dream symbols is valid, even though not every dream contains symbols.

Dr. Nathaniel Kleitman evolved a theory from his experiments in the early 1950s that dreams might act as sentinels to guard the sleeper from awakening. At that time scientists believed that all dreaming took place in the upper stages of sleep only, and Dr. Kleitman suggested that perhaps, as the sleeper went from stage three up into REM sleep, dreams interposed in order to halt the rise all the way toward wakefulness.

The theory was that dreams safeguarded sleep in two distinct ways. One was to incorporate outside stimuli, thus preventing the stimuli from arousing the sleeper. For instance, a sleeper might fight off being awakened by a banging on the door by dreaming he is doing a carpentry job. In the dream the banging noise is explained by his hammer pounding nails, and since this explanation is entirely satisfactory to his unconscious mind, there is no necessity for him to get up and answer the door. His mind has absorbed the disturbance, so that it is no longer an outside stimulus, but an integral part of his dream.

William Dement and Edward Wolpert tested this theory in an experiment at the University of Chicago sleep laboratory. Sleeping subjects were sprayed with cold water and had lights flashed into their faces and buzzers sounded in their ears. The researchers deliberately designed these stimuli so that they were not quite attention-getting enough to wake the subjects. The spray was a fine mist, the lights were only briefly flashed, and the buzzers were low toned.

Nearly 50 percent of the time the subjects incorporated these outside stimuli into their dreams, but whether or not that safeguarded their sleep cannot be stated with certainty. It seemed to have that effect, however.

The second way in which Kleitman—and also later experimenters—theorized that dreams safeguarded sleep was based on the observation that the mind always seems to make a subconscious effort to continue a dream as long as possible. Kleitman thought that this desire to extend the enjoyment of a dream had the effect of postponing awakening.

Of course, this theory presumes that all dreams are pleasant, and its proponents insist that, with the exception of nightmares, that is the case. Recent theory ascribes a possible, entirely different sort of protective function to nightmares, but we will discuss that later.

Even a dream that, after awakening, may be recalled as unpleasant could very well have been an enjoyable experience while it was occurring, the theorists say. They go back to the Freudian theory of dreams to explain why. The symbolism in a dream, though perhaps unpleasant in retrospect, is enjoyable at the time because it represents gratification of thwarted and suppressed desires that the dreamer's inhibitions allow him to gratify *only* in dreams. Thus the previously mentioned Victorian maiden who, upon awak-

ening, recalls her dream of being bayoneted by a soldier as
a nightmare, actually was enjoying the dream experience
while she slept.

According to Kleitman's theory, then, in the periodic
rise from delta sleep upward through the various higher
stages toward wakefulness, dreaming interposes to arrest
the rise just before the sleeper fully awakens. The mind's
resistance to ending the dream keeps the sleeper from
awakening long enough for the sleep cycle to start over
and allow him to slip back downward again into the lower
stages of sleep.

This theory remains unproved, but so far it has never
been disproved, either. It has both adherents and detractors
among the recognized authorities on sleep.

The biggest single argument against it is that it is based
on the premise that dreaming takes place only during REM
periods, whereas it has now been established that dreams
occur during all levels of sleep. Those who believe in the
theory counterargue that dreams during REM periods may
well be of a different type from those during stage three
and delta sleep. They say that dreams in the deeper stages
of sleep may be unpleasant, and that such dreams bring
about the periodic rise toward wakefulness. Then, just
before complete awakening, dreaming alters its nature so
that the sleeper's unconscious desire to rid himself of his
unpleasant dream by awakening changes to a struggle to
remain asleep and enjoy his new and more pleasant dream.
Perhaps this alternation between unpleasant (and largely
unremembered) dreams during deep sleep, and enjoyable
dreams during REM periods, is what causes the rhythmical
rise and fall through the various stages of sleep.

Whether the theory that dreams safeguard sleep is correct or not, even its proponents generally agree that this is
probably not their sole function.

Nightmares obviously don't fit into this theory, because
they often awaken people. A plausible, but again unproved
explanation does account for them, though, and it still

leaves the sleep-safeguard theory intact. But first some background is necessary.

In 1971 the husband-wife team of Doctors Joyce and Anthony Kales made a study of the sleeping patterns of coronary and ulcer patients at the University of California at Los Angeles sleep laboratory. One of their findings was that nighttime angina and peptic-ulcer attacks occur during REM sleep. They then concluded that disturbing dreams might bring on such attacks by increasing the blood pressure, pulse, and respiration to unusually high levels.

The pair experimented with a number of hypnotic drugs and an antihistamine drug, all of which were known to suppress dreaming. The drugs seemed to reduce the danger of attacks while sleeping, but when they were stopped, the patients did the same thing as in earlier experiments with REM sleep deprivation: they made up for it by enormously increasing the proportion of REM sleep they got for a few nights.

Other researchers have suggested that nightmares, instead of bringing on such things as heart attacks, may be safety devices to prevent them. They theorize that perhaps exciting dreams, but not necessarily unpleasant ones, dangerously raise the blood pressure and increase the respiration and pulse, and that a nightmare will then intervene to awaken the sleeper so he can calm down.

The Freudian psychoanalysts theorize that a nightmare is a dream in which the symbols that conceal from us our suppressed thoughts and desires begin to become too easily translatable, and we are suddenly in danger of having to face the truth about what is buried in our subconscious. When that happens, the Freudians say, we run from such unwanted self-revelation by waking up.

In the 1950s Dr. Calvin S. Hall, Jr., at that time a professor at Western Reserve University in Cleveland, tabulated ten thousand dreams reported by "normal" people to various researchers. That is, while many of the dreams sent him had been reported by patients in psychoanalysis, he carefully screened out all who were described as suffering from psychoses or severe neuroses.

Dr. Hall found that young people dream more than older people, that women dream more than men, and that the higher the intelligence quotient, the more one dreams. About a third of the subjects reported dreaming in color; the rest dreamed in black and white. Color dreams were more common to women than men, and to young people than old people.

More recent studies indicate that about half the population dreams at least occasionally in color. However, Dr. Hall's somewhat lower tabulation did not enumerate the number of subjects who dreamed in color, but only the number of dreams in color, and in many cases several dreams were reported by the same subject.

Dr. Hall found that the commonest emotion experienced in dreams was hostility. In 63 percent of the dreams reported, subjects committed unfriendly or violent acts against other dream characters. In 2 percent of the dreams, hostility was so great that the dreamers committed murder.

Though this study encompassed a large sample, people were reporting dreams, in most instances, that they recalled having at home in their own beds. Little of the dreaming took place in sleep laboratories, where a subject may be awakened while dreaming and asked to describe his dream while it is fresh in his mind. Because dreams are so quickly forgotten, obviously the ten thousand tabulated by Dr. Hall had to be the more vivid ones dreamed by the subjects, and may well have represented only a fraction of the total number dreamed.

Dr. Hall later became director of the Institute of Dream Research at Miami, where he and his associates have made many additional studies. One was in conjunction with Dr. Robert L. Van de Castle, now director of the Sleep and Dream Laboratory at the University of Virginia Medical School, but at the time Dr. Hall's assistant.

While the study involved a much smaller sample of

subjects—five hundred males and five hundred females, all college students—the data collected are considered much more reliable. That is because Hall and Van de Castle developed a more sophisticated technique than used in the first study for ensuring that the dream reports were reasonably accurate and for scoring them on the basis of content.

Accuracy is extremely important in recording dreams scientifically. Everyone has a tendency to impose some kind of rationality on a dream when recounting it, even though the dream itself may have been totally irrational. Most dreams you hear recited at the breakfast table have been thoroughly, but probably unconsciously, edited before being reported.

In reality, dream "story lines" are often so distorted as to make no sense at all, and our more logical waking minds attempt to rectify the distortion in order to make them understandable. One moment in a dream you will be talking to a friend; then, inexplicably, the friend will suddenly become someone quite different. Or perhaps you will be peacefully drifting in a canoe on a calm lake, when with startling abruptness you find yourself clinging to a flimsy raft in dangerous river rapids.

When you awaken with a dream memory fresh in your mind, your usual first impulse is to try to make some sense out of it. Often the only way to do that is to cull out some of the absurdities and straighten out the story line. Most of the time you do it quite unconsciously, through an understandable desire to twist the dream action into an order that is comprehensible to your waking mind.

Similarly it is not uncommon for a person to "finish" a dream after awakening by continuing it in fantasy to some satisfactory ending. Then, in recalling the dream, he forgets that an ending was added afterward, and the whole sequence is remembered as dreaming.

In either event, the result of this unconscious editing is to fix in your mind a dream sequence that often bears little resemblance to what you actually dreamed. You are unaware of what you are doing and are not deliberately attempting to deceive either yourself or anyone else. The person who reports dreams that move logically from incident to incident, as though created by a professional short-story writer, is seldom deliberately lying. More likely he has merely done some subconscious editing and revising.

Because of this tendency, subjects whose dreams are to be studied have to receive explicit instruction in dream reporting if the researchers are to get reliable reports from them. They must learn to recall a dream exactly as it occurred, no matter how illogical events were, and to fix it in the memory in its original form, without making any attempt to mold it into a rational story.

Another factor making the Hall–Van de Castle data more scientifically valid was that the subjects reported their dreams directly to the researchers or to their associates. It was not merely a tabulation of dreams from many sources.

One of the most interesting findings of this study was that the things women dream about are so different from what men dream about that the researchers could easily tell whether a man or woman was the subject simply by reading a report of the dream.

Women were more often indoors than outdoors in their dreams and were usually in familiar surroundings, such as their homes, dormitory rooms, or classrooms. There were more characters in women's dreams than in men's, and slightly more of them were women than men. The central characters, however, were about equally divided between male and female. That is, the extra women were more or less bystanders.

The central characters in the women's dreams were usually known to the dreamers, who tended to recall their appearance and dress vividly. The women did not have quite as many aggressive dreams as men, and when they did, they tended to be nonviolent. Instead of striking people in their dreams, they settled for bawling them out. The victims of their dream aggressions were more often other women than men. In general their dream relations with men were friendly, and they were usually platonic. Women sometimes have dream sex-encounters, but not nearly as frequently as men do.

Again it was found that women dreamed in color more often than men.

In the men's dreams there tended to be more outdoor settings and a lot more physical action. A large number of dreams featured hostility, although not as many proportionately as in Hall's first study. In about half of the hostile dreams the dreamer physically attacked another man, usually a stranger.

There were twice as many male characters as female in the men's dreams, and the male characters were quite often identified by their occupations. That is, instead of the dream characters just being other men, they were barbers or cabdrivers or store clerks, and quite often they were serving the dreamer in their occupational capacity. Even when that wasn't the case, though, male dreamers still tended to be aware of other men's occupations. At a dreamed-of cocktail party, for instance, the dreamer would know that one guest was a doctor, another a lawyer, and so on. This tendency was interpreted by the researchers as indicating that men may be more status-conscious than women.

Just as women exhibited more friendliness to male characters than to other women in their dreams, the male subjects were more friendly to women than to other men. Except for dreams involving overt sex acts, male dreamers usually knew the women they dreamed about. For some reason as yet unknown, most female partners in men's dream sex-encounters are utter strangers. Women, however, almost invariably, know their dream sex partners very well.

Other studies have shown that physical and emotional changes have marked effects on dreaming. This effect is particularly striking during pregnancy.

During early pregnancy, it has been found, a woman

frequently dreams about her husband, but as the months pass, her husband appears less and less in dreams and her mother becomes a more frequent dream character. She also has many dreams about babies. During the last three months, seven times as many baby references appear in pregnant women's dreams, on the average, as during the first three months.

Fear that the baby will not be "normal" is a frequent factor in such dreams. There are dreams of stillbirths and child deformities. It is not uncommon for a pregnant woman to dream she has given birth to a litter of cats or dogs. As Dr. Van de Castle once phrased it: "It appears that most mothers harbor deep fears that they are secretly carrying Rosemary's Baby and that some monstrous fate is to befall them."

There are a number of modern theories about dreaming that are at variance with those already reported. Dr. Berger of the University of California at Santa Cruz has suggested that one of the purposes of rapid-eye-movement sleep may be to exercise the eyes so that they will continue to coordinate properly. He does not suggest that it is the sole reason for dreaming, however.

One of the most recent dream theories has been advanced by experimental psychologist Christopher Evans, principal research fellow in the Autonomics Division of the National Physical Laboratory in England. Evans thinks that dreams may serve the function of "reprogramming" the mind, much in the same way that computers periodically have to be reprogrammed.

In order to understand this theory, it is necessary to understand at least the basic principle of the electronic computer.

When computers first came into common use, they were often called "mechanical brains." The term is apt, because in many ways an electronic computer functions in the same way as a human brain. Both have memories, both can "learn," and both are capable of applying their learning to the solution of problems presented to them.

The average computer in business or industry is "programmed" to perform numerous functions. That is, it contains a number of individual sets of instructions, each enabling it to perform a different type of task. For instance, the computer of a manufacturing company might be programmed to make out the company payroll, bill customers, record payments, keep inventories, and operate various sets of automatic machinery.

New material is periodically inserted into a computer's memory bank for either of two reasons. Changes may have to be made in an existing program. For example, a new union contract providing for a general pay raise will require revision of the program that controls the payroll. Or a whole new program may be added in order to give the computer an additional task.

When such reprogramming is done, it is necessary to take the computer "off-line" while the new data are being added. In other words, it is simply unplugged. Actually the entire device is not ordinarily shut down, only the part that is being reprogrammed. However, the analogy to the brain can be better understood if you visualize the plug for the whole machine being pulled, so that, in a sense, it is sleeping.

Programming could be said to be the computer's learning process, inasmuch as that is the way it absorbs new data into its memory.

According to Evans's theory, the purpose of sleep is to take the brain off-line while it is being reprogrammed. And he believes reprogramming is done by dreams.

Evans thinks that dreams represent a sort of passing-in-review of all the new data absorbed by the brain during the day. Much of it is trivial information, which the mind rejects as too unimportant to store in its memory bank. We therefore have no recollection of these useless dreams unless we happen to be awakened by some outside stimulus while having one. Then some bit of trivia sticks in the memory. But otherwise only "useful" information is accepted and stored.

There are some logical arguments in favor of this analogy between reprogramming and dreams. It would be appalling if we had total recall, so that *everything* we experienced were permanently stored in our memory. With our mind cluttered with every word we had ever heard or overheard, with the memory of every face we had ever seen, even fleetingly, with the record of every minor act, no matter how trivial—such as brushing our teeth, for instance—embedded in our memory forever, it would be hard to remain sane, let alone to think coherently.

We *do* remember a good deal of trivia, of course, but perhaps that is because we were awakened at the wrong time.

Christopher Evans points out that computers whose programs are not regularly modified perform less and less efficiently. Human beings deprived of sleep suffer equal loss of performance ability. He suggests that the cause in both instances may be that the memory-reviewing process has been interfered with.

The most provocative experiments with dreams today are being conducted at the William G. Menninger Dream Laboratory at Maimonides Hospital in Brooklyn. Since 1962, when the Dream Laboratory was established, a major study of extrasensory perception of subjects in dream states has been going on.

Extrasensory perception, or ESP, as it is commonly abbreviated, concerns three separate types of mental phenomena that may not even exist. The first is *thought transference,* more commonly called mind reading. The second is *precognition,* which means being aware of what is going to happen at some time in the future. The third is *clairvoyance,* which is the ability to "see" an event that is taking place somewhere else.

Folklore about all three abounds, but unfortunately most of it has never been proved.

Following every great tragedy, such as the sinking of the *Titanic* or the burning of the *Hindenburg,* there is at least one story about someone who canceled a reservation because he had a vision of impending disaster. Over the years at least a thousand newspaper stories must have appeared about clairvoyant mothers who in dreams "saw" their sons die in shipwrecks or plane crashes or battle at the precise moment the tragedy occurred.

Because the evidence accompanying such tales is often less than convincing, ESP has never been in the best repute in the scientific community. However, it has always found enough acceptance for at least a few researchers to consider it worthy of investigation. One group of these researchers is at Duke University at Durham, North Carolina.

For many years psychologists at Duke have been studying ESP under waking conditions in the laboratory. Experiments on thought transference usually involve things such as one person staring at cards from a special pack while another person guesses which cards he is looking at. Experiments with precognition customarily involve having the subject guess what number is going to come up before each throw of a pair of dice. To test clairvoyance, subjects are asked to guess what cards had been sealed in envelopes when even the researchers don't know.

By using statistical tables of probability, the Duke researchers are able to rate the subjects' actual performances in all three types of experiment against what they should have been according to the laws of chance alone. For years they have been insisting that the percentage of "hits" as opposed to "misses" in these experiments is statistically significant and strongly indicates that ESP is not merely a folklore superstition. However, the statistics haven't been startling enough to convince the majority of psychologists, some of whom summarily dismiss them as hogwash.

An interested but unconvinced member of the scientific community was Dr. Montague Ullman, a New York psychoanalyst. In 1950 he had a woman in psychoanalysis who reported to him two dreams that occurred to her the same night.

In the first dream she was at home with her ex-husband, and there was a bottle on the table containing part alcohol and part cream. She described it as some "white, foamy stuff." Her ex-husband wanted to drink it, but she said, "No, you can drink it later." She looked at the label and it read: *Appealing Nausea.*

In the second dream she had a small leopard, which she wrapped up and put in a large bowl. Her mother told her to take the animal out or he would die.

Ordinarily Dr. Ullman would have attempted to decipher the symbolic significance of such dreams. But in this case he was struck by the similarity of the dreams to an educational film he had been watching the same night the patient dreamed them. The film had been shown as part of a lecture on animal neuroses at the New York Academy of Medicine.

In the film two groups of cats were shown in a laboratory. One group was normal; the other had been taught to become addicted to alcohol. Two bowls, one containing only milk, the other containing a mixture of half milk and half alcohol, were offered to the cats. The normal cats chose the former, the alcoholic cats the latter.

The similarity between what Dr. Ullman had been viewing and what his patient had been dreaming at the same time was startling. The possible explanation that occurred to the psychoanalyst was even more startling.

It is routine in psychoanalysis for a close mental rapport to develop between the analyst and his patient, so that they sometimes almost seem to be able to read each other's thoughts. It is akin to the sort of thing that often develops between marriage partners who have a particularly close relationship. One spouse frequently startles the other by expressing the identical thought the first was just getting ready to say, suggesting some kind of ESP.

Such rapport had long been established between Dr. Ullman and this particular patient, who had now been in analysis for a full year. Dr. Ullman wondered if perhaps the incident were evidence that being in a dream state made people more receptive to ESP. The question so intrigued him that he has been involved in trying to answer it ever since.

In 1953 Dr. Ullman and Mrs. Laura Dale of the American Society for Psychical Research agreed on an experiment where they attempted to transfer thoughts to each other every night. They kept diaries of their dreams and met once a week to compare notes. Unfortunately, although they sometimes had dreams on the same night that were oddly similar, the experiment on the whole was not a success.

Meantime Kleitman and Aserinsky had established the first sleep laboratory and had developed the technique of being able to tell by EEG graphs when subjects in the lab were dreaming. Now that it was possible to awaken subjects during dream periods and have them report dreams while they were fresh in their minds, dream research suddenly began to arouse the interest of foundations that made research grants.

However, ESP was still widely regarded as a form of charlatanry by many scientists, and although a lot of money poured into sleep research during the next few years, little of it was earmarked for ESP dream research. As a result, not until 1960 were any experiments in this area conducted in the sleep lab, and the first ones did not prove much of anything.

Then, in 1962, the Ittleson Family Foundation and the Society for Comparative Philosophy provided funds to the Menninger Foundation to set up the present Dream Laboratory at Maimonides Hospital, where Dr. Ullman is head of the Department of Psychiatry. As Dr. Ullman was involved in too many other things to devote full time to the laboratory, Dr. Stanley Krippner was appointed director of the lab. The techniques employed there are largely the brain-children of Dr. Ullman, however—particularly in the area of thought transference, which, until relatively recently, has dominated the research.

The basic technique used in these experiments has been to have the subject sleep wired up to an EEG machine in a special soundproofed room. In addition to the technicians in the control room, there is an "agent" in a third room, which is also soundproofed. In the first experiments the agent's room was about thirty feet from the subject's. Later it was moved to the opposite end of the hospital corridor, about a hundred feet away, and it is now in an entirely different building.

The agent has an intercom over which he can communicate with the control room. He can also hear what the subject says but cannot talk to him.

The agent is supplied with a dozen envelopes, each containing a color reproduction of a famous painting. When the control room informs the agent over the intercom that the subject has gone to sleep, the agent selects one of the paintings and begins to concentrate on it. He concentrates on it all night, drawing pictures of it, writing down comments about it, and all the time consciously trying to communicate his thoughts to the sleeping subject.

In the first experiments the reproductions were the only things used, but in later tests all sorts of props were added. For instance, the packet containing Max Beckmann's "Descent from the Cross" also contained a crucifix, another picture of Christ, and a red-ink pen for the agent to color Christ's wounds. It was felt that handling and thinking about these additional items allied to the main prop would heighten the agent's involvement with the picture.

When the EEG graphs indicate the subject is beginning to dream, the dream is allowed to run about ten minutes, then he is buzzed awake. Over the intercom one of the technicians in the control room asks him to describe his dream. The description is taped, so that it may be typed up the next morning.

This procedure is repeated all night every time there is a dream period.

The next morning the subject is asked to make any

comments he cares to about his dreams, and these comments are also taped. The researchers then show all twelve painting reproductions to the subject and ask him to pick the one that most reminds him of his dreams. After he chooses it, they ask him to rank all the rest in descending order down to the one he thinks is least like his dreams.

If the subject ranks the painting used among the top six, it is scored as a "hit." Among the bottom six, it is a "miss."

If the factor of ESP were entirely missing, by the law of averages there should be an equal number of hits and misses. But right from the beginning a rather startling statistical pattern emerged. Among the first twelve subjects, ten made hits and only two missed, a statistical average of 83.3 percent hits. Over the ten-year period that experiments have been conducted, the percentage rate of hits has ranged up and down from this figure, but it has consistently remained far too high for coincidence alone to account for it.

To make sure that some factor other than pure thought transference was not somehow influencing results, the experimenters have added all sorts of controls and double checks over the years. For instance, when the painting reproductions are shown to the subject in the morning, it is not the agent who shows them, but another experimenter who does not know which painting the agent used. Another control was to have independent judges come in to evaluate the records.

In addition to the statistical evidence that ESP can affect dreams, there have been a number of hits so remarkable that they can only be described as bull's-eyes. There was, for instance, the cabdriver subject whose agent picked George Bellows's painting "Dempsey and Firpo" to concentrate on. The painting depicts the moment Jack Dempsey knocked Luis Firpo out of the ring in their 1923 heavyweight bout. To one side of the boxers is the referee, and in the lower foreground can be seen the heads of some ringside fans.

Here are excerpts from the tapes of two of the dreams the cabdriver had that night:

From the tape of dream one: "Something about posts . . . There's some kind of feeling of moving . . . Ah, something about Madison Square Garden and a boxing fight . . ."

From the tape of dream two: "I'm unclear if there are two or three people in the dream, because there seems to be the presence of other people. . . . These people seem to have met in a social situation, but they were there for some other purpose anyway, and they came together. . . . Now it seems to be clearer. . . . There's one older figure of an old man and two younger ones. . . ."

An equally direct hit with another subject occurred with Van Gogh's "Boats on a Beach." The subject reported dreaming of "being on a boardwalk or beach . . . the seacoast. The place is slightly elevated. It makes me think of Van Gogh."

There have been too many other bull's-eyes to write them off as mere coincidences. A young boy described repeated dreams about a large gray church with a little old lady in front of it, an exact description of Van Gogh's "Church of Auvers," which happened to be the painting chosen by his agent that night. Another subject dreamed of people building sand castles. The painting was of people doing just that. Dozens of other bull's-eyes could be listed, but these few should be sufficient to illustrate the point.

The Dream Lab experiments with precognition and clairvoyance are too recent for any such dramatic developments to have yet been reported, but already the evidence indicates that the other two areas of ESP merit further research in depth.

2.   The Meanings of Dreams

Gay Gaer Luce and Julius Segel

IN 1911, A policeman's wife dreamed that someone had broken into her house. She called out for a policeman but he had gone up several steps into a church, behind which stood a hill capped by a thick wood. The bearded policeman was accompanied by two tramps wearing aprons. Using this example in *The Interpretation of Dreams,* Sigmund Freud offered a paradigm to suggest its hidden meaning. The church was the female genital, the steps a symbol of copulation, the hill a Venus's mound, surmounted by the wood, or pubic hair. Freud's brilliant compendium of case histories and theory revolutionized the treatment of psychological ills, for he saw in dreams the clues to the individual's unconscious. There lay the expressions of primary instincts, the symbols of unrecognized fears and wishes. However innocuous or bewildering, the drama had a meaning. The real meaning of the dream, if it could be unveiled at all, required the kind of guided personal search into its associations that is the basis for psychoanalysis. Almost no modern person is untouched by this theory, yet as Freud's writings were successively abbreviated and restated in popular form, they were mistakenly used as a simple lexicon by which any dream, out of context, could be understood. Most people yearn for some shorter route than psychoanalysis, some quick and simple formula that will disentangle their dreams.

The search for meaning might be called one of man's intellectual and emotional instincts. Throughout history he has pursued the meaning of dreams, usually relying upon some outside person, priest or oracle. Are dreams departures of the soul as the primitive Fiji Islander imagined, or are they portents of reality? The Chester Beatty Papyrus in the British Museum, a document almost 4,000 years old, contains the instructions whereby an ancient Egyptian could know that his dream of a gliding moon signified grace with his god, but a dream of distant crowds meant impending death. There was faith in dreams as portents and their transparence to the interpreter. A pharaoh's haunting dream might place on the interpreter the burden of state decisions. Joseph's interpretation of the fat kine and the lean led to an economic strategy in Egypt that was comparable in magnitude with a modern five-year plan. The Greeks used oracles to prophesy from dreams, and also dream rites to heal the sick. The Iroquois understood dreams as commands to be followed. During the twelfth to sixteenth centuries, Western Europeans lived in fear of an international conspiracy of witches and demons that could invade human thralls in their dreams. The Inquisition judges used their handbook, the *Malleus Maleficarum (Hammer for Witches)* to interpret dreams in a period when they could mean burning at the stake. Dreams and their meanings have been influential in the world's religions. Bertrand Russell once asked whether there was a difference between the statement "An angel visited me last night," and "I dreamed I saw an angel last night." The interpretation of dreams has wielded power in human history. Early Talmudic rabbis said, "A dream that is not understood is like a letter that is not opened."

The Romantic era gave dreams a new importance. They were the fire wheels of imagination. They inspired great poetry. They gave Robert Louis Stevenson the plots for his fiction. Frederich Kekule, the organic chemist, made the important discovery of the structure of the benzene ring in a dream of a snake eating its tail. They reveal a man's own mind to himself. Still, people are lured by the romantic appeal that dreams transcend them, even into the supernatural, lending clairvoyance. Historians repeatedly write that Abraham Lincoln was deluged with crackpot letters; Lincoln knew that threats on his life might not be staved off indefinitely. Yet it is part of our dearest legend that Lincoln's dream of his death was a prediction of his actual assassination.

The yearning for instantaneous and spectacular interpretations of dreams must be widespread. Today, at any large newsstand one can purchase a 25-cent dream book that contains remnants of the ancient Egyptian papyri, indiscriminately mixed with brief excerpts from Freudian paradigms. The numbers gambler may discover that his dream of peanuts means that he should bet on number 345. The introspective reader may find that his dream of guns reveals an undue preoccupation with masculine virility. A dozen or so dream books on the market offer this odd mixture of ancient omens, oracles, prophecy, diagnoses, and psychological advice—a sample of man's attempts throughout the ages to understand his dreams.

Since the 1900s, when Freud's theory was first promulgated, psychoanalysts, psychiatrists, and psychotherapists have become our chief interpreters of dreams. Dreams were mirrors of the dreamer, not god-sent visions nor forecasts of external reality. In ancient times a chill of foreboding might have spread through the family if a youngest son dreamed that his father walked around carrying his head on a plate; but after 1900 it was more likely to be seen as a castration wish. A dream of plunging into water suggested the relief of pain to a Babylonian, but a Freudian interpretation might have suggested a fantasy of birth. In the shorthand of colloquial speech, Freudian interpretation endowed dreams with the forces of primary and often repressed instincts. Freud's more mystical contemporary Carl Gustav Jung saw in dreams a self-transcendence that expressed the collective nature of humankind. Erich Fromm has observed that dreaming man can be irrational and beastly, and also unusually wise and sensitive.

None of the great theorists saw dreams as any one kind of event. The theories derived from long experience with patients, from hearing their dreams, the emotions the dreams evoked, and the patients' train of associated memories. Freud, still the dominant dream theorist, was a neurophysiologist by training and a complex thinker. The oversimplification of his theory has created a popular myth that dream events can be equated with symbolic meanings independent of the dreamer, and that universal and cultural symbols are so uniformly imbedded in men that any dream may be understood *in vacuo*.

The patent foolishness of such an endeavor, like the patent foolishness of the dream books, can be demonstrated in any living room. One need only turn on a televised movie for a minute and watch a single film clip. What does it mean? A young man rises from the sofa and shoots an entering stranger. Without the context of the story, how is anybody to decide whether this was murder, an act of self-defense, panic, justice, or revenge? The psychiatrist is in a similar quandary when somebody tells him an isolated dream and asks its meaning. An honest analyst is not likely to venture a curbstone opinion, for he must know the person and his associations. Even then his chances of full understanding are about fifty-fifty.

Have a dozen years of laboratory dream research given us a shorter route to dream interpretation? Have they altered the psychoanalytic theories about the meanings of dreams? The analysis of literally truckloads of dream stories, and the use of laboratory methods lend no hope that there will ever be a quick formula for understanding dreams, but they are beginning to modify our notions about the nature of dreaming. There are a few analysts who resist the incursion of laboratory findings upon theories delineated by Freud. As one analyst has said, "There is no dream beyond the dream Freud described in his early work. I simply question the findings of the laboratory." In his mind the sole avenue to the heart of a dream is the long probing of morning recollections by a trained analyst, according to his discipline. On rare occasion laboratory experimenters, familiar with the biases of psychoanalysis, have gone to the other extreme. "Now that we are able to examine what is more nearly the raw material of the theories, their failures are becoming obvious."

In point of fact, both methods contain discernible biases. The psychiatric patient or analysand from whom theories have been derived is not a representative sample of the population. Nor, indeed, is the laboratory a normal place to sleep. The rarity of nightmares and nocturnal emissions in the laboratory indicates that the experimenters may be able to tap many more dreams than the psychiatrist, but that the psychiatrist may hear about certain kinds of dreams that do not occur in the laboratory. If a person's rapport with his psychiatrist will affect his degree of candor, a subject's rapport with the experimenter is in the same respect very influential. Experimenters cannot force candor, but they can watch certain physiological changes from the outside, and some of these are being correlated with specific kinds of dreams and feelings. The best example, perhaps, is a male subject's lack of erection, or detumescence, during a rapid-eye-movement dream. Charles Fisher's researches strongly suggest that these signs almost always indicate an anxious or aggressive dream. Whatever the subject describes, these negative emotions are almost invariably imbedded in the dream. Today, as the psychiatric and laboratory methods of dream study are used simultaneously, we may hope to see the differences more clearly, and modify our conception of the actual dream.

The dreams from which theories have arisen have not

been dreams, of course, but memories. There is no way of checking dream reports against dreams. However embroidered and shaped, however censored and skewed, we have only human recall to work with. Quite a number of psychiatrists have been interested in seeing how the dreams reported in the laboratory match with dreams reported to the analyst. Roy Whitman of the University of Cincinnati Medical School found, in a study of two patients, that there were some dreams told to the experimenter that were withheld from the analyst, and the reverse was also true. Some of the dreams told the analyst were not mentioned to the experimenter. The male patient told only the psychiatrist certain hostile and sexual dreams about the experimenter, but he told the experimenter about homosexual scenes that he did not tell the psychiatrist in the morning. The woman withheld from the experimenter dreams which implied that she knew more than he did and was seductive toward him, but she withheld from the psychiatrist seventeen dream scenes about the relationship of psychiatrists and patients, and also her sexual dreams.

Neither the psychiatrist nor the laboratory experimenter can be quite sure that they are recording exactly what a person remembers. The dream is filtered through inevitable shyness, self-consciousness, fear of judgment, and even deliberately distorted. Calvin Hall and his associates at the Institute for Dream Research in Miami, Florida, have tried to eliminate the sterile hospital aura from their dream laboratory. It is located in a frame house, offering as homey an atmosphere as possible. Even so, when monitored records of laboratory awakenings were compared with written reports by the same volunteers as they recalled dreams in their own homes, the dream narratives were strikingly different. Laboratory reports were long and incoherent, and less intense than the highly organized dream reports from home. Perhaps volunteers were self-conscious about their intensity when they talked directly with the experimenter, and perhaps the rules of the waking mind prevailed as they worked over their reports at home, so that they came out in the manner of short stories. In another laboratory, the problem of deliberate censorship and distortion was enunciated with touching candor when the volunteer told the experimenter, "All the way over here, I worried about what would happen if I dreamt certain things—if it got too hairy, you know. I made up this story, all ready to use it in case—but I'm glad I didn't have to use it." Even if the individual were to report his dreams with dispassionate truthfulness, the laboratory technician knows that his subject is not quite so free in his actual dreams as he might be at home.

Edward Wolpert at the University of Chicago Medical School has recalled a striking example of the manner in which a sleeping person can control his own dreams for self-protection. The volunteer was one of Wolpert's first experimental subjects, a sophisticated young man who had just previously finished a psychoanalysis. He began with some reservations about the sleep study, doubting that the researchers could actually pinpoint his dream periods, and on the other hand, fearing that if they did he might disclose too much about himself. His analysis made him hypersensitive to the interpretations one might put upon a dream and he did not intend to spill his guts in public. For three hours in the laboratory he tossed and turned, unable to fall asleep. Then finally he drifted off and his first REM period soon followed. It was an elaborate and vivid dream. As he related the events he began to feel psychologically naked, and embarrassed about the meanings of the dream. He went back to sleep, and for the rest of the night, each time a REM interval appeared on the EEG script, it lasted only a minute or two and then ceased before anybody could awaken him. In the morning when he awakened, the researchers asked him if he remembered his aborted dreams. He did. He had dreamed that a television set had been switched on. He let it play for a little while and then got up and shut it off. The screen went blank.

Judging from thousands of laboratory nights it is obvious that dreams recalled in the morning comprise only a tiny fraction of the nightly fare. By repeatedly awakening volunteers in all phases of sleep, experimenters have demonstrated that the majority of vivid, memorable episodes occur within the rapid-eye-movement periods, and that everyone has four or five of these intervals a night, occupying about an hour and a half of their sleep. Some people enjoy vivid dreams as they are falling asleep, and others have reported remarkable dramas when awakened from the quiescent stages of slow-wave slumber. Even the most prolific dream recallers emerge from the night with but a small portion of this experience in mind. Our general notion about dream content and the meanings of dreams would appear to be based upon REM dreams, and probably upon particular ones, at that. Although a person may occasionally awaken from a dream in the midst of the night, he is more likely to recall dreaming as he wakes up in the morning, and it may be this last REM period that we have been referring to as dreaming in general.

Not all the dreams of the night are alike, nor do people seem to dream alike. David Foulkes and Gerald Vogel have confirmed in a University of Chicago study that many people slip into sleep along a sluice of reveries and vague thoughts. In an extension of this study at the University of Wyoming, Foulkes and his associates have tracked some individual differences in the dreams of sleep onset. Some people dream so vividly that it might be hard to distinguish these border-state dreams from REM experiences, yet other people do not dream as they drift off to sleep. According to a variety of psychological tests the volunteers in the study appeared to segregate by personality characteristics too. The people who reported dreaming as they drifted into sleep seemed to be less constricted and anxious than those who apparently indulged in no fantasy as they lapsed into sleep.

Early dreams appear to be somewhat harder to remember than the dreams later in the night. Arthur Shapiro, internist and sleep researcher at Downstate Medical Center in Brooklyn, has summed up what appears to be a trend in nightlong dream studies. The early REM periods are somewhat colorless, mundane, and thoughtlike; the later REM dreams exude more vigor and imagery. Indeed, toward the end of the night even the thoughts and fragments reported between REM intervals take on some of the coloration and vividness of REM episodes. Laboratory volunteers have themselves commented that the first dreams of the night did not make a firm impression on their memories. The frustrated experimenter, in addition, may be left listening to the yawn of his dreaming subject who has slipped back to sleep in mid-recital, and when reawakened recalls nothing of his dream.

The issue of memory has been nettlesome to sophisticated analysts as they have tried to theorize about the rules governing content. At the same time, while therapists may be interested, the validity of patients' dream reports is not essential for their use in analysis. Dreams as used in therapy are like a vague sketch that must be fleshed out with trains of personal associations and memories. It is this process, not so much the dream, that is crucial. For theorists, however, the problem of memory and distortion remains an issue. Ernest G. Schachtel, expressing a common sentiment, has sadly remarked that few dreams are recalled upon awakening, and that these are fragmented and transformed very rapidly. Freud said: ". . . the forgetting of dreams depends far more upon the resistance than upon the fact stressed by the authorities that the waking and sleeping states are alien to each other." Dreams were not so much forgotten as repressed because their contents were too disturbing to be consciously confronted. A few people adamantly believe that repression is the sole cause of poor memory for dreams, but laboratory studies have indicated that the forgetting of dreams may be more complicated than that.

During the first years of laboratory dream research at the University of Chicago, William C. Dement and Nathaniel Kleitman observed that the incidence of dream recall dropped sharply after the ending of the REM period. Edward Wolpert and Harry Trosman, also in this laboratory, began awakening volunteers at various intervals after REM periods. When awakened directly from REM dreaming, the volunteers remembered their experiences, but if several minutes had elapsed after the close of the REM period it was gone like the trace of the evanescent neutrino. Again and again the laboratory researchers almost literally watched dreams evaporate. A subject who had slipped away in the midst of reciting a dream, and who was reawakened, might say, "I remember being woken, but I don't remember what it was about. . . ." The sleepy subject makes an effort to unscramble his thoughts and the English words to describe them, and the experimenter, now several minutes too late to affix the dream details, has watched them slip into the bog of the forgotten. The particular stage of sleep and the timing of awakening appear to influence the recall of dreams. But the memory problem is knottier than that. Everyone knows that people differ in their ability to recall dreams.

Ten years ago it was possible for a person who rejoiced in his plentiful morning memories to pity the impoverished soul who said, "I never dream." Such people have been observed in the laboratory, passing through the usual number of REM intervals, and when awakened, have often exclaimed, "Oh—so *that's* a dream!" Why do some people habitually remember their dreams and others fail to recall anything? Psychoanalytic patients have high incentive, and often begin to remember more dreaming. Another aspect of memory may be attention. Introspective people seem to recall dreaming more easily than people who rarely contemplate their own emotions and thoughts.

If the time of awakening is important, the speed of awakening appears to influence dream memory in the person who usually does not recall dreams. Since questions about dream recall lie at the vortex of research into the nature of dream content, they have become the focus of a concerted study by a large research team at New York Downstate Medical Center. Donald Goodenough and Arthur Shapiro have been directing various aspects of the research. When they compared people who rarely remembered dreaming at home with people who called themselves dreamers, they found a number of factors at play. The volunteers with poor dream memory, if awakened very abruptly during a REM episode, would recall more details than they would if awakened slowly. If they were awakened gradually as they might awaken at home, they were apt to say they had been thinking rather than dreaming, even though they were drawn out of a REM state.

On a first sorting, there seemed to be at least three explanations for the inability to recall dreams. At home, of course, a person's alarm clock might awaken him outside of the REM interval or he might awaken too gradually. He might, of course, be repressing unpleasant memories. On the other hand, the laboratory studies indicated that some of these nonrecallers might be physiologically somewhat different from the recallers. Some volunteers who awakened from REM sleep feeling they had been in a dreamless oblivion gave physiological signs of dreaming in a deeper state of sleep than others. It took a real blast to awaken them and when they did awaken, it was a slow process. Other subjects, when awakened from a REM episode, would assert that they had been awake and thinking. They may have been in a physiological state of sleep very near the threshold of waking. Occasionally, however, what they would label as waking thought might reasonably cause incredulity in the experimenter. Some of these dialogues between the experimenter in the monitoring room and the sleepy volunteer in his darkened bedroom have a charming humor:

"I was awake and thinking of going over to a candy machine. I began to put the dime into the machine, and more dimes—3 more came out in the front, so I took the dime back out and put it in again and 3 more dimes came to the front. I did this 4 or 5 times. The I put the dime almost all the way in and all of a sudden this pile of pennies came flowing out, an endless stream practically. I put the pennies in my pocket. This soda machine was in the classroom. I asked the teacher if she minded and she said no. I just sat and put the pennies in. This classroom was what you call a student seminar which they have at college. It seems the machine was built over an oil well and there were two bubbling wells in there."

"You say you were awake and thinking this?"

"Yes. It's very hard to tell whether you're awake or sleeping. I thought I was awake."

"Any more details?"

"I didn't want to share the pennies with anybody so I asked a girl if I could borrow her hat and I was going to pour everything in. Except it seems the hat was made of some sort of rubber and I couldn't pour it in because there was no room—it came all the way up to the top. It was a white hat."

It may seem implausible that this fellow thought he was awake and thinking yet many people who typically claimed to be awake when aroused from REM intervals seemed to be in unusual contact with the outside world. They tended to awaken easily, and to show less than usual eye movement during their REM dreams. It appeared that they might be dreaming in a lighter than usual stage of sleep. They often gave terse dream reports and said the memory was rapidly fading.

There are, however, instances in which a person awakened will say that he was dreaming but he cannot remember what. Sometimes the Downstate team has noticed that these REM intervals look particularly intense by physiological measures, yet the volunteer says his dream content has crumbled away or that his mind is a blank. These have looked like instances of repression, and the team has been studying the phenomenon by presenting subjects with very stressful films and neutral films on alternate nights before sleep. After a stress film there are more instances than after a neutral film in which a person fails to recall a dream. Sometimes the repression does not seem to take the form of total memory failure but of a kind of dissociation of feeling. One man, for example, had seen a medical film on the birth of a baby just before sleep. During his first REM interval his respiration was notably wild, yet his reported dream of hammering studs into a two-by-four was relatively unemotional. On his next awakening, however, he said that there had been something else in his mind. "I found the word 'murder' in the back of my mind."

Repression is common enough in waking life. It is rather easier to pinpoint during waking than sleep, for there are witnesses to events, whereas no outsider can enter the brain to share a dream. The Downstate approach to the problem has been to obtain many nights of dreams from people who ordinarily recall with ease, and spot those memory failures that occur on nights when they have been subjected to stress. Unconscious repression, time of awakening, speed of awakening, and physiology may not be the only factors determining our recall of dreams.

Of course, forgetting spares our minds from a clutter that might interfere with the events and thoughts at the center of our focus. Focused attention and action necessitates eliminating all distractions. In our daily lives we do not recall most of our dreams, but then we do not remember every reverie, monologue, or thought we composed in the shower each morning. During waking activity our "poor memory" protects our concentration, for we do not have access to the detailed memories that appear to be available in dreams.

The magnitude and richness of this lifetime memory hoard, which seems to lie outside of conscious retrieval yet landscapes and populates our dreams, has been suggested occasionally under hypnosis. Just as an indication of the amount our brains manage to store, Warren McCulloch gave this example to a Cybernetics conference in 1952.

> We tried this sort of trick. We took master bricklayers who laid face brick and had them recall the seventh brick in the row—in a given year. They were able to recall any one such brick—thirty or forty items at the most. That was a brick that had been through their hands some ten years before.
>
> These things are verified by checking the bricks. They are master bricklayers. That means they are laying face bricks. That means that even ten years later you can go to that row and look at the brick.
>
> The kinds of things men remember are that in the lower left-hand corner, about an inch up and two inches over, is a purple stone which doesn't occur in any other brick that they laid in that whole wall. . . . The pebble may be about a millimeter in diameter. . . .

One member of the conference inquired how a man could possibly remember thirty such features on one brick, to which McCulloch replied, "Oh, they do." In fine detail the unnoteworthy features of our surroundings seem to be physically filed away within the brain, and we may reasonably assume that these billions of "inconsequential" memories form part of the raw material of our dreams.

We are, of course, the authors of our dreams—as Erich Fromm has phrased it, playwrights drawing upon a vast store of materials. They are created out of our emotions, cultural values, and perceptions, and also our biology, our chemistry, our inherited physical structure. These factors also appear to influence our recall of dreams, a recall that appears to be chancy and imperfect. The complex issue of dream memory can be explored and defined by new methods today, as theorists seek to discover or confirm the psychodynamic rules that may dictate the significance of dream content and, indeed, the nature of dream content.

Laboratory methods are allowing us to re-examine some of the old mythology about the nature of dreams. Do they happen in a flash or in real time? Louis Ferdinand Alfred Maury, an ingenious nineteenth-century empiricist, had himself tickled, scorched and sprinkled in order to see how it affected dreaming. His famous dream of the French Revolution has been repeatedly cited as the evidence that dreams occur in the space of an eyeblink. It was an elaborate dream that culminated in his own beheading. As he was taken to the block and felt the guillotine sever his head from his body he awakened in fright. The headboard of his bed had fallen on his neck. Maury concluded that the entire dream occurred between the instant of impact and moment of awakening, and never considered the alternative explanation that the collapsing headboard just happened to coincide with the beheading situation in his dream. Although this dream was reported ten years after it happened, and the alternative explanation was never offered, many people believed that Maury had demonstrated the instantaneousness of dreams. Unfortunately, a great deal of our historical evidence about the nature of dreams is similarly anecdotal. As in clairvoyance, the positive coincidence of prediction and real event is likely to be remembered and offered as proof, but the many negative instances are forgotten. Many dogmatic opinions about dreams have been inspired by a relatively few coincidences.

Laboratory studies now suggest that most dreams probably take place in real time, although "flash" dreams can occur. Foulkes and his associates have obtained reports of very rapid dreams that seem to occur in scenes without intervening continuity, like a series of rapidly flashed photographs. Kleitman, Dement, and Wolpert long ago revealed that the preponderance of our REM dreams probably unfold at about the rate it would take to live out the sequence in waking life. One early subject recalled this scene:

"I was standing by the record player . . . listening to some music, and intending to go home. The doorbell rang and she [a girlfriend] asked me if I would answer it. I hesitated for a moment and . . . it rang again."

The experimenter's finger had accidentally slipped and he had sounded the arousing bell twice, about three or four seconds apart. When the subject was later asked to act out the dream, it took about three seconds. This procedure has been repeated in a number of ways, confirming that dream events often—perhaps usually—take place in ordinary time.

Another myth about dreams has been the notion that they are almost always in black and white, and that the person who dreams in color must be intensely emotional and is exhibiting certain vagaries of personality. Edwin Kahn, William Dement, Charles Fisher, and Joseph E. Barmack studied 38 subjects, whom they awakened from dreams. Apparently, most people pay little attention to color and would not mention it unless asked. If a volunteer never offered a color description, a member of the experimental team would probe. One subject mentioned that she saw a bar of soap in the bathtub with the baby. When later asked what the soap looked like she said, "Like any bar of soap looks. It was round, it was pink, and the baby was playing with it in the bathtub." Another subject mentioned a dream that included girls in bright red bikinis. When the experimenter later asked how he knew the bikinis were red, he replied, "How did I know? I saw them. They were red." Out of the 87 dreams taped in this study only 15 contained no particular reference to color. The old myth about colorless dreams may simply indicate that people do not mention qualities they take for granted. It should not

be surprising that the problems of deciphering t
dreams from the reports of dreamers are at least a
as discovering what transpired in an accident f
testimony of witnesses.

A very old theory about dreaming suggested that dreams
were caused, and assuredly influenced, by sensory stimulation from outside or within the body. The nineteenth-
century experimenters had themselves tickled and scorched
during sleep, but they had no means of gaining access to
all their dreams. Surely, throughout a dreamer's self-
immersion air continues to circulate around his head, there
are sounds, lights may go on or off, and innumerable
events occur within his body. Freud postulated that the
dream protects a person from awakening by incorporating
these outside events. Today, of course, we are acutely
conscious of statistics, and would more likely speculate
that this happens in a certain percentage of dreams. Dreams
may, indeed, wake a person up. Gemini astronaut Gordon
Cooper related an interesting nightmare to Dr. Howard
Minners of NASA after his eight-day voyage around earth.
While in space he dreamed that he had failed to perform
one of his tasks in the spaceship. The dream awakened
him, whereupon he checked the instruments, and found
that he had actually done his assigned task before he fell
asleep.

In their early experiments, Dement and Wolpert systemati-
cally waited until their subject had entered a REM interval.
Then they would sound a humming tone, flash a light, or
spray the person's face with cool water, subsequently
awakening him to hear what he dreamed. About 25 percent
of the time the dreams bore the obvious impact of the
stimuli. After noise people said, "There was a plane flying
overhead," or "There was a noise like Niagara Falls."
Other experimenters have applied heat or cold to dreaming
subjects, and obtained references to temperature in about
25 percent of the dreams. It should not be surprising that
external stimuli do not show a direct impact 100 percent of

the time. Indeed, neurophysiologists have shown us that the dreaming brain, while in some ways as responsive as the waking brain, tends to censor external distractions as it does when a person is focusing his attention upon a difficult problem.

Similarly, thirst, hunger, a need to urinate, and other bodily states produce a noticeable impact upon only a certain fraction of our dreams. Freud ate anchovies and reported dreaming that he drank water, but we will never know what other dreams he dreamed that night. Dement and Wolpert found references to drinking in about 30 percent of the dreams of their thirsty subjects in one study. Edwin Bokert at New York University added a Machiavellian fillip to enhance thirst in his 18 subjects. They were deprived of food and liquid for 8 to 9 hours and presented with a highly spiced meal upon arrival in the laboratory. At least one of their dreams referred to thirst. On one night, in addition, a tape recorder played during sleep, repeating the phrase "a cool delicious drink of water." Interestingly enough, this suggestion was incorporated into dreams directly. Also, the number of dreams about liquids increased and the subjects who dreamed of gratifying their thirst drank less in the morning than did the subjects who dreamed that they were frustrated. These people were thirstier when they awakened, a first tentative laboratory confirmation of Freud's theory that dreams may satisfy drives and wishes.

There have been a number of attempts to discover how drugs may influence dream content. Several venturesome experimenters have slugged themselves with alcohol before bedtime, with various antidepressant or tranquilizing drugs—and found no perceptible trend in their own subsequent REM reports. Since drugs that alter mood or perception presumably act upon the dreaming brain, it is reasonable to expect that they cast some hue or inclination into dreams, but such trends undoubtedly require more than a casual screening of a few nights' dreams. Roy Whitman and his associates at the Cincinnati College of Medicine have detected a trend toward aggressive dreams under the influence of the antidepressant imipramine.

The characteristic nightmares of the alcoholic may reflect a state of toxicity. Milton Gross and his associates at Downstate Medical Center in Brooklyn have heard a vast number of these alcoholic nightmares. Typically, the dreamer is in a truck on a collapsing bridge, or being chased by a cop, shot and borne away dying in an ambulance; he is stomping on screaming hordes of rats, watching doctors dissect living animals, or waiting to be beaten with chains. In general these sick gentlemen arrive at the hospital in a state of hunger, dehydration, and some animal discomfort.

Their dreams appear to reflect this bodily state. One man, in withdrawal, who dreamed of pulling the plug out of a bathtub and continually hallucinated water on the floor, soon thereafter went to the urinal in considerable need. Another bunched up his bedsheet and tossed it onto the floor in his sleep. When he awakened he explained that he had tossed out some spoiled frankfurters. Several men in withdrawal spent their dreaming periods chewing, salivating, making the gestures of someone who is ravenously finding, preparing, and eating food.

Messages from the body do, indeed, seem to penetrate the dreaming mind. A preliminary study of a large group of nurses suggests that women may often have anticipation dreams, dreams of waiting for a bus or train, before the onset of menstruation. On the first day or two of menstruation, however, the dreams may be fantasies of destruction. This is only a tentative conclusion, from a study by Robert Van de Castle at the Institute for Dream Research in Miami. Members of the Institute have postulated that a careful screening of dream content might permit early detection of physical ailments whose pains or symptoms have been overlooked during waking. The difficulty in establishing correspondence between body symptoms and dream content will be considerable. It is indeed difficult to establish correlations between concrete and clear-cut life events and dreams in order to confirm some of the major points of dream interpretation theories.

Perhaps the best established, out of all the factors that influence our dreams, is the role of events in the preceding day. Freud long ago elaborated the hypothesis that dreams were ignited and molded around this day's residue, and this current experience would begin to evoke associations and memorable childhood events. Laboratory records have supported this hypothesis to a remarkable extent. An initial demonstration was made by Paul P. Verdone at the National Institutes of Health. He found that the early dreams in the night tend to surround current happenings in a somewhat more bland and vague fashion than later dreams. As the night wears on and the dreamer's temperature drops to its daily low point, the dreams seem to recede toward past events while also becoming more intense and vivid. As the temperature begins to rise before waking, there is some indication that dreams also move again toward the events of the present. This trend has been observed in numerous laboratories. Not all protocols are alike, yet the unwinding skein of night memory can be exemplified by this transcript:

1st Awakening: "I'm trying to remember if I was dreaming or not. I was thinking in terms of the job—a ten-car train that had to get moved from the shop—thinking where I would put it. . . ."

2nd Awakening: "I was thinking of getting those cars I mentioned—what to do with this train that was getting released from the shop and these ten extra cars. . . ."

3rd Awakening: "This time I finally started dreaming—I was sitting at a desk in the office where I work, figuring out what I was going to do with these cars. . . ."

4th Awakening: "Seems I was in a little vegetable stand in downtown Manhattan. I'd been looking for a place to park—to do my shopping . . . a block away I saw this stand where the merchandise sits out on the sidewalk. . . . The proprietor handed me two or three pieces of fresh, crisp lettuce from a nice head and asked me to take it inside to wash it off—he had three kids sitting there and he was going to give it to them to pacify them. . . . The guy inside was going to put it into a bag—he misunderstood—and the proprietor called out: 'Hey, Eddy, this lettuce is for the kids. . . .'"

5th Awakening: "Seems I was sitting in the living room in this house, when a dump truck came up with this pile of sand. Seems the people were planning to use it for a brick wall or something. It was a woman with the dump truck. She dumped it out front and we stood out there passing the time of day—saying the kids were going to have the time of their lives, and people were going to track sand all over their carpets. . . . She was a woman in white coveralls, with her hair tied up in a scarf. . . . We were laughing and joking. . . ."

Many of the later dreams could be mistaken for descriptions of reality, they are so richly detailed and so natural. Nobody has suggested a physiological reason for the increasing vividness of fantasy, but the progression away from the immediate present fits with the speculations of some neurophysiologists. Dreaming, they feel, is a kind of filing procedure within memory stations in the brain. It occurs in sleep when there is a lull in the flood of incoming information, a time when the day's events can be recycled for proper filing by drawing out the memory folders of the past and linking present with past according to some hierarchy of importance, association, similarity of emotion. Presumably the new information will be filed in a number of forms so that there is a cross index for recalling pertinent events.

The impact of the day's residue has inspired empiricists, even in Freud's time, to try to create a direct impact upon dreams by deliberately generating some of that residue.

Posthypnotic suggestions were used to encourage subjects to dream of specific happenings, and in the morning their dream memories were sifted for traces of the suggestion. Johann Stoyva of Langley Porter Neuropsychiatric Institute in San Francisco and Charles Tart at the Laboratory of Hypnosis Research of Stanford University have used laboratory methods to demonstrate that hypnotic suggestions do crop up in dreams. Stoyva found a curious side effect among his best subjects. Those who would dream of climbing a tree or close facsimile, upon direction, would also seem to cut down on their REM time, yet the less suggestible subjects, who resisted intervention in their dream content, continued to show as much REM dreaming as before. Tart found that hypnotic subjects could be instructed to awaken themselves before or after REM periods. Moreover, one fellow could be instructed to dream all night and would thereupon increase his REM time by 20 percent.

As people have begun to use a variety of techniques to influence dream content, a crucial question has remained at the heart of their endeavor: How does one know when a dream reflects laboratory manipulations? If dreams did no more than parrot reality they would not be difficult to interpret, but their meanings are often hidden in symbols. Some are believed to be common to large cultural groups, some possibly universal, but many cannot be deciphered except by questioning the dreamer, who himself holds the key. The search for the relation between dream symbols and real events might be likened to the anthropologist's work in a newly discovered tribe. He must determine how the strange sounds uttered by tribesmen compose words, and then what objects the words refer to, and finally how the language is organized by grammar and syntax.

An early and well-known program was devised by psychoanalyst Charles Fisher of Mt. Sinai Hospital in New York. He demonstrated that subliminal images—slides flashed before the viewer for only 1/100th or 1/200th of a second—would make an impression even though they were not consciously perceived. In a number of experiments with patients and physicians, Fisher would flash a slide, ask his subject to draw a picture of what he had seen, and then report his dreams in the morning. Since this predated the advent of EEG awakenings, his yield of dreams was small, but the technique seemed to work. One bedtime stimulus, for example, was a slide showing a vase in lines bold enough to be seen by a person with normal vision; however, in very faint outline there was a swastika emblazoned on the vase. The slide was flashed for a split second, only once. In the morning one young man remembered a dream that began, "I was in a totalitarian prison camp . . ."

P. W. Wood at the University of North Carolina has, in a sense, done the opposite. Instead of supplying a small and localized stimulus, he· has removed stimulation by taking over the entire daytime environment of his subjects. His five volunteers were young college graduates who spent five nights in the laboratory. Their second day was lived out in total isolation, perhaps simulating the environment of monotony and loneliness of the aging invalid, prisoner, or future man in space. Wood found that people spent 60 percent more time in REM dreaming after isolation. Although their dreams were longer they exhibited less rapid eye movement than usual, hinting that they might be less intense. The day of experimental isolation was inactive, and the subsequent dreams were inactive. On the other hand, the dreams suggested a kind of wish fulfillment, for they were very sociable, dreams of groups standing around talking, as if to compensate for the previous day empty of human companionship.

The impact of the environment on dreams has been witnessed repeatedly in laboratories, where subjects have reported long dreams about the laboratory and experimenters. Donald Goodenough heard a dramatic instance of a laboratory dream that the subject, when awakened, did not recall. He had been sitting in the control room when the sleeping subject suddenly began to broadcast an unusually coherent dream conversation. The tape recorder was turned on as the man proceeded to answer standardized questions of a post-dream interview: "Quiet? Uh, no. Jittery? No, I wasn't jittery. Placid? No, I wouldn't say so. . . ." It was a replica of a conversation held on many occasions with Dr. Goodenough following awakening from a dream. Dreams of the laboratory are not always such literal translations of the actual procedures as this one appeared to have been.

David Foulkes and Allan Rechtschaffen examined the effects of two bedtime television programs on a number of subjects and found that the different effects of the two films could be seen in the qualities of the subsequent dreams, rather than a mimicking of events. Their procedure may interest parents, who have watched children spend a transfixed hour before the television screen, watching the favorite bedtime program of monsters or crime or conspiracy. The films used in the laboratory were network shows, one a violent Western with some vicious scenes of brutality, the other a romantic comedy about a female con artist. Actual elements from the two programs were rarely apparent in the dream content, but the team found that the dream narratives differed in a striking fashion. Dreams following the violent Western were more vivid, imaginative, more intense than the dreams following the comedy.

More perceptible effects are being obtained by Herman Witkin, Donald Goodenough, and a sizable research team at Downstate Medical Center in Brooklyn. The emphasis of this mammoth project differs from the television studies. Since dreams do not simply mirror reality, researchers are looking beneath the surface to see how a person's dreams transfigure his experience, and how people cope with stress in dreams. This group has collected a number of bedtime films, powerful enough to affect the strongest stomach. The usual television fare, despite its violence, seems to make little impression on sophisticated viewers. The films seen by volunteers in this study may be neutral travelogues on some occasions, but on others they may be close-ups of gruesome automobile accidents, a traffic safety polemic prepared by highway police. Goodenough has remarked on this film, "I went out the next day and bought safety belts and new tires for my car." There have been medical training films, among them one showing the birth of a baby in detail. Another is a famous anthropological documentary taken among Australian aborigines as they perform, in the desert dirt with sharpened stones, a painful rite of subincision on young boys.

After seeing these stress films the subjects have seemed to take longer to fall asleep and often begin dreaming earlier than usual. On these nights, the experimenter more frequently hears when he awakens his subject from a rapid-eye-movement period, "I was dreaming—but I can't remember anything." If this memory failure is what we mean by repression, the forgetting of the unpleasant, the stress films appear to encourage it. The analysis of these dreams is being attacked for effects than can be summarized numerically and also by a psychological evaluation. Psychoanalyst Helen B. Lewis has been collaborating with psychologist Witkin to assess the emotionality of the dreams and the fashion by which they incorporate, transmute, and restructure elements from the films. Internist Arthur Shapiro has been following the physiological patterns that accompany the dreams. The difficulty in the project can be illustrated by the fact that the traffic film that caused Goodenough to go out and buy safety belts and tires nevertheless failed to make any straightforward appearance in the dreams of subjects who had seen it. This was not to say that the film made no impact, for by other criteria the dream narratives reveal qualitative reactions hinting that the stress films have a huge wallop.

Unlike the volunteers of many sleep studies, the Downstate subjects come from all walks of life. There have been factory workers, bakers, subway dispatchers, telephone engineers, airline mechanics, students, writers, and other professionals. Quite a few have been night workers who report to the laboratory after leaving the job. This makes the dream laboratory on top of the large modern hospital a 24-hour operation. The films are projected for the volunteer while he is comfortably settled in bed, already decorated with elecrodes. Then the lights go out, and he will be awakened from each REM period. After he has described his dream over the intercom system, a slide will be projected onto the wall before his bed. It is a chart of adverbs and adjectives, a matrix he can follow in defining the emotions he felt during his dream. Did it make him feel jittery, placid, kindly or fearful? The experimenter, checking off the responses to this chart, will now be able to categorize some of the overt reactions. How does this matrix of feelings change as the night progresses? How do the dream feelings compare with those evoked by the film? Some people have persistently shown the emotions inspired by the film even though their seemingly innocuous dreams bore no obvious relationship to the movie they had seen. The categories of dream feelings as they are graphed over many laboratory nights may reveal some but not all of the film's impact.

The same film means different things to each subject. In morning discussions, one man puzzles about the anthropological film, wondering what those natives were doing. Another is mainly horrified by the filth and unsanitary surgical conditions. Another emphasizes the excruciating pain and marvels that the initiates could dance around after surgery with none of the usual marks of suffering. In his fourth REM period one man dreams:

> "I'm back to that native business again. . . . Let me see, what the heck was I doing? I guess it was on the outskirts of a uh native village. I, uh, was supposed to go someplace with the chief I guess. . . ."

Such explicit references are rare. Another man dreams of a crash and a smoky form like a turtle arising from it. Could this reflect the grayed quality of the old film and the shape of the kneeling men on whose backs the boy initiate lies during surgery? After seeing the birth film, with its close-ups of the baby's bloody expulsion from the womb, a young man dreams of a volcano erupting and red-hot lava pouring down its sides. Only the morning interviews and subsequent biographical interviews begin to show that moments on the film struck off reverberations, and however innocuous the dream, the echoes often travel as in a long tunnel, back to some intense childhood associations.

To an extent that is frequently overlooked in theories of dream interpretation, Witkin and Lewis are finding that people transfigure the films and reality in a characteristic and personal style. One young man, for instance, who consistently reversed reality in dreams, remarked on the bloody gloves of the obstetrician in the birth film—and then proceeded to dream of girls in a park in dim light. The girls all wore long white gloves, and one might say the dream had cleaned up the mess. In a study of the dreams at sleep onset, in which subjects were asked to keep talking after the film until they were asleep, some people exhibited an unusual incorporation from the films and also open reveries about the laboratory and experimenters. These are people who depend heavily upon their surroundings for self-definition. Witkin and Lewis have used a number of tests. If placed in a tilted room and told to straighten his body, will the subject line up with the tilted room or with gravity? People who line up with the tilt of the room and adjust to their surroundings on analogous tests seem more prone than others to incorporate the films into their reveries. Whether or not dreams express instincts and gratify wishes, the individual has a characteristic manner of handling wishes and instincts in dreams as in life. Too quick a generalization about a dreamer's symbols may overlook important meanings. Following the sub-incision film, for instance, one might expect that dreams of castration and apprehension would be frequent. One man dreamed that he was abducted by gangsters in a car and was going to be exterminated. To him, however, the word "exterminate" had a special meaning. He had commented about the film that it appeared to be a circumcision but the natives did not look Jewish. In his dream recollection he was thinking about the extermination of the Jews. Thus the stress film seems to act like a fuse, igniting in different individuals diverse trains of association.

The dream, like an iceberg, shows on the surface only the barest glimmer of the reality that preceded it. Below lie most of the meanings, and it is clear that the correlation between dream symbol and real events and feelings is a subtle one. If one is inclined to generalize too easily about the meanings of symbols, an individual's very special association adds another hue. Even when the laboratory reality is a truly gruesome film, the experimenters are aware that its impact may be muted by many hidden variables. A man may come to the laboratory after an argument with his boss or his wife. Sifting out and sorting these various influences cannot be accomplished quickly. Laboratory studies of dream content are very young, and while they have suggested modifications of our traditional interpretations, they have not yet contributed a new theory.

Years before the dream hunters had electronic equipment or any means of predictably awakening people in dreams, Calvin Hall founded the Institute for Dream Research in Miami, Florida. He was asking very similar questions about the nature of dreams, and the rules they employ to represent the reality of the dreamer, but he used a very different method. He went about his assay in a manner similar to that of the sociologist, polling opinions and surveying population behaviors. By amassing a staggering number of dream reports, and assaying them statistically, Hall was able to see that certain kinds of dream content typified certain groups of people. Among the 30,000 dream reports in his files, about 5,000 were collected from other cultures, Nigerians, Mexicans, Peruvians, from citizens in other countries and members of tribes. Hall and his associates would select items that recurred in dreams and classify them, the dramatis personae, the settings, objects, predominant emotions. How frequently did particular events occur in the voluntarily remembered dreams of a large group? In 7,000 dreams they discerned a difference between dreams of men and women. Men tended to dream about men generally, but women dreamed about equally of men and women. A thousand dreams from college students, when put to analysis, suggested that young adults are frequently fearful. In about two out of five there were sequences of fear, often of being pursued. A similar assay implied that every dream of good luck was counterbalanced by seven dreams of misfortune, and that the dreamer more often felt himself a victim of circumstance than a beneficiary.

The natural language of the brain is often said to be symbolic, and it need not abide by the artificial logic by which we are educated as we mature. If dreams speak our hearts in a symbolic language, are some symbols universal to all humankind? Are some cultural symbols identifiable throughout a nation? Do these symbols really mean the same things in the dreams of different people? Freud revolutionized our attitudes toward dreams by emphasizing that they had symbolic meaning, that they were communications to ourselves.

The quests of the last decade in dream laboratories seem to confirm that dreams must be as rich in language and meaning as everyday life and behavior. Their contents reflect influence from multifarious sources, and on close inspection may eventually prove diagnostic. Thomas Detre of Yale Medical School, in exploring the relationship between sleep disturbances and mental illness, has the impression that we may find characteristic trends in dreams. Very depressed people who are entering a suicidal stage, for instance, report peculiar nightmares that are often uniquely empty of people and actions, dreams of natural scenes, a desolate rocky beach, a mountain crest, a plateau conveying an ominous and isolated sensation. Certain recurrent nightmares among children have been suggestive of temporal lobe abnormalities.

A child's nightmare differs in its force from an adult's. Sometimes, without ever awakening, a terrified youngster will continue screaming for his mother although seated on her lap and embraced. Dreams are not mere figments of imagination to children. Young children have eidetic imagery, and can count the buttons on a remembered shirt. Dreams have a similarly direct quality. While attempting to study his son's dreaming, Joe Kamiya got the boy to sleep in his laboratory at Langley Porter Neuropsychiatric Institute in San Francisco. He would awaken the child after some minutes of REM activity and ask if he had been dreaming. The boy invariably answered, "No." However, when his father rephrased the question and asked, "What were you doing just now?" the child would say, "Oh, I was playing with a tire out on the back porch. . . ."

At what point in life do dreams begin? The strong physiological markers of the REM cycle have been detected in infants ten weeks premature, occupying about 80 percent of sleep. Studies of Arthur Parmelee and his associates at UCLA have been adding to the evidence that this percentage shows a predictable decline. Indeed, the rate of decline has been thought to be a possible sign of brain maturation, suggesting that infant sleep patterns may provide an index of normal or abnormal development at a time when the infant does little but sleep, and there is not much other behavior to evaluate. By about two years, the vigorous sucking, kicking and waving of fists has subsided, and the REM phase has dropped to 30 percent or less of the child's sleep time. It declines to about 20 to 24 percent during the next few years and throughout early adulthood, appearing to decline somewhat after age forty-five, and dropping until in some aged persons REM sleep occupies only 13 percent of sleep time. Infant animals also show an enormous proportion of REM sleep that begins to diminish soon after birth. Judging from the work of Parmelee and others, this REM state evolves in the womb. Is the infant in the womb dreaming as he sucks his thumb and gives his mother perceptible kicks?

The starting age of dreaming depends in part upon our definition of dreams. Even in the womb there is presumably sensation. A newborn infant feels changes in temperature, the satisfaction of hunger, the discomfort of cramped position, the solace of being held or rocked. An infant's nightmare might be the diffuse memory of hungrily sucking while being held uncomfortably, the frustration of an instinctive need. Visual dreams would not seem likely in the womb or for some time after birth, but the congenitally blind dream without vision. The blind and deaf, who live in a changeless dark silence, also dream. One such patient at Albert Einstein Hospital in New York had never heard of the concept of a dream when questioned by an interpreter, but she recalled that a pet bird had died and weeks later she awakened in inconsolable sorrow having re-experienced the shock of reaching into the bird's cage and finding his lifeless body.

Helen Keller, who was deprived of sight, hearing, and smell by an attack of scarlet fever before she was two years old, managed to learn through language to replace this sensory world. She wrote a great deal about her dreams, commenting that she dreamed little before Miss Annie Sullivan became her tutor. Her dreams had been purely physical, inchoate, instinctive.

. . . something was always falling suddenly and heavily, and at times my nurse seemed to punish me for my unkind treatment of her in the daytime. . . . I would awake with a start or struggle, frantically to escape my tormentor. I was very fond of bananas and one night I dreamed I found a long string of them . . . all peeled and deliciously ripe, and all I had to do was stand under the string and eat. . . .

Later she was able to see, in her dreams, with her mind alone.

Once in a dream I held in my hand a pearl. I have no memory-vision of a real pearl. The one I saw in my dream must, therefore, have been a creation of my imagination. It was a smooth, exquisitely moulded crystal . . . dew and fire, the velvety green of moss, the soft whiteness of lilies. . . .

Dreams may start before speech or clear vision. For some period in the womb and early infancy the REM state appears to provide the baby's most active exercise in what are to become the motions of survival—sucking, kicking, erections. This may be a biological exercise required to establish the expression of instinctual drives, helping the infant to develop sucking strength, genital sensation, muscular reflexes, the first exercise of his apparatus for survival. His memories of sensation may, indeed, recur in sleep. From the point of view of the analyst, as Charles Fisher has aptly stated, this activity hardly seems to constitute dreaming until outside influences come to bear upon the evolving personality. At some unspecified day in infancy, sensory perception is sufficiently clear so that impressions from outside can begin to generate coherent internal experience. The rudiments of diffuse dreaming, sensory change, may begin back in the dark waters of the womb, but this is hardly what most of us call dreaming.

The early REM activity of the infant, the movements, the grimaces, the erections, are the first manifestations of the instinctive behavior around which childhood education centers. The first disciplines of the infant and child focus upon the control of instincts. Niceties of civilization demand that adults not urinate whenever and wherever they feel the urge, not instantly satisfy hunger, and the punishment for directly following sexual impulses is usually severe. These are the basic impulses that Freud saw emerging in dream forms. Surely, drive centers would seem to be somewhat charged during REM intervals, and it is interesting that humans and animals deprived of REM sleep for long periods begin to show a loss of waking control over their impulses. Dreams, on the other hand, do not often reflect these impulses straightforwardly, and this fact led Freud and dream researchers since his time to examine the symbolic language of the sleeping mind.

Raul Hernandez-Peón has represented the Freudian theory of dreams as symbolic release of repressed wishes and instincts in the language of neurophysiology, suggesting that we may someday see anatomical reasons why the state of sleep represses thoughts and the punished wishes of childhood. Perhaps, again, viewing our growing library of dreams, we may begin to see in what percentage of our dreams these points of theory hold. Not all dreams protect sleep, or fulfill wishes, or exhibit a covert form of repressed behavior. Sometimes dreams seem to follow a sequence and develop a theme. Sometimes memory fails. Dream researchers are not seeking a single formula to describe all dreams, and indeed in the laboratory they must analyze far more than merely dreams. The experimenter at the controls hears the voice on the intercom system, and he detects a style in the yawns, the pauses, sudden inflections, reticences, the timbre of the speaking voice. Several nights of dream recollections amplify the subject's personal qualities. Interviews begin to relate dream fragments to his life and feelings. The experimenter sees him dressed and awake, and also sleepily arising in the morning. As in the psychiatric clinic or analyst's office, the dream itself is but the first strand in a web of associations and memories gravitating about certain points. The meaning lies within the person, and all that he has become in the history that has molded him, and which he bears within his brain.

3. Learning to Keep a Dream Diary

Patricia Garfield, Ph.D.

YOUR DREAM LIFE can provide you with many marvelous gifts: creative products, delightful adventures, increased skill in coping with waking life, and a personal laboratory to develop any project of your choice. The party is held several times each night. You are the guest of honor. All you need to do is attend, enjoy, pick up your presents, and return to waking life. Of course, you need to be aware. Otherwise, unconscious and tipsy, you'll forget who was there, what they said, what you did, and lose your gifts before you reach home. *You can develop almost total recall for your nightly dream parties and become able to record and use your gifts in waking life.*

Skill in remembering your dreams begins with your attitude. Value your dreams. Don't reject any one of them. The dream you dismiss as ridiculous or trivial, like an orphan child, may be the very one with great potential to blossom beautifully when it's more developed. Accept each dream you remember. Treat it with respect. Write it down. Give it permanent form. You will be amazed to find, after you keep a dream diary for a few months, that seemingly unimportant symbols appear again and again. They change in shape and size but are clearly recognizable when written down. They literally grow. You can trace their development over time. Each dream you have is a child of your own. *Attend patiently to all your dreams and they will provide you with remarkable insights about yourself.*

Let's assume that you already value your dreams and are willing to accept them as they come, silly or fragmentary. How can you get in touch with them close enough to recall and record them in order to relate to them in the exciting ways that are possible?

Your attitude immediately prior to sleep is important: Plan to remember your dreams. Suggest it to yourself. One student found it helpful to drink half a glass of water before sleeping, determining while drinking that she would recall her dreams. In the morning she drank the remainder of the water while trying to recall. The same effect can be achieved by self-suggestion: "Tonight I will remember my dreams." *Remind yourself before going to sleep that you will remember your dreams.*

If you are not already a vivid dream recaller, the best time to begin developing skill in dream recall is *in the morning from a natural awakening.* When you awaken spontaneously in the morning (not by an alarm clock, not by phone ringing, not by children's calls), you are awakening directly from a REM period. Any time that you awaken by yourself you awaken from a dream. The morning dream, however, is the longest of the night's series, sometimes lasting a half to three-quarters of an hour. You have much more to catch hold of. If you ordinarily must wake up by alarm clock and you begin thinking about the day's activities even before opening your eyes, you are likely to lose all trace of the night's dreams. You will find it helpful to begin catching hold of your dreams by arranging a time to sleep in and awaken naturally. A weekend or peaceful vacation time can give you an opportunity to start. I personally prefer this method to artificial awakenings designed to catch a dream because it is possible to develop it into the special system described below. It also allows your dream to come to a natural conclusion rather than intruding into the theme with bells or buzzers. (These methods may be necessary, however, with chronic nonrecallers of dreams.) *Arrange a time when you can spontaneously awaken.*

Knowing that you have just completed a dream, the next step is crucial: Don't open your eyes! *Lie still with closed eyes and let images flow into your mind.* Don't begin thinking about what you must do for the day. You've chosen a peaceful unpressured time. Just let yourself feel. Very often this is enough to allow the images of your just-ended dream to return. The tiniest fragment of the last dream can serve as a hook for the whole night's series. I often recall the last dream scene first. I wake up hearing the words that I or some other dream figure is speaking, dancing the dance, laughing at the joke. It is the closing scene of the play. By reviewing it in my mind, the scene before that flows back, then the preceding one, and the one that preceded that. In reverse order the scenes of the last dream appear. It is not like a film run backward; the whole scenes, in complete sections, line up in reverse order. "Oh, before that so and so happened. And before that. . ." Occasionally the dream will return *in toto,* but it more commonly comes with the last scene first. Some small scrap that seems inconsequential, when considered, is found to be attached to a richly woven intricate garment. In a similar way, remembrance of the last entire dream will stimulate association to previous dreams of the night. *When you awaken naturally from a dream, close your eyes (preferably don't open them at all), lie still, and let the dream images flow back.*

Suppose there is not even the slightest fragment of a dream to let your mind wander on. You may sense that you dreamed or have a vague feeling without an image or there may be nothing at all. Don't give up. If a couple of minutes produces no dream recall, try this: Let your mind wander over images of the people close to you, your family, your intimate friends. Like riffling the pages of a book you may hit upon the image you seek in passing. You will *know*. There is a feeling of certain recognition that you dreamed something about that person that is inescapable. It's like trying to recall a forgotten name. The shape and rhythm and even initial sound may be there, but the whole name is elusive. When you hit upon the correct name yourself or someone supplies it, you recognize its accuracy. *Run through the important people in your life in your mind; it may trigger associations to your recent dream.*

Strange as it may seem, the position of your body in the morning is important in recalling your dreams of the preceding night. Hermann Rorschach, who invented the famous "ink-blot" test, observed that it was necessary to lie still when awakening because any quick motor movement like jumping out of bed disrupts memory of the dream. This is true, but you can go beyond it. Allow yourself to recall whatever dreams come to you in the position in which you awake. Lie still and let the images flow. *Then roll over.* If you find yourself lying on the left side, roll over to the right; if you are on your stomach, roll over slowly onto a side or onto your back. For some as yet unknown reason, additional dream recall often comes when you move gently from one position and settle into another. One contemporary theorist speculates that dreams may be stored in codes that are more readable when we are in the original posture in which the dream occurred: "Trying to recall a dream while in an inappropriate posture feels something like trying to write left-handed." When we recreate the original sleeping posture in which the dream occurred, memory of it often flows back. *When you feel as though your dream recall is complete in the position in which you awoke, move gently into other sleeping positions you use, with eyes still closed, and you will often find additional dream recall.*

You may find yourself recalling scraps of dreams during

the day. Some incident, some tone of voice, something someone says to you, something you hear yourself say, or something you see may trigger the response, "Oh, I dreamed about that last night!" Just as with morning dream recall it is important to capture these birdlike wisps of dreams, to put them into cages of writing or tapes or drawings before letting them go. No matter how vivid and accessible they seem at the moment, you will find they have vanished completely in a day or two and your memory of them, if you have any at all, will be a pale, distorted reflection. Recorded, even in fragmentary form, they can become extraordinarily useful to you later. Dream recall triggered by some stimulus in the environment may even occur several days after the dream in question. However, the sooner you can catch hold of it after the dream, the more complete and accurate your recall will be. Timing is crucial.

One research team clearly established that *dream recall is richest and most detailed immediately after a REM period ends*. Researchers awakened sleepers at four different times: (1) when the EEG machine showed they were experiencing REM: sleepers reported, as expected, an ongoing dream story; (2) during a body movement immediately after REM stopped: sleepers awakened at this point described complete, vivid, specific dream stories; (3) sleepers were awakened five minutes after REM stopped: they reported vague snatches of dream stories; and (4) sleepers were awakened ten minutes after REM stopped: most of these sleepers had no dream recall or only a blurry impression of a dream. Thus, only *five minutes* after a dream finishes, recall of it breaks up into fragments, and ten minutes after a dream, recall is almost, if not completely, gone. If you are going to catch an ordinary dream in its full expression, you must get hold of it quickly. Lucid dreams, in contrast, are vivid enough to stay in memory because you were there—conscious—just like an exciting event in waking life. Nightmares, too, are often vividly recalled. The ordinary dream, however, needs immediate attention to capture it.

Now, you may believe it is impossible to capture a dream within five minutes of its completion. It can be done. I am not speaking of artificial awakenings. Of course, if you sleep in a dream laboratory and an experimenter watches the unfolding record of your brain waves, he can see when the pattern of dreaming occurs and can wake you. Although an interesting experience, it is hardly convenient and not one you would wish to employ every night. You could also arrange with a good friend to stay up all night and watch you sleep. An alert observer can see the rapid eye movements indicating a dream state without an EEG machine. In one of my dream seminars, a student with poor dream recall made such an arrangement with his girlfriend. She passed the long hours of the night by reading at her friend's bedside and apparently missed some of his REM periods, much to their mutual frustration. Those she caught were interrupted too near the beginning of the dream story so there was not much to recall. Having a friend watch you sleep and wake you at appropriate times can be done but is tedious and uncertain. Another artificial awakening method involves setting your alarm clock at approximately the time you would expect a dream to occur—about ninety minutes after falling asleep and every ninety minutes thereafter. Again, this method interrupts an ongoing dream story, if it catches a dream at all. Otherwise, sleep is disrupted. Another student of mine, who underwent surgery, was subsequently waked by a nurse for shots throughout the night while she was in the hospital. She was delighted to find herself in the midst of dreams and busily recorded them while getting her shot. Generally, however, I do not recommend artificial awakenings of any sort unless other methods of capturing dreams do not produce results.

You can actually train yourself to awaken after a dream story is completed naturally. As you develop the habit of valuing your dreams, taking time to recall them in the morning, and recording them regularly each day, you will find that your memory for dreams increases dramatically. This is how it happened for me.

I became interested in recording my dreams when I was about fourteen. People in my family were discussing Freud's views on dreams, then much in vogue. I wanted to check for myself. I had been a heavy dream recaller all my life (and still recollect some unrecorded childhood dreams). At fourteen, I began to write down my dreams that seemed striking. I recorded the date, a description of the dreams I recalled in the morning, often adding events of the preceding day, feelings and associations, and sometimes drawings and attempts at analysis. I was mainly curious about the symbolism. The records I made were sporadic. As I grew older and went through typical teenage trauma, I found that dream recording was cathartic; it helped me understand my shifting feelings and cope more effectively. My descriptions were more complete and I kept steadier records. As a clinical psychology doctoral student I became aware of the considerable possibilities of a scientific examination of the record spanning several years. Dreams, unless examined by EEG, were in some disrepute at my university, however, so I did my dissertation in an area more concrete and measurable. Records from this time forward were comprehensive, with additional data and rare gaps. As I made daily records, I found I had developed extraordinary dream recall. There was rarely a morning wakening without a vivid dream in mind.

Suddenly, during this time of regular recording, I found myself awake in the middle of the night. This was a rare event and I puzzled, "What am I doing awake?" Nothing had happened to arouse me. Then I realized I had just been dreaming. I was waking from a dream in the same way as I did in the morning. How to remember it? At first, I tried reviewing it in my mind with the intention of recording it in the morning with the most recent dream. Anyone who has attempted this knows how futile it can be. Two or even three "replays" of the dream seem to have it firmly set and you return to sleep, only to discover in the morning that a ghostly trace of the once vivid dream is all that remains. This method was useless and time wasting for me. Yet, I continued to wake during the night following a dream. How to record it? Too lazy to get up, unwilling to turn on the light and disturb my husband by writing in bed, I scribbled a few short phrases on my ever-present bedside pad and returned to sleep. Again I woke. Another dream. Another scribble. In the morning the scrawls done in the dark were hard to decipher because they often overlapped. And so I hit upon a special way to capture these fleeting dreams so they would survive until morning.

When I self-awaken from a dream, during the night or in the morning, I remain still with my eyes closed. I pick up the 5″ x 8″ pad on my night table with the pen that lies on top of it and record the dream *with eyes still closed* in the following special way: I grasp the notepad with the 8″ side held horizontally with my left fingertips. I brace the pad on the bed or night table beside me (lying on my left side) or upon my chest (while lying on my back). I hold the right hand in normal writing position except that the little finger is extended upward in order to feel the top edge of the pad. I write a complete description of the dream (not just phrases) across the pad making the line straight by feeling the top edge of the pad as a guide. When I reach the end of a line, I lower my left hand fingertips to indicate the starting position of the next line and return the pen in my right hand to the spot marked by my left fingertips by tactual contact. It's rather like a typewriter carriage returning to the next line. Keeping the little finger extended while writing corrects for the tendency to write in a downward curve in the dark. This method virtually eliminates superimposition of lines. After one page is filled with writing I turn the page, press it flat, and continue the same process, using both sides of the paper until recall is complete.

Each new entry is marked with a paragraph symbol to

indicate clearly that it follows a period of sleep. I have already noted when I retired the approximate time of falling asleep and I note the time of awakening. In the morning I have several pages of wobbly notes which usually describe three or four dreams, but may range from one to seven dreams.

This method may sound very complex, but it quickly becomes easy and automatic with practice. At first it requires tremendous effort to pick up the pad and pen, but this, too, soon becomes simple. The method provides a record of dreams immediately following REM periods. I checked this point by spending several nights in a dream laboratory attached to an EEG machine and verified that I do, indeed, awaken following each REM period (and occasionally outside of REM). Once the written record is made I can easily dismiss thinking about the dream and return quickly to sleep. There is no need to "rehearse" the dream or exert effort to remember. I believe recall is more complete with this method. Opening your eyes and sitting up in bed, however gently, and turning on a light, however dim, break into visual imagery of the dream. As the dream is recorded with eyes shut, previous dream scenes flow back into mind. Experimenters who use tape recorders to describe the dream also disrupt total recall, in my opinion. The drowsy dreamer must rouse considerably to speak clearly and loudly enough to record immediately after a dream. Such arousal is very likely to disturb dream recall as well as a bed partner. My personal preference is for the writing technique described above. It gives, for me, the most complete recall with the least effort. You may wish to experiment with it. Each dreamer, however, should use the method that is most comfortable and appealing to him or her. *Whatever method you use, record your dreams, preferably with eyes closed, in the order that you recall them.* This practice will enable you to maximize your dream recall.

If you want to try my dream recording technique, the

equipment you choose is important. Select unlined 5″ x 8″ notepads that are sealed with string embedded in the plastic binding. Pages on pads with only a plastic edge break off as the page is turned, rather than remaining firmly attached. It's impossible to write legibly on loose, moving paper. Pads with spiral bindings or thick tops with perforations are bulky and hard to handle. It's better to choose a standard size pad and stick with it, because each change requires accommodation and is confusing. Pencil is too light for sleepy note taking; use a high-quality inexpensive ballpoint pen such as an accountant fine point. Become aware of the feel of writing with the pen with ink flowing. Alert yourself to the draggy, scratchy feel of writing with a pen out of ink. Many pages of notes can be lost in the dark if this escapes you. Keep a second pen within easy reach in case you run out of ink during the night.

If you happen to know shorthand, as I do, you will have to guard against lapsing into it. For several weeks I found my midnight dream entries partially or entirely in shorthand when I awoke, even though I had determined not to use it. Transcribing is too difficult a task to add to deciphering the shaky notes. On a few occasions I found the first entry in longhand and later entries on the same night in greater amounts of shorthand until the last entry was *entirely* in shorthand, although I had no awareness of writing in that form. Extra effort has eliminated the appearance of shorthand.

Another aspect of this technique that requires attention is to be certain you are actually recording on the pad with the pen. When I first evolved this technique I often dreamed I was recording the dream (so there was no necessity to wake to do so). Occasionally, however, I felt certain I was actually recording because I could feel myself writing with what I believed to be the pen on what I believed to be the pad. On rousing further, I discovered I was actually tracing the words with my fingers on my skin. In one case, the thigh of my right leg served as a pad and in another my right cheek. Now, after long use of the method, this does not happen. In fact, my dream state cooperates with the intent to record. For example, at the end of one dream segment, I saw a dark-haired, moustached reporter holding a pen and notepad. He was looking at me and pointing to the right. Turning my head to see what he was pointing at, I opened my eyes and saw my own pad and pen. It was as though the dream image were saying, "It's time to write now." In another dream, a character said, "Now it's time to pause for a commercial." I found myself awake obviously for the purpose of writing. *As you establish a habit for dream recording and work on building dream friends, you will develop a more cooperative dream state.*

I mentioned above the importance of writing down your dreams in the order that you recall them. There is one exception to this rule: Always record a unique verbal expression immediately. If I awaken with a dream poem in mind and I also recall the entire preceding scene, I dare not describe the scene first and then the poem in the order that the images appeared and were recalled. I write the poem itself immediately, then describe the story that led up to it. When I come to the place where the poem originally appeared I often write it again, if possible. Later when I have my eyes open and am fully functional, it is interesting to compare the first recording to the second. Within the few minutes it took to describe the dream scene, several words of the poem may have changed. *When you record a unique verbal expression immediately you have a better chance of preserving it in its original form.* You will find it helpful to follow this practice with unusual phrases, names, or impressive quotations, too. Such dream-concocted expressions as "Scandia Rose," "Engrabble," "Emmanual Styles," and "Wemberly" would have escaped me long before their proper place in the story had I not recorded them first. *Note your unique productions first.* The story will come back with association to other elements in it, the strange dream creations may not.

As I record my dreams during the night and in the morning, I also make note of any unusual occurrences. For example, on rare occasions I may be so tired that I start to fall asleep for a few instants while writing. When I rouse, I note "F.A." (falling asleep) or even "fell asleep," if that's the case. On other rare occasions I may begin to dream again—probably hypnogogic experiences—while recording the just finished dream. When I become aware of this fact, I record "O.D." (overlaid dream) and a description of it in parentheses. Again, the telephone may ring and disrupt recording and recall of the dream. (With four children this can happen even in the middle of the night.) Such a fact is also noted. *Note any unusual happening that may affect your record.*

There is one *common* happening that I often note: The dream imagery that occurs as one drifts off to sleep is technically called hypnogogic visions or hypnogogic experiences. You have perhaps experienced these with a startle response that sometimes occurs at the onset of sleep. Hypnogogic experiences are not usually dream stories but more images or scenes that one is aware of while still semiconscious. One researcher studied this type of imagery extensively. He observed the moment of transition from abstract thought to concrete imagery. The more you become aware of this type of visual thinking, the more you notice its occurrence as you drift off to sleep. In fact, Hervey de Saint-Denys found that it was so frequent he asserted, "There is no sleep without dreams, just as there is no waking state without thought" (my translation). He woke himself completely each time he had a hypnogogic vision in order to capture and record it. I choose to note only one or two of these hypnogogic experiences with "D.O." (drifting off) if the images seem particularly interesting but do not count them as dreams or attempt to keep track of them. They are endlessly available and I prefer to concentrate on the dream state *per se. You may wish to make note of interesting hypnogogic experiences. They, like your dreams, will help you understand your own symbol system.*

There are some aspects of dreams that seem impossible to describe. Most dreamers have experienced changing from one form into another—you turn into a bird and escape, or the cat becomes a pig. Sometimes the setting shifts while you and the action continue—you are inside a house doing something and the area around you becomes a marketplace while you continue just as before. However, other shifts are subtler. Sometimes the texture of a dream is complex beyond ability to express. Everything seems to be happening simultaneously; or there are several levels of dream action, intricate beyond Lawrence Durrell's *Alexandria Quartet,* and all occurring at once; or a story repeats two or three times in different versions. When a dream is impossible to describe, I state what I can of it and add "complex" or "many-layered," as the case may be. *Try to at least identify the elusive elements of your dreams.*

Many people find that telling a dream to a friend helps them to recall it. The very act of putting the dream into words and trying to explain or express it seems to stimulate both recall of the dream and insight into aspects of it. Sometimes, if you "forget" (suppress or repress) the dream, your friend can recall it readily. However, it's tempting not to record a dream once it has been told, so be sure to write it down, too. *Share your dream experiences with a friend, if possible, as well as record them.*

Let us assume that you have collected your dreams in some way in the morning and during the night (or just in the morning). You have written them complete, or in phrases, or taped them. Now you need to give them permanent form to get the most benefit from them.

I take the several pages of wobbly notes that I have collected during the night and morning and copy them over sometime during the day into a standard form with date, location (I often travel), dream description, time of retiring and rising, waking state recall or lack of it, associations to the dreams, and facts of the day preceding the dream. Sometimes I add sketches of unusual images and analyses. These dream record forms, on one side of plastic-reinforced loose-leaf notebook paper, are kept in chronological order, with monthly dividers, in yearbooks. The current collection covering twenty-five years is contained in twelve volumes filling a three-foot bookshelf. There are over 10,000 dreams recorded. The latest are most complete, with approximately 1,000 entries each year. (With the method described above, for example, the 1971 record has 900 entries from 362 nights of dreaming—no sleep on three nights—with a typical month of about 75 dreams and an average of 3.12 dreams each night.) You may not wish to bother with so complete a record. There is much to learn from it if you do. However, if you merely record those dreams you recall in a systematic method where you can examine them, in chronological order, you can gain a great deal of insight. Here is another way written records are, I believe, superior to tapes (unless the tapes are transcribed). You can *see* the changes. You may wish to keep an extensive record for a limited period of time. *Keep a written record of your dreams and you can learn a great deal about yourself.*

In examining my own record and making comparisons I find it helpful to use the suggestion of one of my students to give titles to the individual dreams as though they were stories. Thus, it is much easier to recall a specific dream by the title "Dancing Vegetables" than by date. I choose distinctive elements of the dream for its title. Idiosyncratic elements of a dream are believed to be emerging parts of the dreamer's personality. By selecting one of the unique aspects of a dream for its title, you will not only be increasing your ability to recall it but also will be identifying elements in it which deserve special attention. *Select titles for your dreams from their unique characteristics.*

When you have your dream record in a permanent written form, you can examine it from many points of view. In my permanent record, I have written a description of the dream in the main section of the form. In the right-hand column, I have noted associations to the dream imagery. In this approach to working with dreams, I now make a "translation." I take the dream plot as it appears and substitute my associations to the symbols. For example, my dream as originally recorded may read: "I am with my husband outside at the foot of some hills when an attractive woman with her hair in a long brown braid appears. I see that she is blind. She has come to consult with him, so I leave them alone." Assuming for the moment that all parts of the dream are parts of myself, my "translation," incorporating the associations, would read: "The wise part of me is near some rough terrain (difficulties). The old-fashioned part of me cannot see something. It needs help." Or suppose my record reads: "I am with — (my daughter) in a living room. I want her to help me put out a small fire that has started. I yell at her to get some water. She is unbelievably stubborn and annoying." The "translation," again using my associations, might read: "There is a small problem that needs attention. The childish part of me resists cooperating. I feel angry at myself." I proceed through a dream record sentence by sentence "translating" in this fashion. The resulting document can lead to amazing insights. It is important to incorporate associations of current feelings. My daughter, for example, can represent childishness, vulnerability, betrayal, potential talent, or emerging strength, depending on the relationship of the moment of her current condition. Of course, she may also represent herself. In one dream I was holding on to her at the edge of a ledge. She was about to fall over and I yelled at her to do something. I couldn't support her weight if she didn't help. In this case, the dream image of my daughter represented my conception of *her* and her need to perform in a specific situation rather than a part of me. However, it is always informative to first try a "translation" from the point of view that all dream images are parts of yourself.

Dreams are perhaps the most highly personal expressions you have. No one else can tell you what your dreams mean. *Try translating some of your dreams in their entirety with your current associations to the symbols in them. You can learn much about yourself.*

Some people are able to recall their dreams easily and often (high dream recallers) while other people remember their dreams only rarely and with difficulty (low dream recallers). Researchers have tried to discover why. Are there personality differences between high dream recallers and low dream recallers? Results of current studies are inconclusive. However, researchers seem to agree that, in general, low dream recallers are more likely to repress (keep from conscious awareness) or deny important psychological experiences. Low dream recallers seem to be conformist, self-controlled, and defensive; they are likely to be more confident and less self-aware than habitual high dream recallers. Conversely, high dream recallers tend to be more anxious, less self-confident, yet have more self-understanding.

I have observed, in my many conversations with dreamers around the world, a difference between high and low dream recallers that is striking enough to mention: Females seem to recall dreams more often and more completely than males. Let me emphasize that I did not make a careful study of this; it is purely an impression. There is, however, one study that may support my observation. Researchers collected written dreams from a large sample of schoolchildren. Records of dreams from female students were clearly longer and more complete than those of male students. It may be that this finding is a variation of the usual finding of female superiority on verbal tests. Another possible explanation is that greater female dream recall, if it is found to exist, could be a result of attitudes taught by our culture. It is considered all right for females to be interested in dreams, but men are more practical and work-oriented. The man who must get up and go to work often begins planning his projects for the day while still in bed. Plans calling for assertiveness, competition, and problem solving may be well under way before eyes are open. We noted earlier that distraction immediately following a REM period disrupts recall of the prior dream. The man who is involved in rational thinking from the moment he wakes up is very likely to disrupt dream recall. A less pressured woman with less immediate distractions may have greater recall simply because of leisure to contemplate the night's dreaming. Male-female roles are taught; they are in the process of change. Perhaps life-style plays a more important role in dream recall than sex *per se*. *If you regard your dreams as important and take time to recall them, they will come to you more easily and more often.*

Regardless of your current level of dream recall, you can learn to increase its quantity and enhance its quality. Ordinary dreamers can learn to establish extraordinary dream recall. In one study, researchers found that dreamers who have trained themselves to self-awaken from REM periods can do so with remarkable accuracy. In another study, students learned to substantially increase their dream recall during the first two weeks of keeping a regular dream journal and meeting with a group three hours a week to discuss dreams. When they were given a special task one night to use their dreams to creatively solve a problem there was *four times* as much dream recall as on other nights. Dreamers who were usually low in dream recall showed the most improvement in amount of dream recall. Dreamers who were usually high in dream recall showed more qualitative changes as they intensified efforts to re-call and record their dreams: Their dreams became more detailed, more colored, and they remembered other sensa-tions and emotions more clearly. Many dreamers in this study felt that as their acceptance of dreams increased they felt more accepting of themselves. *As you practice valu-*

ing, recalling, and recording your dreams, you will increase your recall. Your dreams will become more vivid, complete, and relevant to waking life.

I believe that low dream recallers can benefit by increasing their dream recall. By using methods suggested above they can learn to recall and record their dreams on a regular basis. Motivation will increase dream recall. *If you are a low dream recaller, you can learn to increase your dream recall and, with it, reach a greater understanding of yourself.*

High dream recallers can increase color, vividness, and detail of their dreams. By employing creative dream techniques outlined in this book, high dream recallers can reduce anxiety and learn to become more self-confident in waking life. *If you are already a high dream recaller, you can get even more learning from your dreams and at the same time increase skills and confidence.*

Recalling your dreams and then recording them in a permanent form will give you an invaluable document from which you can both contribute to knowledge in general and learn, in depth, more and more about yourself. You can not only learn *about* yourself, but also *from* yourself.

4. How to Interpret Your Dreams

Erich Fromm

ONE OF THE most significant and often most difficult problems in the interpretation of dreams is that of recognizing whether a dream is expressive of an irrational wish and its fulfillment, of a plain fear or anxiety, or of an insight into inner or outer forces and occurrences. Is the dream to be understood as the voice of our lower or our higher self? How do we go about finding out in which key to interpret the dream?

Other questions relevant to the technique of dream interpretation are: Do we need the associations of the dreamer or can we understand the dream without them? Furthermore, what is the relation of the dream to recent events, particularly to the dreamer's experiences on the day before he had a dream, and what is its relationship to the dreamer's total personality, the fears and wishes rooted in his character?

I should like to begin with a simple dream which illustrates the fact that no dream deals with meaningless material:

A young woman, interested in the problems of dream interpretation, tells her husband at the breakfast table: "Tonight I had a dream which shows that there are dreams which have no meaning. The dream

81

was simply that I saw myself serving you strawberries for breakfast.'' The husband laughs and says: ''You only seem to forget that strawberries are the one fruit which I do not eat.''

It is obvious that the dream is far from being meaningless. She offers her husband something she knows he cannot accept and is of no use or pleasure to him. Does this dream indicate that she is a frustrating personality who likes to give the very thing that is not acceptable? Does it show a deep-seated conflict in the marriage of these two people, caused by her character but quite unconscious in her? Or is her dream only the reaction to a disappointment caused by her husband the day before, and an expression of a fleeting anger she got rid of in the revenge contained in the dream? We cannot answer these questions without knowing more about the dreamer and her marriage, but we do know that the dream is not meaningless.

The following dream is more complicated though not really difficult to understand:

A lawyer, twenty-eight years of age, wakes up and remembers the following dream: ''I saw myself riding on a white charger, reviewing a large number of soldiers. They all cheered me wildly.''

This dream is very simple, and for this reason permits us to study the various elements that are significant in the art of dream interpretation. Is this a dream of wish-fulfillment or is it an insight? The answer can hardly be in doubt: this is the fulfillment of an irrational wish for fame and recognition which the dreamer had developed as a reaction to severe blows to his self-confidence. The irrational nature of this wish is indicated by the fact that he does not choose a symbol which in reality could be meaningful and attainable. He is not really interested in military matters, has not made and certainly will not make the slightest effort to become a general. The material is taken from the immature daydreaming of an insecure, adolescent boy.

What role do his associations play in the understanding of this dream? Could we understand it even if we had no associations from the dreamer? The symbols used in the dream are universal symbols. The man on the white charger, cheered by troops, is a universally understood symbol of splendor, power, admiration (universally, of course, in the restricted sense of being common to some cultures but not necessarily to all).

The following dream is an illustration of dreams to be understood in terms of wish-fulfillment. The dreamer, a man, thirty years old, unmarried, suffered for many years from severe attacks of anxiety, an overwhelming sense of guilt, and almost continuous suicidal fantasies. He felt guilty because of what he called his badness, his evil strivings; accused himself of wanting to destroy everything and everybody, of the wish to kill children, and in his fantasies suicide seemed the only way to protect the world from his evil presence and to atone for his badness. There is another aspect of these fantasies, though: after his sacrificial death he would be reborn into an all-powerful, all-loved person, vastly superior in power, wisdom and goodness to all other men. The dream he had was as follows:

I am walking up a mountain; right and left beside the road are the bodies of dead men. None is alive. When I arrive at the top of the mountain, I find my mother sitting there; I am suddenly a very small child and am sitting on my mother's lap.

The dreamer woke from his dream with a feeling of fright. At the time of his dream, he was so tortured by anxiety that he could not associate with a single part of the dream nor discover any specific event of the preceding day. But the meaning of the dream is transparent if we consider the thoughts and fantasies the dreamer presented before the time of this dream. He is the older son, a younger brother having been born a year after him. The father, an authoritarian, strict minister, had little love for the older boy—or for anyone else, for that matter; his only contact with his son was to teach, scold, admonish, ridicule and punish. The child was so afraid of him that he believed his mother when she told him that had it not been for her intervention his father would have killed him. The mother was very different from the father: a pathologically possessive woman, disappointed in her marriage, with no interest in anyone or anything except the possession of her children. But she had fastened herself particularly on this first-born son. She frightened him by telling about dangerous ghosts, then offered herself as his protectress who would pray for him, guide him, make him strong, so that one day he would even be stronger than his dreaded father. When the little brother was born, the boy was apparently profoundly disturbed and jealous. He himself had no memories of that period, but relatives reported unmistakable expressions of intense jealousy shortly after the brother's birth.

This jealousy might not have developed to such dangerous dimensions as it did after two or three years had it not been for the attitude of his father who picked the newborn baby as *his*. Why, we do not know; perhaps because of the striking physical likeness to himself or perhaps because his wife was still so preoccupied with *her* favorite son. By the time our dreamer was four or five years old, the rivalry between the two brothers was already in full swing and it increased from year to year. The antagonism between the parents was reflected and fought out in the antagonism between the two brothers. At that age the foundations of the dreamer's later severe neurosis were laid: intense hostility against the brother, a passionate wish to prove that he was superior to the brother, intense fear of the father, greatly increased by the guilt feeling because of his hate against brother and the hidden wish to be stronger than the father eventually. This feeling of anxiety, guilt and power-lessness was increased by his mother. As already men-tioned, she instilled him with even more fear. But she offered him also an alluring solution: if he remained her baby, possessed by her and with no other interest, she would make him great, superior to the hated rival. This was the basis for his daydreams of greatness as well as for the tie that kept him closely bound to his mother—a state of childish dependency and a refusal to accept his role as a grown-up man.

Against this background the dream is easily understand-able. "He climbs up the hill"—his ambition to be superior to everybody, the goal of his strivings. "There are many male bodies—every one is dead—none is alive." The fulfillment of his wish for elimination of all rivals—since he feels so powerless he can be safe from them only if they are dead. "When he arrives at the top"—when he achieves the goal of his wishes—"he finds his mother there, and he is sitting on her lap"—he is reunited with his mother, her baby, getting her strength and protection. All rivals are done away with—he is alone with her, free, without reason for fear. Yet he wakes with a feeling of terror. The very fulfillment of his irrational wishes is a threat to his rational, grown-up personality, which is striving for health and happiness. The price of the fulfillment of infantile desires is that he remain the baby, helplessly tied to and dependent on his mother, not permitted to think for him-self or to love anyone else. The very fulfillment of his wishes is terrifying.

The two dreams represent the fulfillment of irrational desires, dating back to childhood, the first arousing satis-faction because of the wish's compatibility with adult con-ventional aims (power, prestige), the second arousing anxiety because of its very incompatibility with any kind of adult life. Both dreams speak in universal symbols and can be understood without associations, although, in order to un-derstand fully the significance of each dream, we need to know something about the dreamer's personal history. But then, even if we knew nothing about the dreamers' histories, we would get some idea about their characters from these dreams.

Here are two brief dreams, the text of which is similar and yet the meaning of each is different from that of the other. Both are dreams of a young homosexual. The first dream:

> I see myself with a pistol in my hand. The barrel is strangely elongated.

The second dream:

> I hold a long and heavy stick in my hand. It feels as if I were beating someone—although there is nobody else in the dream.

If we followed Freud's theory, we would assume that both dreams express a homosexual wish, one time the pistol and the other time the stick symbolizing the male genital. When the patient was asked what came to his mind of the events of the preceding days, respectively, he reported two very different occurrences:

In the evening preceding the pistol dream he had seen another young man and had felt an intense sexual urge. Before falling asleep he had indulged in sexual fantasies with this young man as the object.

The discussion of the second dream, approximately two months later, elicited a rather different association. He had been furious with his college professor because he felt he had been treated unfairly. He was too timid to say anything to the professor but had an elaborate daydream of revenge in the period before falling asleep, which period was frequently devoted to daydreaming. Another association that came up in connection with the stick was the memory that a teacher whom he disliked thoroughly when he was ten had once whipped another boy with a stick. He had always been afraid of that teacher, and this very fear had prevented him from giving expression to his rage.

What does the symbol of the stick mean in the second dream? Is the stick also a sexual symbol? Does this dream express a well-hidden homosexual desire, the object of which is the college professor and perhaps, in his childhood, the hated teacher? If we assume that the events of the preceding day and especially the mood of the dreamer just before falling asleep are important clues for the symbolism of the dream, then we shall translate the symbols differently in spite of their apparent similarity.

The first dream followed a day in which the dreamer had homosexual fantasies, and the pistol with the elongated barrel must be assumed to symbolize a penis. It is not accidental, though, that the sexual organ is represented by a weapon. This symbolic equation indicates something important about the psychic forces underlying the dreamer's homosexual cravings. To him sexuality is an expression not of love but of a wish for domination and destruction. The dreamer, for reasons we need not discuss here, had always feared not being adequate as a male. Early guilt feelings because of masturbation, fears that he was thus harming his sexual organs, later fear that his penis was inferior in size to that of other boys, intense jealousy of men—all had combined in a wish for intimacy with men in which he could show his superiority and use his sexual organ as a powerful weapon.

The second dream had a quite different emotional background. There he was angry when falling asleep; he had been inhibited in expressing his anger; he was even inhibited in expressing his anger directly in his sleep by dreaming that he was beating the professor with the stick; he dreamed that he held the stick and had the feeling of beating "someone." The particular choice of the stick as a symbol of anger was determined by the earlier experience with the hated teacher who beat the other boy; the present anger at the professor became blended with the past anger at the schoolteacher. The two dreams are interesting because they exemplify the general principle that similar symbols can have different meanings, and that the right interpretation depends on the state of mind that was predominant before the dreamer fell asleep and hence continued to exercise its influence during sleep.

Here follows a short dream which also represents a fulfillment of an irrational wish and is in extreme contrast to the feelings the dreamer is aware of:

The dreamer is an intelligent young man. He is considered a good, even a brilliant worker. But this external picture is deceptive. He has a constant feeling of uneasiness, feels that he does not do as well as he could (which is true), feels depressed in spite of his apparent success. Particularly troublesome to him is his relationship to his boss, who tends to be somewhat authoritarian although within reasonable limits. The patient oscillates between attitudes of rebelliousness and submission. He often feels that unfair demands are made upon him even when this is not the case; he then tends to sulk or become argumentative; sometimes he makes mistakes unwittingly in the performance of such "forced labor." On the other hand, he is overpolite, close to being submissive to his boss and other persons in authority; quite in contrast to his rebellious attitude, he overadmires his chief and is inordinately happy when praised by him. The constant alternation between these two attitudes causes quite a strain and aggravates the depressed mood. It must be added that the patient, who came from Germany after Hitler's rise, was an ardent anti-Nazi; not just in the conventional sense of an anti-Nazi "opinion" but passionately and intelligently. This political conviction was perhaps freer from doubt than anything else he thought and felt. One can imagine the surprise and shock when one morning he remembered clearly and vividly this dream:

I sat with Hitler, and we had a pleasant and interest-ing conversation. I found him charming and was very proud that he listened with great attention to what I had to say.

When questioned as to what he did say to Hitler, he replied that he had not the faintest memory of the content of the conversation. Unquestionably this dream is the ful-fillment of a wish. What is remarkable about it is that his wish is so utterly alien to his conscious thinking, and that it is presented in the dream in such undisguised form.

Surprising as this dream was for the dreamer at the moment, it is not quite so puzzling to us if we consider the total character structure of the dreamer, even though only based on the few data communicated here. His central problem is that of his attitude toward authority: he exhibits an alternation of rebelliousness and submissive admiration in his daily experience. Hitler stands for the extreme form of irrational authority, and the dream shows us clearly that, in spite of the dreamer's hate against him, the sub-missive side is real and strong. The dream offers us a more adequate appreciation of the strength of submissive tenden-cies than the evaluation of the conscious material permits.

Hitler is a symbol for someone else; he stands for the young man's hated and admired father. In the dream the patient uses, as it were, the convenient Hitler symbol to express feelings which belong not to the present but to the past, not to his existence as a grown-up person but to the incapsulated child in him.

The blend of rebelliousness and submissiveness came into existence and developed in the relationship to the patient's father. But the old attitude still exists and is felt in reference to people with whom the patient comes in contact. *He* is still prone to rebel and to submit; he and not a child in him or "the unconscious" or whatever name we give to a person allegedly *in* him but not *him*. The past is significant—aside from a historical interest—only inasmuch as it is still present, and this is the case with the authority complex of our dreamer.

Dreams are like a microscope through which we look at the hidden occurrences in our soul.

Here is a "crossing the river" dream. The dreamer is an only, spoiled child, a boy. He was pampered by his parents, admired by them as a future genius, everything made easy, and no effort expected—from the breakfast, which his mother brought to his bed in the morning, to the father's talks with teachers, which always ended in the expression of his conviction of the boy's wonderful gifts. Both parents were morbidly afraid of danger for him; he was not permitted to swim, to hike, to play in the street. He wanted to rebel sometimes against the embarrassing restrictions, but why complain when he had all these wonderful things: admiration, affectionate caresses, so many toys that he could throw them away, and almost complete protection from all outer dangers. He actually was a gifted boy, but he had never quite succeeded in standing on his own feet. Instead of mastering things, his aim was to win applause and admiration. Thus he became dependent on others and—afraid.

But the very need for praise and the fear engendered when it was not forthcoming made him furious and even cruel. He had entered analytic treatment because of the uneasiness that was constantly produced by his childish grandiosity, dependence, fear and rage. After six months of analytic work he had the following dream.

I am to cross a river. I look for a bridge, but there is none. I am small, perhaps five or six. I cannot swim. [He actually learned how to swim at eighteen.] Then I see a tall, dark man who makes a sign that he can carry me over in his arms. [The river is only about five feet deep.] I am glad for the moment and let him take me. While he holds me and starts walking, I am suddenly seized by panic. I know that if I don't get away I shall

die. We are already in the river, but I muster all my
courage and jump from the man's arms into the water.
At first I think I'll be drowned. But then I start swim-
ming, and soon reach the other shore. The man has
disappeared.

The preceding day the dreamer had been at a party, and it
had suddenly dawned upon him that all his interests were
directed to the goal of being admired and liked. He had
felt—for the first time—how childish he really was and
that he had to make a decision. Yes, he could go on being
the irresponsible child, or he could accept the painful
transition to maturity. He felt he must not kid himself any
longer that everything was as it should be and mistake his
success in pleasing for real achievement. These thoughts
had quite shaken him, and he had fallen asleep.

The dream is not difficult to understand. Crossing the
river is the decision he must make to cross from the shore
of childhood to that of maturity. But how can he do it if he
thinks himself five or six, when he could not swim? The
man who offers to carry him stands for many persons:
father, teachers, everyone who was ready to carry him—
bribed by his charm and promise. So far the dream symbolizes accurately his inner problem and the way he has
solved it again and again. But now a new factor enters. He
realizes that if he permits himself to be carried again he
will be destroyed. This insight is sharp and clear. He feels
that he has to make a decision, and he jumps into the
water. He is aware that he really can swim (apparently he
is no longer five or six in the dream) and that he can reach
the other shore without help. This again is wish-fulfillment
but, as in the previous dream, it is a vision of his goal as
an adult; it is a keen awareness of the fact that his accus-
tomed method of being carried must lead to ruin; furthermore, he knows that he actually can swim if he only has
the courage to jump.

Needless to say, as the days went by the vision lost its

original clarity. The daytime "noises" suggested that one must not be "extreme," that all was going well, that there was no reason to give up all friendship, that we all need help and that he certainly deserved it, and so on—these and many other reasons which we manufacture in order to befog a clear but uncomfortable insight. After quite some time, though, he was as wise and courageous during the daytime as he had been in the night—and the dream came true.

We often wish things that are rooted in our weakness and compensate for it; we dream of ourselves as famous, all powerful, loved by everybody, etc. But sometimes we dream of wishes which are the anticipation of our most valuable goals. We can see ourselves as dancing or flying; we see the city of light; we experience the happy presence of friends. Even if we are not yet capable in our waking life to experience the joy of the dream, the dream experience shows that we are at least capable of wishing it and seeing it fulfilled in a dream fantasy. Fantasies and dreams are the beginning of many deeds, and nothing would be worse than to discourage or depreciate them. What matters is the kind of fantasy which we have—does it lead us forward or does it hold us back in the chains of unproductiveness?

One type of dream for which we have given no illustration is the nightmare. In Freud's view, the anxiety dream is no exception to the general rule that the latent content of a dream is the fulfillment of an irrational wish. There is, of course, an obvious objection to this view, which will be raised by anyone who ever had a nightmare: If I go through the terrors of hell in a dream and wake up with an almost unbearable fright, does it make any sense to say that this is a wish-fulfillment?

This objection is not nearly so good as it seems on first glance. For one thing, we know of a pathological state in which people are driven to do the very thing that is destructive to them. The masochistic person has a wish—

though an unconscious one—to incur an accident, to be sick, to be humiliated. In the masochistic perversion—where this wish is blended with sex and therefore less dangerous to the person—the masochistic wish is even conscious. Furthermore, we know that suicide can be the result of an overpowering impulse for revenge and destruction, directed against one's own person rather than against someone else. Yet the person driven to a self-destructive or other painful act may, with the other part of his personality, feel genuine and intense fright. This does not alter the fact that the fright is the outcome of his own self-destructive wishes. But a wish may create anxiety, so Freud observes, not only if it is a masochistic or self-destructive impulse. We may wish something but know that the gratification of the wish will make other people hate us and bring about punishment by society. Naturally, the fulfillment of this wish would produce anxiety.

An illustration of this kind of anxiety dream is offered by the following example:

> I have taken an apple from a tree while I am passing an orchard. A big dog comes and jumps at me, I am terribly frightened, and I wake up yelling for help.

All that is necessary for the understanding of the dream is the knowledge that the dreamer had met, the evening before the dream, a married woman to whom he felt greatly attracted. She seemed to be rather encouraging, and he had fallen asleep with fantasies of having an affair with her. We need not be concerned here whether the anxiety he felt in the dream was prompted by his conscience or by the fear of public opinion—the essential fact remains that the anxiety is the result of the gratification of his wish—to eat the stolen apple.

However, although many anxiety dreams can thus be understood as disguised wish-fulfillment, I doubt that this is the case with all or perhaps even most of them. If we

assume dreaming to be any kind of mental activity under
the condition of sleep, why should we not be as genuinely
afraid of danger in our sleep as we are in our waking life?

But, someone may argue, is not all fear conditioned by
our cravings? Would we be afraid if we had no "Thirst,"
as the Buddhists say; if we were not desiring things?
Therefore, may it not be said that, in a general sense,
every anxiety in waking and in dream life is the result of
desires?

This argument is well taken, and if we were to say that
there is no anxiety dream (or no anxiety in waking life)
without the presence of desire, including the fundamental
desire to live, I do not see that any objection could be
made to this statement. But this general principle is not the
one Freud meant with his interpretation. It may clarify the
issue if we talk once more about the difference between
the three kinds of anxiety dreams we have already discussed.

In the masochistic self-destructive nightmare, the wish
is in itself painful and self-destructive. In the second type
of anxiety dream, as the one with the apple, the wish is not
in itself self-destructive, but it is of such a kind that its
fulfillment causes anxiety in another part of the mental
system. The dream is caused by the wish—which as a
by-product generates anxiety. In the third type of anxiety
dream, where one is afraid because of a real or imaged
threat to life, freedom, etc., the dream is caused by the
threat, while the wish to live, to be free, etc., is the
all-present impulse that does not produce that specific
dream. In other words, in the first and second categories
the anxiety is caused by the presence of a wish; in the third
category, by the presence of a danger (real or imagined),
although not without the presence of the wish to live or
any other of the permanent and universal desires. In this
third category the anxiety dream is clearly not the fulfillment of the wish but the fear of its frustration. Dreams that
are particularly interesting and significant are those recurrent dreams which some people report as going on for a

period of years, sometimes as far back as they can recall. These dreams usually are expressive of the main theme, of the *leitmotif,* in a person's life, often the key to the understanding of his neurosis or of the most important aspect of his personality. Sometimes the dream remains unchanged, sometimes there are more or less subtle changes, which are indicative of the inner progress of the dreamer—or of a deterioration, as the case may be.

A girl of fifteen who grew up under the most inhuman and destructive conditions (father who beat her, alcoholic, violent; mother running away periodically with other men; no food, no clothing, dirt) tried to commit suicide at the age of ten, and after that five times more. She has had the following dream many times as long as she can remember:

> I am at the bottom of a pit. I try to climb up and have already reached the top, which I hold with my hands, when someone comes and stamps on my hands. I have to let go and fall back to the bottom of the pit.

The dream hardly needs any explanation; it fully expresses the tragedy of this young girl's life—what happened to her and how she feels. Were this a dream occurring once, we would be entitled to assume that it is expressive of a fear, which the dreamer feels once in a while, stimulated by specific, trying circumstances. As it is, the regular recurrence of the dream makes us assume that the dream situation is the central theme of the girl's life, that the dream expresses a conviction so deep and unalterable that we can understand why she has tried to commit suicide again and again.

A recurrent dream in which the theme remains the same but where there is, nevertheless, a considerable amount of change is one of a series which began with the dream:

> I am in prison—I cannot get out.

Later on the dream was:

> I want to cross the frontier—but I have no passport and am held back at the frontier.

Later still:

> I am in Europe—am at a port to take a boat—but there is no boat, and I don't see how I can leave.

The latest version of this dream was:

> I am in a city—in my home—I want to go out. When I open the door I find it difficult—I give it a hard push—it opens and I walk out.

The theme underlying all these dreams is the fear of being shut in, of being imprisoned, incapable of "getting out." What this fear means in the dreamer's life is of no importance for us in this context. What the series of dreams shows is that throughout the years the fear remained but became less intense—from being in prison to having difficulty in opening the door. While originally the dreamer feels incapable of escaping, in the last dream he can—with a little extra push—open the door and walk out.

5. Common Dream Themes

Ann Faraday, Ph.D

THERE ARE EIGHT common dream themes that crop up time and again in lectures, correspondence, TV and radio shows, and even in casual conversation—namely, falling, flying, nudity, taking an examination, losing teeth, losing valuables, finding valuables, and sex. Statistical surveys have shown them to be among the commonest dream topics in Western civilization, and although there are many others equally common I have chosen these eight themes to illustrate how dream interpretation works. Novices at the dream game who have collected a few recent dreams may be able to make a start at understanding them by following the basic principles laid down here and even old hands and professionals should find some useful hints here, since my own empirical approach does not depend on any theory of dream symbolism, as most schools of dream interpretation have done in the past.

The basic rules of the dream game at this stage are:

1. The dream should always be considered literally in the first instance and examined for signs of objective truth, such as warnings or reminders, before moving on to metaphorical interpretation.

2. If the dream makes no sense when taken literally, then (and only then) should it be seen as a metaphorical

statement of the dreamer's feelings at the time of the dream.

3. All dreams are triggered by something on our minds or in our hearts, so the primary objective must be to relate the dream theme to some event or preoccupation of the previous day or two.

4. The feeling tone of the dream usually gives a clue as to what this particular life situation is. For example, if the feeling tone of the dream is miserable, then the dream was sparked by some miserable situation in the dreamer's current life.

5. Common dream themes like those discussed in this chapter are likely to indicate common areas of human feeling or experience, but within these broad limits each theme can mean quite different things to different dreamers according to the individual's life circumstances at the time of the dream.

6. The same dream theme may recur from time to time in the dreams of the same dreamer and have a different specific meaning each time, according to his life circumstances at the time of each dream.

7. Dreams do not come to tell us what we know already (unless of course, it is something we know but have failed to act upon, in which case they will recur, often in the form of nightmares, until we do), so if a dream seems to be dealing with something you are quite well aware of, look for some other meaning in it.

8. A dream is correctly interpreted when and only when it makes sense to the dreamer in terms of his present life situation and moves him to change his life constructively.

9. A dream is incorrectly interpreted if the interpretation leaves the dreamer unmoved and disappointed. Dreams come to expand, not to diminish us.

The following examples of common dream themes aim to show how to put these principles into practice in understanding your own dreams, by giving the feel of how dreams work without forcing any particular interpretations.

My discussion by no means exhausts the host of possible alternate interpretations you may find to your own dreams —in fact, the point is to stimulate you to look for your own meanings in the dreams you have collected, in the light of your own current life experience.

DREAMS OF FALLING

The first step is to see whether or not the dream contains some kind of warning of a possible literal fall in your life because of something you have been neglecting or have failed to register consciously during the previous day or two. For example, when I dreamed of falling off the balcony of our new seventh-story apartment, I immediately examined the guardrails on waking and found them distinctly rickety. This information had obviously registered at the back of my head the previous day, but I had been too preoccupied to take conscious note of the potentially dangerous situation. The same rule applies when we dream of someone else falling. For example, our neighbor dreamed that his son fell off a ladder, and having talked with us about taking dreams literally in the first instance, he examined their ladder and discovered a loose rung. Once again, the watchdog of the psyche helped prevent a nasty accident.

However, if a falling dream carries no literal warning message of this kind, the next step is to ask what kind of metaphorical "fall" the dreamer could currently be concerned about. Looking through my dream collection, I find the following examples: a colleague who dreamed of falling down the college stairs at a time when he feared demotion on account of poor work, reflecting his fear of loss of status; a schoolboy who dreamed of falling down the school stairs the night after he presented his parents with a poor report card, reflecting his feeling that he would now fall in their estimation; the wife of a radio station director who reported a series of falling dreams soon after her husband had been promoted, reflecting her feeling that she could not keep *up* with him; a teenage girl of a Catholic background who related a series of very unpleasant falling dreams soon after she started sleeping with her boyfriend, reflecting deep guilt feelings about her "fall from grace and virtue" in the eyes of God.

In all these dreams, the falls were experienced as unpleasant, but this is not always the case, in which event the dream is showing that some "fall" we have experienced, or are anticipating in waking life, is seen by our hearts as less fearsome than perhaps we think, or maybe even downright pleasant. For example, when I appeared on the TV program *To Tell the Truth,* Peggy Cass, the actress, related a dream she had some years previously in which she fell from the top of the Empire State Building onto a beautiful soft bed of pine needles. Having ascertained that the falling sensation was pleasurable, and bearing in mind that she landed on a *bed,* I suggested that she saw herself as a "fallen woman." Amid the laughter, she was heard to protest, "Not any more . . ." This dream disposes of the widespread myth that you will die if you hit the bottom in a falling dream; the whole idea is nonsense, for quite apart from the fact that thousands of people who have hit bottom in a dream, including Peggy and myself, are still alive and well, how can we ask those who died in bed whether or not they had a falling dream at the time of death?

DREAMS OF FLYING

Since dreams of flying under one's own power cannot have any literal significance (except perhaps for astronauts), we have to look for their meaning by converting the picture into an idea or thought—that is, they express the dreamer's feeling of being "high" or "on top of the world" in his life at the present time, or perhaps his struggle to "rise above" circumstances or avoid restrictions. Once again, the feeling tone—elation or anxiety—gives the clue to how you really feel about these events in your life. For example, Johnny Carson, host of the *Tonight* show, often dreams of flying and performing acrobatics in the air after a good day in the studio. He thoroughly enjoys these dreams, which indicates that he really "gets a lift" out of showing off his verbal acrobatic skill. And I myself flew for days in my dreams after the publication of *Dream Power,* which came as quite a revelation as to how very delighted I felt to become an author.

Some years ago, I experienced a series of flying dreams in which I was trying to escape from a threatening situation. I was pursued by an enormous green, shapeless monster, and I would usually awaken in terror as the thing enveloped me. The dreams occurred at a time in my life when I was battling jealous feelings about my first husband, so I had no difficulty in identifying the "green-eyed monster" of my nightmares, and the message was clear. Whereas my head was quite convinced that I had these feelings under control, the thoughts of my heart showed quite clearly that my efforts to "rise above" them had failed and that I was still "consumed" with jealousy. The dreams continued, with variations according to the events of the previous day, until I faced the unpleasant truth that I was not as uninvolved as I believed and discussed the subject openly with my husband. Only then was I able to get myself together and view the situation rationally.

The height to which you fly in dreams is important, as well as the feeling tone. Jimmy Dean, the comedian, told me a dream in which he was flying along at medium height, having discovered that he felt distinctly anxious if he ventured higher. When I asked how he felt about "flying high" in his life, he replied, "Funny you should ask that. I've just been offered my own show on Broadway but turned it down because I didn't feel quite *up* to it." His heart and head were obviously together on the subject of ambition.

Psychoanalysts tend to reduce all pleasant flying dreams to sexual desire, but this is at best a gross overgeneralization and can be a put-down of one of the most extraordinary phenomena of dreams. My research has shown that when flying dreams have erotic overtones they are usually forerunners of an out-of-the-body experience. I have found that very often a flying dream is initiated by sexual energy circulating in the region of the lumbar plexus at the base of the spine or around the sexual organs. If the energy manages to flow up the spine to the top of the head, the dreamer takes off into flight which culminates in an out-of-the-body experience. If the energy remains blocked in the low-back or genital region, then the dreamer finds himself indulging in an ordinary sex dream of his own making. I find this a fascinating discovery, since yogis have for centuries used such disciplines as yoga and meditation to raise the "serpent power," or kundalini as it is called, from the base of the spine right up to the highest energy center, or chakra, situated at the top of the head, where it can be used for all kinds of higher spiritual activities.

DREAMS OF NUDITY

It is very widely believed that dreams of being naked or scantily clad in public are indications of sexual feelings or guilt about sex, but the truth is that in most cases such dreams have no reference to sex at all, and even those that do often have only an incidental concern with it. In the first place, such dreams can be literal warnings of something wrong with your clothes—and if you dream of finding yourself naked at the airport, do check that you have packed your pants for tomorrow's journey! If all is well at this level, then you must ask in what way you feel naked, revealed, vulnerable, exposed, or open in your life at the present time.

A university lecturer I know has a recurring dream in which he is walking through the college grounds or reading in the library, when he suddenly senses all eyes upon him. Looking down, he discovers to his dismay that he is naked or clad only in shoes and socks. As the dream takes place at college, it obviously refers to some aspect of his work, and he is able to relate it to the fact that he blatantly uses other people's ideas to advance himself, a habit he consciously considers rather clever. The dream, however, which usually occurs soon after he has published a paper, expresses his heart's fears that this time he is sure to be found out and "exposed" as a fraud—and the dream will no doubt recur until he gets head and heart together on this issue.

Sara, a research subject, reported a similar kind of "exposure" dream, but for her this was an isolated occurrence and not a recurring theme, for the simple reason that she did not live in almost constant fear of exposure, as did the lecturer. After meeting us at a dream group in Pennsylvania, she asked us to let her know when we were coming north again so that she could arrange a private group session. We arrived in Baltimore unexpectedly, and Sara offered to arrange a small group at very short notice. That night she dreamed she was standing naked in a hospital room, when the door was flung open and a procession of people led by a guide filed through the room on a tour of the hospital. Taken by surprise, Sara tried to hide her nakedness by running to her bed, stopping to pick up a small piece of paper lying on the floor as she did so, and complaining bitterly to the guide of the unannounced invasion of privacy. The dream showed in beautiful picture language Sara's ambivalence about our unexpected arrival. While she was consciously delighted to have the chance to work with dreams, her heart was angry, for she would now be exposed as the fraud she felt herself to be—she had not been writing down her dreams as she had promised at our last meeting, and the most she could hope for now was to pick up one small dream (the piece of paper) before the weekend. The knowledge of her heart's thoughts put her in touch with her anger, which if left unrecognized might have sabotaged or spoiled the weekend for all of us.

Young men often ask me what it means to dream of being without trousers in public, and questioning usually reveals a concern with convincing the world of one's sexual prowess when underneath there lurks a fear of being exposed as sexually inadequate. A member of one of our dream study groups dreamed of seeing her teacher in the nude and being struck by his tiny penis. Her conscious mind admired him but the dream revealed her heart's feeling that underneath he was not much of a man.

Feeling tone is particularly important in getting to the meaning of nudity dreams. For example, one of our young college students dreamed that he disrobed in front of a cheering crowd of college friends. Here there was a reference to sex in that he had just experienced his first sexual intercourse with a girl, but even so this was only incidental to the dream's meaning, which was that he had managed to "shed" his moral prohibitions and felt delighted about it. Had the onlookers in the dream been disapproving, this would have indicated guilt feelings, for in the objective world, his fellow students would certainly have approved. On the same principle, a dream in which you find yourself embarrassingly exposed but no one takes the slightest notice, is a message from your heart that some disclosure you are consciously very concerned about is really nothing extraordinary.

Honesty, openness, and vulnerability are often symbolized in dreams by nudity. I recently fell asleep debating whether or not my small daughter was telling the truth about something and dreamed of her standing in front of me quite naked. The dream corroborated my conscious feeling that she had told the truth, and my heart was confirming my hunch about her honesty. By this, I am not implying that the heart is necessarily always correct: I am simply saying that in this case it had not picked up contrary vibes during the course of our encounter. As a general rule, however, I have found that when head and heart agree on any issue, there is a good chance of their being correct, whereas if they disagree you had better start asking questions.

EXAMINATION DREAMS

The commonest type of examination dream is one in which we sit down at a desk, look at the paper, and realize to our horror that we cannot answer a single question. Less frequent are the dreams in which we feel we have passed the examination successfully. The first question to ask on waking from an examination dream is whether or not there really is an impending examination or test confronting us in the near future, for if there is, then the dream is a clear warning to do more study or survey the situation more carefully. This can be very useful if we consciously feel quite confident of our chances.

The majority of examination dreams, however, are metaphorical, expressing our heart's thoughts that we are "under examination" or being "put to the test" on some issue in our present life, usually with the fear that we shall not make the grade. It is not at all surprising that such dreams recur time and again in the lives of most people in our society, for we are taught from the cradle to view life as "one big test" in everything from getting our parents' approval, to passing real tests and examinations throughout our schooldays and beyond, to making the grade in a competitive adult society, and living up to our own inner ideals. So it is not enough to say that a particular examination dream shows the dreamer feeling tested in his life generally: he would be very unusual if he did not. It is essential to relate the dream to specific circumstances, for this will enable him to see in what particular area of life he feels strained and hopefully point the way toward some constructive solution.

For example, I recently dreamed of passing a history examination and failing an English test on linguistics. As I was totally absorbed in writing this book at the time, I had no difficulty in relating the history examination to my review of the history of dream research in *Dream Power,* and the linguistics test to the next chapter, on puns, slang, and metaphor. My heart was warning me in no uncertain terms that while I had done a good job on the former, there was quite a bit to be desired on the latter, so I called a professor of English to check out my facts. I was exceedingly grateful to my dream, for I had been inexact on several points. So while it would be perfectly true to say that I feel myself under examination on this book—hardly surprising when one bears the reviewers and critics in mind—such a general interpretation would never have inspired me to "pass" the specific linguistics test, which was the purpose of the dream.

On the evening prior to giving a lecture on dreams last year, I dreamed that I walked into an examination hall to take a biology examination. It suddenly occurred to me that I hadn't done any biology for years and would probably fail the test. So, with an unusual spurt of dream confidence, I confronted the biology instructor and said, "I will look at the questions, but if I can't answer them I shall leave." The significance of this dream did not dawn on me until the start of my lecture when a woman biologist interrupted with what I considered irrelevant questions about the biology of the dreaming process. Realizing that my dream was a specific warning on this issue (we had already been in conference for two days, so my heart had time to pick up subliminal vibes from the other participants), I at once told the dream to the group, adding that I would answer any questions if I could but reserved the right to leave them if I could not. My dream saved much time and energy that day, and I felt really good about my newfound firmness and boldness in dealing with my "examiners."

To religious people, examination dreams often reflect their feelings of failing or "passing the test" in their spiritual growth, and this is probably what lies at the back of the widespread belief that dreams of being unprepared for an examination indicate the dreamer's unpreparedness for death and the "final judgment." I regard this whole way of thinking as thoroughly unhealthy, indicating that religion has been overtaken by the very disease it is meant to cure. True spiritual progress involves learning to sit lightly to the world's demands for competition and becoming as unconcerned with working for approval as the lilies of the field. On this basis, the best indicator of spiritual growth would be a reduction in the number of examination dreams we experience, not whether we pass or fail them.

DREAMS OF LOSING TEETH

If you dream of losing your teeth, check your mouth carefully first to discover whether or not your teeth really need attention. So often in its replay of the day's events in depth, the dreaming mind throws up subliminal perceptions of wobbly or decaying teeth, or of developing abscesses which we have been too preoccupied to notice or which may even be too subtle to be consciously registered by the waking mind. I take such dreams very seriously as literal warnings, for I have more than once been saved serious embarrassment by doing so.

If, however, your teeth are in good order, then you must ask yourself what feeling your dream is expressing, and this will depend on what teeth mean to you. My own loss-of-teeth dreams almost always reflect my feeling that I have "lost face" or "spoiled my self-image" in some way during the day, usually by giving in to emotions of fear or weakness. To call this "castration anxiety" (fear of losing one's masculinity, or in the case of a woman, her pseudo-masculinity), as the Freudians do, is beside the point, for many other people have loss-of-teeth dreams when they have spoiled their very feminine, passive, nurturing self-image.

To Edgar Cayce a dream of losing teeth meant loose or careless speech, a dream of false teeth signified falsehood, and a dream of infected teeth referred to foul language. But this cannot be taken as a universal rule, any more than the Freudian interpretation. To many people, teeth symbolize aggression, while to Stephen Dedalus, hero of James Joyce's novel *Ulysses,* they stand for decisiveness, and in the novel's dream sequences his loss of teeth symbolizes his loss of the power of decisive action. I have also come across cases where dreams of losing teeth symbolize "growing up" in the sense of maturing to a new stage of life, presumably based on the dreamer's memory of milk teeth falling out in childhood.

So if you dream of losing teeth without real dental trouble, then ask yourself what your teeth mean to you—potency, aggression, appearance (self-image), decisiveness, or whatever—and then try to discover what it is in your current life that is making you feel "toothless."

DREAMS OF LOSING MONEY AND VALUABLES

If you dream of losing your wallet, money, or other valuables, always check the next morning to make sure that you still have them. You may have lost something the previous day without consciously realizing the fact, in which case your dreaming mind is throwing up your subliminal perception in drama form to warn you to take action before it is too late. I dreamed one night of losing my wallet, and the following day discovered that it was in fact missing. I had been on the nearby beach the previous evening, so I immediately searched in that area and found it. Had I not recalled the dream, I should probably not have discovered the loss for several days, by which time it would have been too late.

Another down-to-earth possibility is that such dreams are warnings of likely future loss or theft. A friend of mine dreamed of losing her wallet, but found it safely inside her handbag the following morning. In looking for it, however, she noticed that her handbag was coming apart at the seams and realized that her dream was warning her to repair it before actual loss occurred. She had evidently noticed the tear in the bag without consciously registering the fact.

If, however, you have neither lost, nor are in any danger of losing money, valuables, or possessions, and you dream of doing so, then you should ask yourself what *values* you feel you may be losing in your life. A student who participated in my original research experiment on dream recall in Britain presented me with a dream of losing the rose from her ring. The ring was a treasured possession and she was greatly relieved on waking to find it still intact. Knowing something of Freud, she herself interpreted the dream as a fear of losing her virginity (deflowering), and related it to the fact that she was thinking of moving in with a boyfriend. On further discussion the following morning, however, it emerged that it was not so much the actual loss of physical virginity that worried her, as the sense that student life was making her lose the cherished values of her family upbringing.

In another case, an ex–Miss America told a recurring dream of running across a busy street, dropping her wallet, and dashing back to the curb to retrieve it. While we had no time to discuss the dream in depth, my guess was that she felt herself to be in the process of transition (crossing the street) from unknown girl to celebrity more quickly than she anticipated, and in her hurry to reach stardom felt herself to be in danger of dropping some of her values. These need not necessarily be sexual values: a sudden transition to prominence can threaten the domestic values of home life, moral values on account of the scheming that often seems necessary in a public career, or even spiritual values such as warmth and sensitivity. However, this dream has a happy ending, for it shows her running back to the curb and retrieving the wallet, which suggests that she feels able to "curb" herself in time to save the values in question.

It is important to remember that a feared loss of values may not necessarily be something to be avoided: often old values have to be lost so that we may grow by finding new and deeper ones. In a series of dreams that changed my life I dreamed successively of losing my wallet, handbag, money, books, clothes, and home, and while in every dream I was initially heartbroken about the loss, I found myself reflecting in the dream itself that it was not the end of the world, since I had ample resources to cope with life independently of these things. These dreams marked my slowly growing recognition—arrived at mainly from my work with dreams in my own personal life—that I am not dependent for my essential identity on playing any role, whether that of careful financial manager (as my mother had urged me to be), householder (my father's ideal), author, psychologist, or public figure. This discovery of the essential core of inner selfhood is obviously closely related to what the world's great spiritual disciplines describe as "detachment"—detachment from social roles in favor of a deeper reality which might be called the divine essence—but in my case, this initial realization came not from sitting at the feet of any guru, but from the "guru within" who speaks to us every night in dreams if we take the trouble to listen to him.

DREAMS OF FINDING MONEY AND VALUABLES

Finding money seems to be a major theme of the great American dream, for practically every time I took part in an American TV or radio show, at least one member of the studio staff asked me about a dream of finding money. As they were all invariably short of cash at the time of the dream, they feared it might be mere wish fulfillment, but I assured them that there was usually a lot more to it than that. For example, how much money did they find? Where did they find it? And what did they do with it?

One producer related a dream of finding a pile of gold coins beneath the foundations of a house he was thinking of buying. As there was not much likelihood of real buried treasure, I asked him about the house. "Well, it seems rather expensive at the moment," he said, "especially as we are short of cash and my wife says we can't possibly afford it. I've been trying to tell her that it will rise in value over the years. . . ." His wife and colleagues were inclined to dismiss the dream as wish fulfillment designed to prove his own point, but when we explained that his heart may possibly have picked up vibes about the place, this resonated immediately with his inner conviction that the house's situation would make it a "veritable gold mine" in years to come when waterfront property became scarce. His feeling may, of course, turn out to be mistaken, but this is true of any financial venture; the dream assured him, however, that his heart agreed with his head, which in my experience is sufficient reassurance for following through a particular hunch.

If there is no prospect of literal financial gain facing you, then a dream of finding money or valuables may reflect an inner feeling of your own "value" or "worth" as a person. A ten-year-old girl I know has a recurrent dream of being operated on, but instead of the surgeon's finding some disease, he always finds a precious stone in her body. We traced the last dream of this kind back to a family row in which her mother called her a monster and "rotten at the core," which we gathered was a fairly common accusation. It was obvious that her heart was protesting against this judgment, reflecting her very healthy feeling that she is intrinsically good, despite all outward appearances to the contrary.

The same applies if a dream of finding money or valuables occurs at a time when the dreamer's external life is going through a bad patch. Such a dream is a reassurance from the depths of the psyche that there are "inner riches" and resources in the personality which will insure that any impoverished condition will soon be overcome. In corroboration of this point of view I received this morning a letter from Australia in which a young woman described the anxiety and loneliness she felt on separating from her husband. These feelings were reflected in recurrent dreams of falling from a boat into deep water and waking in fright. She wrote that, in the final dream of the series, "I was on a boat again. This time I was not alone. Lots of people were falling overboard and while I saw them sink down deeply into the water, they did come up again. Then I fell, but instead of waking in fright, I landed safely and found myself happily picking up silver coins! I woke up feeling sure that the level of anxiety about loneliness, which I now recognize as pathological, was cured and that I will not experience it again, even though the outer circumstances of my life may not change."

In all the above examples the dreamers were delighted with the discovered treasure and accepted it gladly, but this is not everyone's attitude to a dream windfall. Often the dreamer feels he has no right to what he has found, or at least not to all of it, and he determines to hand it over to the authorities. Dreams of this kind have nothing to do with the ethics of real treasure discovery: they reflect a psychological problem of self-deprecation, a feeling that one's own worth is so low that any kind of good fortune must be rejected. Such dreams are important warnings of an unhealthy attitude which could lead us to sabotage our own successes.

SEX DREAMS

I am using the term "sex dreams" with its simple meaning here, to denote dreams depicting overt sexual activity or explicit sexual feelings. The fact that some apparently nonsexual dreams turn out to be symbolic representations of sex (poking a cow with a gun, or turning a key in a lock, to take just two commonly cited examples) is a different question altogether, and shows you how you feel about sex in your life (in the above cases, as an aggressive act toward someone you see as a "cow," or as the unlocking of new possibilities and opening up of a relationship).

Popular thinking about overt sex dreams has suffered from the Freudian belief that dreams are wish fulfillments—witness the myth that virile men are always dreaming of having Raquel Welch on a tropical beach. The truth is that we do not dream randomly about sex any more than about other subjects. In fact, sex is like any other dream theme—it has a literal meaning if it reveals something about your actual sex feelings toward real people in your life at the time of the dream, but otherwise has to be understood as a metaphor for being "excited," "worked up," "turned on," "intimately involved," "frustrated," "deflated," or "intruded upon," and may refer to a cause you are "embracing," an idea you are "getting close to," or the "coming together" of two aspects of your personality. In these cases the metaphor does not tell you how you see sex, but how much libido you have invested in something in your life.

If your dream shows you being sexually involved with someone in your present life toward whom you have no conscious feelings of attraction, then it is almost certainly a straight warning dream. This is an area where society has benefited enormously from the Freudian revolution, which has made it possible for us to recognize that everyone has sexual feelings about other people all the time, including those of the same sex, children, and blood relatives. Such feelings and the fantasies that go with them are a normal part of life and do not in the least imply that the person who has them is sick or is a lascivious monster whose "real" desire is to break out into promiscuous or incestuous behavior. It is when we thrust such feelings and fantasies right out of conscious awareness that they become dangerous, by building up tension which can drive us to do things we have no true wish to do at all—and sex dreams often come to alert us to this danger.

A woman asked the meaning of her recurrent dreams of having sex with her next-door neighbor, which disturbed her because she was happily married. Having ascertained that the neighbor was reasonably attractive, I told her the dream meant simply that he turned her on sexually, whereupon she exclaimed in horror, "But I love my husband!" She seemed very relieved to learn that there need be no contradiction between loving a partner and enjoying sexual fantasies about others. I advised her to view the whole thing with a sense of humor, enjoy the dreams, and if possible tell her husband, who might be similarly worried by his own sexual fantasies. The most important thing in cases like this, however, is to become aware of one's own feelings, thereby avoiding the danger of the repressed impulses seeking expression in some devious way, perhaps by outbursts of anger against one's partner or by "accidentally" finding oneself in some compromising situation with the dream lover in waking life.

If you find yourself enjoying sex in a dream in circumstances your waking mind finds shocking, this is a sure sign that you are imposing a life-style on yourself which is at variance with your natural feelings in some way, and your dream is a warning to change it. In many cases the change needed is nothing more than a better sense of proportion about sex which will make you less uptight, and this can often be achieved by becoming aware of the fact that many of the ideas we accept as gospel truth are no more than outmoded and distorted opinions derived from parents, teachers, clergymen, and authority figures of the past. It is perfectly normal to have sexual feelings toward almost anybody, including members of our own family, and the mother who becomes aware of sexual feelings toward her child is in far less danger of becoming a Mrs. Portnoy than one who would ''never dream of having such nasty thoughts.'' Similarly, the girl who is aware of being attracted to her father or brother runs far less risk of expecting boyfriends to be like him than if she were unconscious of her feelings. Many women in our society are shocked to dream of themselves as prostitutes until they understand that this is the heart's view of the way they have been trained from birth to give or withhold sexual favors in return for goods received. This very salutary discovery can bring about a much healthier life-style.

If your dream shows you sexually involved with someone who is not part of your present life, it must be using sex as a metaphor, and this is equally true whether it be a Raquel Welch–type dream or an incest dream of a parent or sibling no longer in direct contact with you. The first point to note in such dreams is what the sexual experience felt like, since this will help you identify the event of the day to which the dream refers. For example, a woman in one of our groups had a vivid dream of her long-dead mother raping her painfully with an enormous, bonelike penis, and said she felt furious at the sense of violent intrusion. Instead of trying to interpret this in terms of some trans-sexual Oedipus complex or similar psychoanalytic notion, we asked her whether she had felt the presence of her mother intruding on her during the course of the day. She resonated at once to this, recalling that she had been playing happily and noisily with her children when she had suddenly felt compelled to stop the game, calm them down, and tidy up the room. Her heart interpreted this experience as being ''raped,'' ''taken by force,'' and ''penetrated'' by her mother's strict views on child upbringing, and she realized how necessary it was to free herself from this piece of outmoded conditioning.

On the other hand, when I dreamed of making passionate love to a famous older man, the experience was unquestionably a pleasant one, but as he was not in my life at the time, the dream had to have a metaphorical meaning. (When we told him the dream later, his comment was, "But, of course—at my age it couldn't be otherwise!") Since he stands in my mind for very traditional Establishment attitudes and is also a frequent public performer, I was readily able to relate the dream to the good feeling I had the day before when I was well received (to my surprise) in a symposium where most of the other participants were rather traditional and uptight in their views. My heart was telling me that I was more "excited" than I realized by this "coming together," as I had feared they would reject some of my more way-out ideas. Similarly, when Sara dreamed of being in bed with a young black civil rights leader whom she had met only once in her life long ago, and of being frustrated because they never got to intercourse, she was able to relate this to her growing feeling of "dissatisfaction" with her job in a civil rights organization, which was concerned with housing low-income families.

Sara provided another example of a metaphorical sex dream which is one of the best in my collection. In the dream she was lying on the floor with a stranger whose name she knew to be Hal, kissing and embracing, and very pleasantly engaged in foreplay. To her horror, she noticed that the walls were made of glass and hundreds of faces were watching them. She was too excited to stop but became frustrated because Hal seemed to be satisfied with merely rubbing his penis between her legs. She tried to help him, but he did not respond. In the end, he got up and walked off down the hall seeming very satisfied. Sara was left bewildered and frustrated by the whole experience, yet inexplicably felt she ought to thank him for the good time!

Sara called me because she could make nothing of this dream. Her only association was that Hal was the name of an impotent church friend, but he was not the man in the dream and she had not seen him for months. When I asked what had happened the previous day, she said that the legal suit she had brought against her organization for nonpayment of expenses had been settled very satisfactorily out of court, and everyone—her lawyer, parents, and church friends—was delighted because this meant that Sara was absolved and the organization admitted its responsibility. When I asked Sara for her own feelings, she said that she was happy too, though it had come as something of an anticlimax. "Like making love with Hal in a public place?" I asked, and we both laughed as the meaning of the dream became clear. Sara had, in fact, been getting very "excited" and "worked up" by the coming case, as she saw it as an opportunity to get her own back on the organization she felt had so mistreated her. She had a great deal of anger to come out, and although she was glad to get the money and be vindicated, she felt somehow "deflated," "let down," "unsatisfied," and deprived of her "orgasm." She was then able to identify Hal as a symbol of her lawyer (who also belonged to the church), revealing her heart's feeling that he had acted like an impotent man in allowing his love of peace to settle out of court and avoid an "un-Christian" conflict, when her need was not just to get the money but to discharge all her pent-up anger. Of course, she had thanked the lawyer after the settlement, but her heart had been fuming with frustration at the "anticlimax" of the whole "affair."

On the night after Sara and I had worked this out I had a vivid short dream of delightful sex with a young student who had been one of my subjects many years ago when I was doing experimental dream research with the EEG machine. A random sex dream? Not at all. It showed that I had been very excited and turned on by the resolution of Sara's dream—or, in the dream's language, I had felt very "sexy" about "my subject," namely dream interpretation. I then recalled how John's business colleagues would often

talk of getting a sexual kick out of some new deal or
scheme, how journalists often referred to feeling sexy
about new ideas for an article, and how Janis Joplin said
that when she performed with a rock band "it was better
than it had been with any man!"

A strict Freudian would probably say that this shows
that all our creative activities are sublimated sex, but I find
it more meaningful and less down-putting to say that all
our energies have an erotic character; the drive toward
reproductive sex is just one of many possible manifestations of the basic life-urge to "pour ourselves into," or
"embrace," or "take into ourselves" whatever excites us
throughout the fibers of our being. Our ordinary waking
consciousness represses most of these erotic feelings, but it
is well known that under the influence of psychedelic
drugs, when the brain's information processing is greatly
speeded up, people can become conscious of relating to
the entire environment in this way, with an experience of
superorgasm whenever life-energy is able to flow freely. I
believe this is why mystics have so often used erotic
language to describe their experiences of total oneness
with reality. It is possible that dreams are able to reveal
this aspect of experience to us because they also involve
the speeding up of the brain's information processing,
which would explain the fact that the sex organs become
excited during REM periods irrespective of dream content.
And when our dreams use sex as a metaphor, they tell us
just how much libido we have tied up in any particular
event in our lives and what experiences set the life-energy
flowing for us.

6. Finding Omens in Dreams

Robert Wayne Pelton

DREAMS AND THE need to uncover their hidden meanings are as ancient as humanity. This desire to discern the unknown is even found among the most primitive peoples on earth. Dream interpretation is interwoven with native religion, a powerful force that is heavily blended with witchcraft and occultism.

Dreams have always been highly regarded in every society. Such is revealed by early writings. Positions of authority were held by prophets and diviners of dreams. Their influence was unmatched in all state business and in the area of religion.

The bible is filled with a multitude of excellent dream prophecies—both in the Old and the New Testaments.

Some authorities claim that the Book of Daniel was written from a dream. The Book of Daniel contains a number of prophetic dreams which were fulfilled to the letter. The insanity of Nebuchadnezzar and his downfall were presaged. So was the eventual overthrow of the despotic Belshazzar.

Dreams play a major role as warnings throughout the New Testament. The Holy Family was advised in a dream to go into Egypt. Pontius Pilate's wife warned him after she had a vivid dream at the time of the crucifixion:

"Have thou nothing to do with that just man: for I have suffered many things this day in a dream because of him!"

Many kings and queens have been given warnings of impending danger through a dream. Ceasar, on the night before he was murdered, continually had the same dream. He saw himself "soaring above the clouds on wings." Caesar's wife also tried to warn him of the impending danger. She, too, had experienced a terrible dream the evening prior to his assassination.

The Emperor Marcian dreamed that he saw the bow of the Hunnish conqueror break. This took place on the same night Attila met his death.

Many strange and wonderful revelations come to us through a dream. Marriage, divorce, a broken engagement, financial losses, sickness, and even death have been foretold with remarkable accuracy through the interpretation of a dream. Many inventions as well as fortunes have had their beginnings in a dream.

Dreams, however, are not always crystal clear. They are quite often symbolic. A dream appearing to be insignificant may contain many omens of good fortune. These should inspire the dreamer to try something new or to push ahead with former plans. Any dire warnings, if considered seriously, could turn out to be invaluable—as proper preparation may help to win out in the final analysis.

The numerous sensations felt by the dreamer when they accompany various dream symbols should be carefully recorded. These include such things as danger, sensuality, nervousness, fear, pleasure, discomfort. Any sounds or noises heard in a dream can have unique psychic meanings. The same is true of any words the dreamer reads, hears, or speaks.

If many different objects appear in a particular dream, the prevailing aspect of them, aside from the state of the weather or physical feelings, is interpreted. The most outstanding items are to be initially examined. Nothing in the dream should be omitted, even when it may seem to be relatively minor. Even an insignificant person or thing may be the solution to what at first appears confusing or contradictory.

To help you find the prophecies in your dreams we have culled the records of the ancients to reveal the dream symbols that have appeared over and over again throughout the ages. They form a catalog of omens—good and evil.

The dreamer, for example, must be ever alert for the presence of impending danger or evil when he or she dreams about a vine that bears no fruit strangling a tree or other plant.

When a dream concerns a tree being chopped or sawed down, it is a prediction of success unless the particular tree happens to carry an unfavorable connotation. Cutting down a tree presaging something good indicates misfortune for the dreamer. Problems will arise because of stupid activities, bad decisions, and so forth. But when the felled tree is a bad omen to begin with, a change of luck for the better will quickly take place. If you dream of falling out of a tree, it is a sign of losing a job, monetary losses, or a decrease in social standing in the community.

Dreaming of a fertile, well-kept orchard is a fortunate sign. If the trees are blossoming, great luck is in store for lovers; and families will experience more stability and bliss. If the trees in the orchard are bearing ripe fruit, it represents gain in every area of life. If the fruit is green, new opportunities are available for the dreamer. If the fruit is small and scarce, success will be less than expected.

Finding yourself in the woods presages a great deal of money for those who do not believe that they are lost. Becoming lost in the woods denotes an abundance of unexpected obstacles in the way of success. Hard times can be expected if the woods appear to have been recently burned.

Just before the famous battle of Waterloo, Napoleon dreamed that two black cats were running back and forth between the opposing armies. One of the cats, his, was finally shredded to ribbons. Napoleon, aware of the deadly omen, suffered a humiliating disaster and lost the battle the very next day.

If a dream concerns an animal that appears to be fat and healthy, it adds much force to the meaning of that particular omen. By the same token, a lean or sickly animal represents a lessening of the influence. When an animal is seen to be starving or in poor health, and this can be changed through better care and feeding, it shows that the adverse sign can be subdued through understanding and effort.

Healthy herds of cattle or flocks of sheep denote good fortune in business matters. If the dream relates to the feeding of these animals, it indicates that the dreamer's work will be highly rewarded.

Dreaming of wild or ferocious beasts denotes impending danger from prominent or influential people. If the dreamer is wounded or even attacked by an animal, danger and problems will befall him or her causing serious mishaps or illnesses.

General farm animals are always a choice sign for marriage. A dream concerning trapping animals, or even seeing one in a snare, is a serious warning of danger through self-indulgence and avarice.

If an animal comes to the dreamer to be petted, it represents that friends are available who truly care. When an animal denoting a bad omen seems to be friendly in a dream, then expect to be deceived and taken advantage of in the near future.

Birds are usually a preferred symbol, especially in matters of love, passion, and domestic tranquility. However, when the birds appear sickly or weak, the dreamer should expect discontentment, disillusionment, and frustration.

If birds are seen flying north and the sky is clear, success is predicted for all endeavors. If, instead, they fly south, depression or a dull, unexciting sense of boredom will envelop the dreamer. If the sky looks stormy when the birds fly over, the future is discouraging. If they happen to be feeding, expect good things to take place. But should they be fighting, it represents unhappiness and disagreement between close friends.

Catching a bird in a dream is a premonition of a wedding. But if a wild bird is caught and then confined to a cage, there will be little marital bliss.

Dead birds seen in a dream always signify disappointment and sadness in all areas of life, but especially in love affairs and marriage.

Dreaming of any rare, valuable, or beautiful piece of jewelry, or a precious stone, is taken as a sign of great favor. The dreamer is warned to be careful if the item happens to be cracked, broken, or disfigured in any manner. In this condition it denotes a loss of friendship, broken love affair, or a divided marriage. However, if the stone or jewelry can be repaired, there is a good chance for lovers to make amends.

An imperfection in any stone or piece of jewelry indicates unhappiness, disgust, and fraud. Any stone attached to a setting which must be pinned on the clothing presages sadness and discontent. If the point is bent, then this state of affairs will not be long lasting.

An interesting example of a dream involving a precious stone is that of a Missouri farmer who lived outside of St. Louis. One night, while fast asleep, a young girl appeared in his dream and took his hand in hers. She quietly led him to an old wooden fence and pointed to a huge ruby laying on the ground in front of one of the posts. She then whispered in his ear: "Come here tomorrow and look for a beautiful reddish stone. Pick it up carefully and set it aside." The girl suddenly disappeared.

The farmer, upon arising in the morning, went out in his pasture to search for the stone seen in his dream. He spotted a large rock with a red hue. Upon rolling the stone away from the area, he found a small metal box underneath in a hole. The box turned out to be filled with old gold coins—a gift from the girl in his dream.

Flowers seen in a dream always presage devoted love, sincere affection, continuous bliss, and free-flowing passions in all personal relationships. Blooming, fragrant, and lovely, they denote everything good. When wilted in a pot or on the stem, they portend passion and sexual experiences soon to be forgotten. Gathering flowers in a dream means success in finding a lover and much joy while together. Seeing a couple of flowers amid the weeds denotes but very little sensual pleasure although the individual exerts much effort in this direction. Dried rose petals or other dried flowers always presage fond memories of past lovers and former sensual experiences.

Fresh, crisp vegetables always denote good health. Enjoyment of simple, everyday things is also evidenced. If the vegetables are wilted, there will be many problems caused through thoughtlessness and oversight. If bruised or rotting, even more problems are foretold—these because of ignorance and procrastination. Gathering vegetables in a dream denotes the saving of money and abundant material things. Placing fresh vegetables in a basket, bag, or box presages a speedy marriage for singles. It also foretells of domestic tranquility for married couples.

Dreams of herbs portend continuing excellent health for well people. Those who are sick will quickly recover. Relief will come to those in pain, or those who suffer mental anguish. If the herbs are wilted, they portend sadness and distress through neglect of the dreamer's health. Dreaming of dried herbs indicates that the individual has provided well for the future.

Grains always presage abundance of material goods and great success in all areas of life. If ears of corn are very full and appear rich, then things in life will be bountiful. Ears of corn appearing haggard denote poverty or at least great need because of laziness and inaction. Entire fields of healthy grain in a dream express huge monetary gains, and enduring peace of mind.

Gardens with healthy, green-looking plants represent great opportunities for love, happiness, and material gain. If the plants are seen to be mature, a rosy and solid future is predicted. Newly budding garden plants portend a happy, well-matched marriage for lovers. If the plants are leafless, or sickly, there will be very little love and lack of mental peace for the time being.

Insects seen in a dream are seldom good omens. They denote minor problems and irritants. There are some exceptions to this rule: The ant (hard work will bring grand achievements), a bee (profit and increase of everything), a cricket (contentment amid happy surroundings assured). Lice and other vermin usually denote a gain of cash, but sometimes they are a warning of impending sickness.

Reptiles are unlucky omens to see in dreams. They normally warn of animosity from friends, deceit in the dreamer's daily life, and selfish enemies surrounding the dreamer.

Shellfish (crabs, lobsters, and so forth) are not signs of good fortune. Most other kinds of fish are portents of luck and better times. Fish being caught in a dream denote many good things to come through the efforts of the dreamer. Dead fish indicate nothing more or less than severe disillusionment and lots of disappointment in love and in business matters.

Dreaming of a crowd of happy people, or a group of fun-loving friends is always a positive sign. This indicates cooperation in business matters, a big gain in social stature, and abundance of pleasures in life. Children seen happily playing in a dream or teenagers dancing at a party signifies bliss and total peace of mind just around the corner. Dreaming of a riot or any other noisy situation denotes involvement in political events and erratic finances. If the people seen in a riot are sickly looking, expect much distress, sickness, and other depressing things.

Any dream of people attending church presages problems in the social area, and the dreamer's conduct must be guarded. Dreaming of ministers or priests signifies unsurpassed lust and ambition, predicting dishonor and unhappiness in store for the dreamer.

Unapproving brothers and sisters appearing in a dream signify arguments and hostility. Scolding mothers and fathers denote dissension and stress. The appearance of other chiding relatives denotes impending trouble. Stepbrothers or stepsisters seen in a dream are indicative of a problem with an inheritance, and arguments over personal possessions.

The general condition of clothing worn by the people in a dream is significant in the overall interpretation of the dream. Also important is the sensation the dreamer feels when touching or seeing clothing. New clothing is a sign of happiness and monetary gain. Filthy or soiled clothing signifies humiliation, disgrace and some degree of infamy. When clothes are torn, attacks on the dreamer's character and reputation are to take place. Clothing that is too heavy denotes that the dreamer spends too much time on outward appearances, and not enough thought is given to emotional development. When the clothing is seen as clean but well-worn or threadbare, a shortage of money is presaged.

When a piece of clothing is seen as a favorable omen, but uncomfortable to wear, expect to be deceived by a friend or business associate. Where an unfavorable omen-bearing piece of clothing makes the dreamer feel good, lying and misleading advice will be freely given. A piece of clothing bearing an unlucky connotation and feeling uncomfortable to the dreamer, denotes problems and discontent. Wearing too few clothes, or being naked in a dream, presages humiliation for the dreamer.

The sounds you hear in a dream also have important connotations. To hear the baying of dogs is a warning of a death in the family. To hear birds singing means there will be nothing but bliss in the future, but the sound of a cock crowing means that a boastful friend will create trouble.

The hooting of an owl presages bad tidings and serious dangers, but the braying of a donkey means that you can expect to inherit some cash. The sound of voices talking presages gossip by those who are supposed to be friends. The sounds of singing, especially if it is pretty, denote much happiness.

Monetary gain and sensual pleasures are indicated by dreaming of any food that tastes delicious. Bad tasting food presages humiliation and dishonor. The omen is even worse if the food is seen smeared on the face, lips, and hands of the dreamer. Any bitter-tasting food denotes an experience usually filled with unpleasantness.

Food with no seasoning and rather tasteless food always portend displeasure with the dreamer's surroundings. This can be readily changed for the better with a little fore-thought and effort on the part of the dreamer.

Ships and boats of any kind signify some sort of business endeavor, love arrangement, or dangerous situation. A vessel's overall fitness is important in understanding the dream's full meaning. The weather condition at sea is also extremely important in a dream. Quiet seas and good sailing breezes connote a happy marriage and favorable love life. A stormy sea indicates the opposite.

A disabled ship wallowing at sea portends impending danger. A ship in excellent running condition presages bliss in marriage and much luck in love situations. This is especially true if the object of the dreamer's affection is also present in the dream.

Neat and clean rooms are good omens when seen in a dream. So are nicely appointed furnishings when seen in a room. Messy rooms denote problems arising from laziness and self-centeredness. If a room is seen empty or sparsely furnished, it is a sign that things are lacking in the dream-er's life. Poverty is also a strong possibility. There is an exception to this rule. When a destitute person dreams of an empty room, it portends no immediate change in their financial status.

Clean furniture and other things found in a room or in a building indicates success and good luck. Rooms in disorder signify mental confusion and haphazard habits. Broken, soiled, or filthy furniture and other items suggest that problems and embarrassment will result from impulsive and evil thoughts. If the room is full of furniture it is generally taken as a good omen unless some of the items otherwise represent a negative sign. If a bad symbol is seen in a full room it means that there will be obstructions to success. If the room of a building is leaking when it rains, there will be financial loss and bad investments. Any object seen in a room that is accidentally broken by the dreamer is a warning to be more cautious in order to gain success and good fortune.

The numbers one through nine are important dream symbols. To dream about the number one is a sign that individuality and success can be expected. The number two indicates that experience in life will bring good fortune, and to dream about the number three is an indication that the arts will bring you success. Number four appearing in a dream is a sign that the dreamer's abilities will bring material success. The number five tells the dreamer to apply sharp mentality to get ahead in life. Dreaming of a six indicates that happiness for the dreamer will come from family and social life. Number seven portends certain poise and accomplishment. The number eight offers a life of much achievement but little cash reward, but dreaming of nine is assurance that inspiration and endurance will bring riches.

Dream appearances of angels, the devil, Christ, ghosts, dragons, and goblins always relate to the moral status of the dreamer. They are often dire warnings of danger and the need to change in certain areas of life.

Christ, angels and God seen in a dream with happy, smiling faces presage approval of the dreamer's chosen lifestyle, and protection in all situations. When their faces show irritation or sadness, it is a warning. The dreamer must change or suffer grave problems and much sorrow.

Gnomes and fairies are a good omen. If they appear to be angry, it is a warning to do something about changing. When a witch appears in a dream, much sadness and bitterness is forthcoming. Greed and envy control the dreamer. When Satan is seen in a dream, temptation is to be avoided at all costs. The dreamer is being told to seek a better way of life—perhaps a new career, a good partner in marriage, and so on. Regret, illness, shame, sadness, and dishonesty are seen to be in the foreground.

Dreaming about heavenly bodies such as the sun, moon, and the various planets presages something unusual and important. Many of these heavenly bodies would not be recognized outside of a dream—except for the color, such as the red of Mars, the white glow of the moon, and certain shaped constellations. The dreamer is given a deep understanding far beyond the usual knowledge of the conscious mind. If you see your own sign of the zodiac in a dream, it simply denotes that you are directly under the influence of that particular planet at the moment.

To dream about an eclipse of the moon is to bring misfortune, divorce, broken engagements or loss of a loved one. An eclipse of the sun portends great disaster, loss of a loved one, public censure, a child who will become famous. Dreaming of a moon that is bright and clear presages that devoted love will be faithfully returned. A clouded moon warns that marriage or love are unfavorable at this time, and a red moon portends universal dissension and possible wars. A dream that includes a rainbow means that sorrow will be followed by extreme joy.

Strong winds in a dream indicate powerful opposition to success. Hurricanes, gales, tornadoes, and other storms of a like nature show numerous difficulties and insurmountable problems. Gentle breezes, on the other hand, are always seen to be good omens, especially for matters pertaining to business and love affairs.

Fire is taken as a warning of rage and discomfort caused by the dreamer's behavior. There is one exception to this rule: a candle flame, burning clearly, presages a state of bliss in both the home and in all love matters.

Clear running water in a dream indicates purification and relief from all problems and distress. Rough water signifies much anguish and many perplexities, while dreaming of muddy or brackish water portends dishonor and misfortune.

This, of course, is merely a sampling of the thousands of omens to be found in dreams. The warnings and predictions are not always as evident as they have been presented here, but even a dream that appears to be insignificant may contain many omens of good fortune.

7. Sex in Dreams

Jeremy Taylor

FREUD ORIGINALLY PROPOSED that the dream is a kind of mask, manufactured every night by the "guardians of sleep" to prevent the spontaneous sexual urges and feelings, which well up when the faculties of conscious self-awareness are relaxed and diminished in sleep, from awakening the dreamer with their unacceptable imagery and intensity. Contemporary medical research has confirmed the deep association between genital sexuality and dreaming by demonstrating that penile erection and clitoral swelling occur regularly during REM sleep. However, if Freud's formulation were wholly correct, then it would be reasonable to expect that this universal "censoring" and "protecting" function would all but eliminate explicitly erotic imagery from remembered dreams, and that when and if explicitly sexual imagery were to somehow evade these controls and appear "unmasked" in dreams, then this occurrence would tend to awaken the dreamer immediately. This is simply not the case. Virtually everyone has sexually explicit dreams from time to time, and far more often than not, these dreams do not precipitate immediate or agitated awakenings.

On the other hand, it is true that "Freudian" dream work, focusing on the possible sexual meanings of com-

mon dream experiences, such as climbing and descending
stairs, encountering long, sharp, penetrating objects, encountering concave, hollow, encircling objects, plunging
into bodies of water, etc., often elicits strong tingles and
aha's of confirmation from people who spontaneously dream
such images and are not consciously aware of their sexual
connotations. Clearly, Freud was exploring one strong
element among the many multiple elements that are always
present to one degree or another in every dream. Every
dream is composed of "masked" sexual imagery and energy in much the fashion that Freud described. However,
Freud's exhaustive demonstration of this fact in no way
addresses the question of what other elements are also
eternally present woven into the fabric of every dream.

Part of the legacy of Freud, even among non-Freudian
dream workers, has been a tendency to view overtly erotic
elements in dreams as "self-evident" and thus to shy away
from further symbolic analysis of sexual metaphors, concen-
trating instead on exploration of whatever waking life
issues of sexual and emotional relationship are brought up
by the dreams. This is always a productive way to proceed, but it is not the only way. When, in addition to
pursuing sexual/relational tensions in the dreamer's personal life, the dream work also includes further exploration
of the symbolic quality of the sexual images themselves,
other, deeper layers of meaning and significance are almost always revealed. The explicitly sexual images in
dreams are as symbolic and multileveled as all the other
images in dreams.

The tendency to perceive physical sexuality as an
"irreducible" element of human life is in keeping with the
general cultural idolization of "science" and the belief
that anything that cannot be "objectively observed" and
measured is somehow less "real" than things that can.
This attitude amounts to an archetype of psychological
repression itself, and as such is largely responsible for the
exploitive and oppressive quality of so many contemporary

sexual mores, just as it is also close to the center of other aspects of our contemporary technological crisis.

However, just as dreams of death often have an archetypal association with the growth of personality, my experience is that dreams containing explicitly sexual and erotic imagery and experience also have an archetypal tendency to be associated with issues of religious, philosophical, and spiritual concern. Most often, overtly erotic imagery contains a level of reference to the desire for direct experience of spiritual reality, the desire to understand directly what's *really* going on beyond the obvious appearances of life, the desire to commune more directly with the energy of the divine. This archetypal resonance between sexuality and spiritual search is also clearly visible in the poetic testimony of the world's avowed and acknowledged mystics. Over and over again the mystical writers of all religious traditions couch their descriptions of their transcendent experience in sexual terms, giving shape to their encounter with the divine as a metaphoric encounter with the "Lover." St. Teresa, Rumi, Julian of Norwich, the anonymous author of *Secret of the Golden Flower,* Kabir, the Nahuatl religious poets of Aztec culture, Mechtild of Magdeburg, the anonymous authors of the *Kama Sutra*—the list of men and women who have employed erotic metaphors to express their deepest religious and spiritual intuitions and experiences is virtually endless.

One reason for this archetypal association between sexuality and spiritual life is that adult sexual encounter always involves a simultaneous stimulation of multiple levels of self-awareness, ranging from the purely physical to the mental and emotional. Even oppressive and exploitive sexual encounters have the effect of simultaneously stimulating these centers of experience in a negative way, while loving, communicative sexual encounters often awaken depths of awareness previously unimaginable. For this reason alone, there is is an obvious archetypal resonance between sexual experience and the experience of more direct communion with the energies of the divine, which also characteristically involves a discovery of previously unimagined depths of awareness and harmonization of all levels of perception, from the obviously physical to the ineffably emotional and intuitive. At the same time, sexual encounter is the course from which each of us springs, and in this sense as well there is a deep archetypal resonance between sexuality and the most profound human religious and philosophical questions and concerns.

Contemporary medical developments, such as artificial insemination, amniocentesis and the ability to predict sex and potential birth defects, *in vitro* fertilization of human eggs, and the invention of increasingly sophisticated life-support systems potentially capable of bringing a human embryo to "birth" without gestation in a woman's womb have all created ethical and moral dilemmas which have no solutions—unless the "unmeasurable" elements of human emotion and love are clearly understood to be as real and as important as the machines that make these medical procedures possible.

Human beings come into existence as a consequence of sexual encounters between individual men and women, no matter how many complex medical procedures may also intervene. Arguments over the use and ethical implications of these procedures often lose sight of the emotionally charged sexual nature of human reproduction. Human reproduction is ultimately sexual and emotional, even when this fact is ignored and "sublimated" into mechanical medical procedures. Perhaps Freud's greatest contribution to the successful continuation of human life on the planet may be his uncompromising demonstration that whatever else we may be, we are sexual beings first—both biologically and psychologically. No matter how far removed our conscious motivations and intents may be from sexual encounter, some aspect of the energy we call upon to think and act is sexual in nature, no matter what else it also may be at the same time.

In my experience in working with explicitly sexual and overtly erotic dreams, I have detected a pattern in which dreams with frightening, oppressive, and otherwise unpleasant sexual feelings and images are often associated on one level with repressed, unresolved, or inadequately resolved religious and philosophical problems. Conversely, my experience with explicitly sexual dreams where the experience is happy, pleasurable, or rapturous is that there tends to be an association between these dreams and the greater recognition and resolution of philosophical and spiritual concerns. Indeed, when the sexual element of the dream appears explicitly, as opposed to being in a "masked" state, it is often an indication that increased consciousness and self-awareness has been brought to the waking life relational tensions, and that the philosophical and religious implications of waking life relational choices are beginning to emerge.

The fact that sexuality and spiritual life are deeply intertwined has been recognized universally. It is at the root of the many prohibitions against spontaneous sexual expression imposed by the world religions on the one hand, and of the seemingly opposite but actually complementary strains in Eastern and Western religious and occult tradition which celebrate the cultivation of sexual encounter as a form of worship, meditation, and spiritual discipline on the other.

In the evolution of human consciousness, the conscious control and suppression of spontaneous, "animal" sexuality is a central event. The myths of the world are filled with stories suggesting this archetypal act of individual self-awareness where the sexual instincts come into conflict with developing ego consciousness and an ambiguous struggle ensues. Among these myths, the story of the birth of Athena and Hephaestos's unrequited passion for her is most interesting and revealing.

Zeus, like his father Chronos and his grandfather Uranos before him, began to fear once he had seized power that his children might grow to overthrow him, just as he had overthrown his father. Again like his father and grandfather, Zeus chose to devour his children the moment they were born, rather than let them grow into whatever they might become. He himself had escaped this fate and grown into maturity only because his mother Gaea had foiled her drunken husband and substituted a stone for her baby son when Chronos came to eat him. Perhaps because of this, Zeus was not fooled by similar attempts on the part of his wife/mother to save her children from his all-devouring desire for eternal, unchallenged supremacy.

At last, however, he developed a terrible pain in his head that could not be assuaged by the power and healing magic of all the gods. Zeus lay in agony on his ceremonial couch, and he finally summoned Hephaestos, the shaman/god of fire, tool craft, and metal work, to split his head open and release him from his torture. At first Hephaestos refused his lord's command, but when he was able to extract prior forgiveness and absolution from Zeus for any and all consequences of the terrible act, he struck Zeus's throbbing forehead with an axe, splitting it open.

Out stepped Athena, "fully armed" we are told, and "shining." Athena was Zeus's child who had continued to grow and develop in his brain even after he devoured her. It was her continued growth inside his skull that had been the cause of Zeus's headache, and once she was released, Zeus was immediately restored to health and vigor.

Hephaestos, however, was so struck by Athena's splendor and beauty when she emerged that he immediately fell in love with her and tried to press his affections on her on the spot. Athena did not return his positive regard, and she repulsed his advances immediately and effectively.

The phenomenon of "love at first sight" as experienced by Hephaestos is not an unknown phenomenon in contemporary life, and is always associated at a deep level with the projection of previously unsuspected unconscious material and energies out onto the "loved one." Thus, at this mythological moment we have a picture of the two simultaneous aspects of repression and projection—in Zeus's "headache" we can discern the interior consequences of repression, and in Hephaestos's "love at first sight" we can see the tremendous emotional power of the complementary projection.

Hephaestos never wavered from his passionate desire for Athena, we are told. Even when Zeus gave him Aphrodite, the goddess of love and sexual passion, for his wife, he still sought after Athena. Indeed, all the stories of Aphrodite's unfaithfulness to Hephaestos take place against the backdrop of Hephaestos's continued unrequited love for Athena, his "unattainable ideal."

Several stories relate how Hephaestos pursued Athena, fabricating all manner of clever mechanical devices as gifts for her—robots, and other "labor saving devices"—all to flatter her and demonstrate to her his cleverness and worthiness to be her husband. Athena spurned them all, and at one point Hephaestos decided to follow her on one of her solitary rambles along the snow-covered lower slopes of Mount Olympus and rape her so that she would be forced to accept him as her husband. When he attacked her, Athena feigned submission, but at the last moment, when Hephaestos was about to impregnate her, she threw him contemptuously aside into the snow. As the sperm spurted from Hephaestos's penis, it fell on the snow and congealed into the shapes of statuary—lifeless but passionately evocative images of Hephaestos's frustrated desire. These figures became the famous "Sculpture Garden of Hephaestos" which Phidias and other classical and later sculptors claimed to have visited in their dreams to receive the inspiration for their greatest work.

In this myth at one important level we can see a representation of the psychological mechanism of "sublimation" of raw sexual energy into creative work which was so important to Freud as an explanation of the creative process. At another level, the Sculpture Garden of Hephaestos and the story of Athena's emergence from her father's head also represent the moment of archetypal struggle and development when sexual desires and instincts come under the increasing control of conscious self-awareness and will.

It is interesting to compare this story with a similar story from the Hindu tradition—the story of the birth of Dawn. It is a similar moment—Brahma sits absorbed in yogic trance. All that is is himself, and as he becomes increasingly aware of his infinite depths, he manifests the forms and existences of the other gods. He is the "Father of All," but even he does not know what he will manifest out of his unconscious depths as he meditates. So he is greatly surprised when suddenly he manifests "Dawn," the first goddess, and the morning light simultaneously. The poems tell us that she is also "shining" and "beautiful" beyond all previous imagining, and Brahma immediately conceives a similar passion for her. He reminds himself, however, of the prohibition against sexual union between fathers and daughters. In other versions, it is Shiva who reminds him with a mocking rebuke. Once reminded, Brahma exerts his will and controls his desire, but the effort is so great that it causes beads of sweat to break out all over his body. These beads of sweat roll down his body and transform into all the "demons of desire." They march off his body shouting and chanting, "Fear! Rage! Lust! War! Greed! Murder! Suicide!" In other versions, it is human beings who are born of Brahma's sweat of repressed desire.

These desire demons fill the myths of Hinduism and Buddhism, and when Gautama sits beneath the Bo tree in his final heroic effort to penetrate the true nature of reality, it is these demons whom Mara summons up to attack the Buddha and prevent him from attaining full enlightenment. When Buddha calmly dismisses Mara's demon army as a mere illusion, unworthy of attention in the midst of his meditation, he redeems Brahma's "original sin" in an echo of Jesus' redemption of Adam and Eve and all their children under somewhat similar circumstances of concerted attack.

The story of the manifestation of Eve from part of Adam's interior and her subsequent association with the source of evil and discord places the Genesis story into the same archetypal scene. All three stories (and many more besides) testify to the central place that the development of conscious influence and control over instinctive, spontaneous "animal" sexuality has in the development of human consciousness. These stories also hint at the possibilities inherent in increasing consciousness of sexual energies for the meditative reconnection of human consciousness with our deepest archetypal roots. The story of Hephaestos and Athena is particularly poignant in connection with the contemporary scene since it pictures the deep schism between Wisdom (personified by Athena) and Technology (personified by Hephaestos). Wisdom does not love Technology, and unless these two archetypal energies in ourselves can be reconciled, we will surely destroy ourselves in particularly nasty and horrible ways.

This story also points to the submerged truth that all the horrors we have created for ourselves with our clever technology and our incomplete wisdom are, at one deep level, frustrated attempts to give love-gifts. In another ironic but by no means accidental coincidence of seeming opposites, the frustrated sexual energies that unconsciously motivate so much of our self-destructive behavior are themselves among the very energies which are necessary for a satisfactory resolution of our current predicament. If sexual energies are only acknowledged and explored with increasing consciousness into the areas of transcendent religious, spiritual and philosophical concern where they inevitably lead, then erotic desire itself can become a meditative means to increasing wholeness, deepened spiritual experience, and vital human reconciliation.

8. Why We Forget Our Dreams

Ann Faraday, Ph.D.

WHY IS IT that some people wake up with a dream in mind almost every morning while others claim to dream no more than once a month, once a year, or never? We know that people do not differ in the number of REM periods they experience each night of normal sleep, and that "nondreamers" report almost as many dreams on experimental awakenings as "dreamers." This led investigators to conclude that the apparent widespread differences in dreaming activity must be variations in the *memory* of dreams rather than differences of dream frequency, and they now refer to those who recall a dream less than once a month as nonrecallers and to all others as recallers.

It has often been suggested that those who awaken slowly have a better chance of recalling dreams than those who are normally awakened by a sudden stimulus, like an alarm clock. This is not so. In fact, the contrary is the case: abrupt awakenings following a loud noise result in much more recall than gradual awakenings produced by means of a soft whisper, which suggests that the dream dissipates rapidly in the time between sleep and full awakening. For this reason, fairly loud buzzers or telephone bells are usually used in dream collection experiments. In my own work, the awakening stimulus was a buzzer which sounded rather like an angry bull. This sometimes upset my subjects, who would declare plaintively, "I'm sure I'd remember more if you used a softer buzzer." In the end, I was persuaded to try this, but with negative results.

The extent to which individuals habitually experience one or the other kind of awakening in their normal sleeping environment, such as always being awakened in the morning by an alarm clock instead of coming to gradually, may account for a small portion of individual differences found in everyday dream recall. As the last REM period of the night is sometimes an hour in length, we all have a good chance of awakening from it, but those who are suddenly awakened will have more chance of catching the dream than others who take their time to wake up.

Other experiments have shown that habitual nonrecallers normally need a stronger stimulus to wake them up than recallers, which suggests that the former are deeper sleepers than the latter. This could mean that one reason some people are recallers is that they wake up more often during the night and catch more dreams than their deeper-sleeping brethren.

However, the general weight of evidence points to the fact that the difference between recallers and nonrecallers is more a matter of the psychological characteristics of their personalities than their depth of sleep or the way they wake themselves up. Several years ago investigators observed to their surprise that nonrecallers showed more actual rapid eye movements per second on their REM/EOG records than recallers, which suggested that they experienced more active dreams. Why then did the nonrecallers usually report shorter, blander, and less vivid dreams than recallers?

This paradox was answered when it was discovered that in waking life more eye movements are executed in *looking away* from an object or scene than in *looking at* it. When pictures were shown to a group of subjects whose waking eye movements were being recorded, it was observed that more eye movements appeared on their records when they glanced away from some of the more distressing and threatening aspects of the pictures than when they looked straight at them. In a further study, when subjects were asked to imagine a particular event, few eye movements were present, but many more appeared on the records when they were asked to try to suppress it. Some subjects looked aimlessly around the room as if trying to distract attention from their fantasies.

The investigators reasoned that it was possible for nonrecallers to behave in a similar shifty-eyed way toward their dreams, particularly if they are unpleasant. This would explain why the nonrecallers usually experience less exciting dreams than recallers. Of course, it could be argued that because the dreams of nonrecallers are rather dull, they are harder to remember than the more interesting dreams of recallers. The bulk of the evidence, however, suggests that nonrecallers are decidedly reluctant to remember their dreams, just as they tend to avoid or deny unpleasant experiences and anxieties in everyday life. In fact, nonrecallers have been shown by means of psychological tests to be more inhibited, more conformist, and more self-controlled on the whole than recallers, who tend to be more overtly anxious about life and more willing to admit common emotional disturbances, such as anxiety and insecurity. The willingness to confront this dimension of experience—some have called it self-awareness—which manifests a close interest in the inner, subjective side of life, is probably the crucial difference between recallers and nonrecallers.

I cannot help being reminded here of Jung's famous classification of people into two types: extroverts, who are more concerned with their relation to the external world than with their inner life, and introverts, whose energies are mainly directed inward. Future research may well show low and high dream-recall to be closely correlated with the personality measures of extroversion and introversion, respectively.

Psychoanalysts would say that nonrecallers "repress" their dreams—that is, they "deliberately" banish all memory of them from conscious awareness because they contain distressing ideas and wishes. Analysts believe that we all harbor infantile sexual and aggressive wishes which, denied expression in waking life because they are incompatible with the high moral code we impose upon ourselves, find a kind of vicarious gratification in dreams. In one way, the analysts argue, we are all repressors of dreams, in that the repressive mechanism functions universally and automatically to disguise these unacceptable wishes in dreams so that we never become aware of them. However, sometimes the disguise is very flimsy, in which case we would then use repression to dissipate all memory of the dream. It is in this sense that nonrecallers can be said to be *more* repressive than recallers—they condemn more of their anxiety-provoking dream life to oblivion than their more courageous brethren, who use it for further growth and self-knowledge.

Many analysts are convinced that their nonrecalling patients fail to remember even their disguised dreams because they are afraid that underlying horrors will be revealed by means of interpretation. A nonrecalling friend of mine became very upset when her analyst kept accusing her of being out of touch with her unconscious mind for this reason. I offered her an experimental session in which we would conspire to take the unconscious by force by waking her from REM periods and obtaining immediate dream reports. The experiment was a failure in that her record showed the presence of three distinct REM periods during the course of the night, yet she was unable to report a single dream when awakened from them, although each time she felt she had been dreaming. She admitted sadly to her analyst that he was right, and became resigned to her "dreamless" existence. Some time later, however, I discovered that she had taken her usual sleeping pill before going to sleep on the experimental night. Suspecting this might have something to do with the failure of the experiment, I asked her if she would be willing to return for a second session, this time without her pill.

Although she was convinced she would never fall asleep without it, she eventually agreed, and the night resulted in three "big" dream reports which she presented triumphantly to her analyst the following day, saying, "Out of touch with my unconscious, indeed! It's just those wretched sleeping pills I've been taking." In her case, the pills probably had the effect of deepening her sleep in some way so that the memory of dreams was lost between the time of the buzzer and full wakefulness. On the other hand, barbiturates have been known to reduce the number of rapid eye movements in REM periods, which may result in more passive and therefore less memorable dreams. On the rare occasions when I take a sleeping pill, I have noticed that I rarely remember a dream.

However, as I said earlier, it does appear that some people really are "out of touch with their unconscious minds" (implying that they are completely unaware of the hidden parts of their personality), and that lack of dream recall is symptomatic of this. I am sometimes approached by psychoanalysts and psychotherapists who ask if I will give their nonrecalling patients a going-over in the laboratory, in order to capture a few dreams for the purpose of analysis. While psychoanalysts can manage to work without a patient's dreams, it makes life a lot easier if they are produced from time to time. While the laboratory methods have been successful in eliciting dreams from chronic nonrecallers, it must not be forgotten that if a patient is really resistant to getting in touch with the hidden part of himself, merely waking him from REM periods and asking him for dream reports is not necessarily going to solve the problem automatically.

For example, it is not unusual for a subject who has been referred to the laboratory because he fails to recall dreams spontaneously at home to produce a dream on the first couple of awakenings and then have nothing more to report for the rest of the night. Or he may be quite successful on the first experimental night and fail to produce anything on subsequent nights, often reporting that he knew he was dreaming but that the dream seemed to slip away as he woke up. One subject became very cross, and said, "Every time you've woken me up, I know I've been dreaming, but I just can't get them back. Is it a defense, do you suppose? I really am interested to know what I'm dreaming about." There is no doubt she was speaking the truth, and I think a psychoanalyst would be correct in assuming that her unconscious mind, having been taken unawares on the first few awakenings and burgled of dreams, became wise to the trick played upon it and was fighting back by causing the dreams to be repressed.

The repression of a dream probably takes place just before waking or even at the moment of waking, so that either the dream is forgotten completely or only innocuous fragments remain. The theory of dream repression is an attractive one for those of us who have witnessed countless unsuccessful struggles on the part of our subjects to hang onto a dream as it is literally being sucked under. But this is not the whole story in dream forgetting, as we shall see later.

Even normal volunteer subjects who are in the habit of regularly remembering their dreams at home often show (unconscious) resistance to remembering their dreams in the laboratory. One apparently keen and willing subject, who said she was really looking forward to the experiment, produced several bland, unexciting dream reports from the first few REM awakenings of the night. On the last awakening, she was unable to remember anything except that she felt she had been in the middle of a long, dramatic dream when I woke her. She expressed considerable impatience that she was unable to remember any of it. She telephoned me the following afternoon to say that the dream had just come back to her but it was too personal to tell. "Even if I'd remembered it at the time," she said, "I doubt whether I should have told it to you. After all, dreams are very private things, aren't they?" They are indeed, and many an enthusiastic volunteer takes part in dream experiments quite unaware of his underlying anxiety about revealing too much either to himself or to the experimenter.

Other subjects sometimes express their unconscious fears and resentments about the experiment in the dreams themselves. One overtly cooperative subject made it clear after the very first dream report that we were in for a trying time. He dreamed he saw a doctor on the landing between the experimental room in which he was sleeping and my room, where I sat recording his dreams on a tape recorder. This doctor, who had a sinister appearance, was apparently trying to cut the wires between the two rooms or in some way stop the experiment. My subject was just going to warn me about this, he said, when he was awakened by the buzzer. As he himself was a doctor, I had little doubt about the real identity of the saboteur, and my fears were realized when, halfway through the night, he developed a migraine and the experiment had to be terminated.

So the psychotherapist looking for dreams to interpret will not find the new laboratory techniques a panacea. Nevertheless, they can be very useful in helping chronic nonrecallers to begin to become aware of their dream life, and this is of value not only to those who are having professional psychotherapy, but to all of us.

For recallers, on the other hand, the new methods may have little to offer, as only a limited number of dreams can be dealt with in the course of therapy—normally two or three a week at the most. Indeed, in professional psychotherapy even this number can be embarrassing. When I first began analysis, I kept a dream diary in which I recorded over 200 dreams during the first year. In the end, I stopped doing this, as neither I nor my analyst could cope with so much material. I later read with interest that

Freud had eventually destroyed his own dream diary: his reason—"The stuff simply enveloped me as the sand does the Sphinx."

Also, as every psychotherapist knows, too many dreams can be as symptomatic of resistance to therapy as too few. I am reminded of a weekly psychoanalytic group I used to attend in which one of the members would invariably pull out a thick wad of dream reports halfway through the session and proceed to bore us to death with them for the following hour. These were his dreams of the previous week, and very long and complex some of them were, too. In the end, the group leader did not even bother to interpret the dreams but interpreted the member's preoccupation with them instead, saying that this was his method of avoiding the deeper issues which he was unwilling to face!

I do not mean to imply that laboratory methods of dream catching have nothing to offer the psychotherapist. On the contrary, many therapists have used them to advantage, particularly in attempts to discover how far repression plays a part in the forgetting of a *once-remembered dream*. As far back as 1900, Freud wrote:

It not infrequently happens to me, as well as to other analysts and to patients under treatment, that, having been woken up, as one might say, by a dream, I immediately afterwards, and in full possession of my intellectual powers, set about interpreting it. In such cases, I have often refused to rest till I have arrived at a complete understanding of the dream: yet it has sometimes been my experience that after finally waking up in the morning, I have entirely forgotten both my interpretive activity and the content of the dream, though knowing that I have had a dream and interpreted it. It happens far more often that the dream draws the findings of my interpretive activity back with it into oblivion than that my intellectual activity succeeds in preserving the dream in my memory.

Freud also noted that many of his patients, while recounting a dream in the consulting room, would suddenly pause and recall a part of the dream they had previously forgotten. He considered that these forgotten fragments were of more importance than the remembered parts of the dream. "Often when a patient relates a dream," he wrote, "some fragment is entirely forgotten. The forgotten part provides the best and readiest approach to the understanding of the dream. Probably that is why it sinks into oblivion."

Professor Roy Whitman and his colleagues at the University of Cincinnati College of Medicine, Ohio, have produced evidence that Freud might be correct in his view that the dream or part of the dream which is *not* remembered is of more significance than that which is recalled. Two subjects who were undergoing psychotherapy were awakened from REM periods on several nights and asked to report their dreams to the experimenter. The following day, they both had therapy sessions with a psychoanalyst. From the early sessions, the female subject reported most of her sex dreams to the experimenter but not to the analyst, while dreams containing sexual and aggressive material directed toward the experimenter were told only to the analyst. Dreams in which she expressed her fears of analysis and denied any need for treatment were reported to the experimenter but not to the analyst. The male subject retold to the analyst all dreams which highlighted his capabilities as a man, but omitted to relate those dreams in which he expressed homosexual tendencies. As the meanings of these dreams were not always immediately apparent, Whitman inferred that the subjects understood at least subconsciously the meaning of their dreams, and therefore kept them from anyone who was likely to see through them. This the subjects did by means of conscious suppression of the dreams or by unconscious repression along the lines we have been discussing.

Whitman writes that "it is usually taken for granted that the dream reported in the t™rapeutic session contains one of the major conflicts with which the patient is struggling at the time. These findings suggest that therapists should maintain a degree of suspicion, for one or more of the major interpersonal conflicts of the patient may well be contained in the dream that is *not* told.'' He believes that modern techniques of dream detection could be clinically useful if used along the lines of his experiment in making *forgotten* dreams available to the analyst in order to increase his knowledge of the subject's deepest fears and resistances. However, I have a feeling that a really repressive patient would soon learn to ''forget'' his dreams at source, as it were, by using some of the methods observed in my own subjects.

While I have no doubt that a certain amount of repression is responsible for the forgetting of dreams, this cannot be the whole story, as Freud believed, since even extremely open and self-aware people find it difficult and often impossible to counteract the almost overwhelming tendency to forget dreams. Even if dreams are remembered briefly on waking, they are gone the moment we allow ourselves to doze. And even the most prolific dreamers do not recall four or five dreams every morning, although the evidence of REM periods suggests that we all experience something like this number during a night of seven or eight hours' sleep. In fact, the evidence suggests that the great majority of dreams are never remembered at all, while others are retained only as fragments. How and why do we forget so many of our dreams?

Kleitman has suggested that the poor recall of dreaming may be attributable to the impaired efficiency of the brain during sleep, and he likens the sleeper's condition to that of the very young, the very old, and the very drunk! Oswald agrees with him: ''The forgetting of dreams is extremely rapid, and it is not necessary to invoke repression to account for the failure of recall of most dream material, any more than it would be in the case of post-traumatic amnesia, amnesia after drunkenness, electroplexy or other states in which cerebral vigilance is impaired for a time.'' In other words, the condition of the brain during sleep is probably quite inadequate for the laying down of memory traces.

At first sight, this seems to contradict the view that the conditions of REM sleep are actually *optimal* for the consolidation of existing memory traces in the brain. But it is one thing to say that REM sleep completes the consolidation of *already-existing* memory traces formed during the course of the day, and quite another to say that it is also capable of laying down *new* traces of the *dream itself* as it occurs during the REM period. The evidence suggests that REM activity does not continue long enough at any one time to allow the formation of a dream trace strong enough to sustain itself beyond the end of a REM period.

Experiments have shown how the dream swirls away from memory, first fragmenting and then completely evaporating. When a subject is awakened from a REM period, he nearly always reports a vivid dream. If he is awakened five minutes after the end of a REM period, he can catch only fragments of it: and if the awakening takes place ten minutes after the end of a REM period, the dream is almost completely lost. Just on the basis of the number of words used to report a dream, there is a straight and dramatic decline.

It is obvious then that unless a subject is awakened during a REM period, he is likely to forget the mental content experienced during it. Much of everyday recall probably arises from spontaneous awakenings from the last long REM period of the night: since we normally do not awaken for any length of time during the night, a natural process of forgetting occurs. One of the great values of the new experimental techniques in dream research is that many of these early dreams, which would otherwise be lost, can be caught and their content recorded.

Further experiments suggest that the chief culprit responsible for the forgetting of dreams is the relatively passive and inactive state of NREM sleep. Subjects awakened at hourly intervals throughout the night and shown a word on a screen above the bed were usually able to remember the word in the morning only if they were kept awake for ten minutes or so after seeing it. If they were allowed to drift back to sleep immediately after identifying it, it tended to be quite forgotten. As a person almost invariably falls into Stage 2 NREM sleep after an awakening, it seems likely that any experience—including a dream—followed by NREM sleep passes rapidly into oblivion. On the other hand, the act of keeping the person awake for ten minutes or more seems to have the effect of strengthening a memory trace so that the incident will be remembered at some future date.

Normally, then, the only dreams we are likely to remember are those from which we awaken directly and stay awake, either in the middle of the night or in the morning. In the ordinary course of events, a sleeper awakens for only very brief periods during a normal night's sleep, and therefore never remembers most of his dreams. We have all probably experienced the strange, uncomfortable feeling of being in touch with two worlds at the same time on restless, disturbed nights after overeating or during fever, our constant brief awakenings resulting in snatches of dream recall, most of which appears meaningless and trivial and is quite forgotten by morning. In these cases, our awakenings are probably not long enough for memory traces of the dreams to be formed so that we remember them only briefly and then they are gone forever. Incidentally, this is one reason why many people think they dream more when they are restless: what really happens is that wakefulness results in more dream recall than normal, but never in extra dreams.

Most of us, like Freud, have also had the experience of waking from a vivid dream in the middle of the night and thinking we must remember it in the morning. We may turn it over in our minds several times and even attempt some kind of interpretation, as he did, but if we doze back to sleep within about ten minutes of waking, the whole lot will probably be gone by morning. I don't believe Freud was repressing the memory of his dreams and their interpretations—at least not on all occasions. I suspect rather that he did not allow a long enough interval between waking and falling back into NREM sleep for the formation of an adequate memory trace of the whole experience.

For this reason, I advise those who are intent on catching their dreams to write them down as soon as they wake up, even if this is in the middle of the night. The effort involved in sitting up, putting on the light, and writing down the dream all help to bring about a state of wakefulness which is necessary if we are to catch most of the details. Incidentally, Freud advised his patients not to write down their dreams, as he believed that this increased the chances of their repression. Dreams, he thought, resist all efforts at capture and the intention to write them down is a sure way of frightening them off. However, as we have been led to conclude that dreams disappear more on account of weakness of memory trace than of wickedness of content, we shall have no hesitation in ignoring Freud's advice on this point.

Most of our spontaneously recalled dreams probably come from the last long REM period just before waking in the morning. The best way to catch these dreams is, once again, to sit up immediately and write them down, instead of either continuing to doze or leaping out of bed and hurrying off to work.

It is reasonable to assume that there is always a better chance of recalling an emotional dream than a bland one, a long one than a short one, and a vivid one than a vague one, just as we tend to remember our more exciting and dramatic experiences in waking life. There is, however, no way of testing this assumption, as we have no access to the original dream material. The most we can do is to collect dream reports from awakenings during the night and com-

pare them with a second recall the following morning. In
my own studies I found that REM dreams reported from
nocturnal awakenings were better recalled the following
morning than NREM dreams reported during the night.
Further analysis showed that this was mainly on account of
their tendency to be longer, more vivid, and more emotionally intense than NREM dreams. Emotional intensity,
irrespective of whether it was pleasant or unpleasant, was
a particularly strong factor in determining whether or not
the memory of a dream reported during the night would
survive until morning.

In a further experiment, I tested the hypothesis that
subjects who were set or motivated to recall their dreams
would do better than those with no motivation. Two groups
of subjects slept in the laboratory, believing that the purpose of the experiment was merely to monitor their eye
movements during sleep. Before going to sleep, one group
was requested to try to remember their dreams the following morning, while the other group received no such instructions. The former group remembered far more dreams
than the latter, indicating that we tend to recall more
dreams when we are in some way set to catch them than
when we take a more casual attitude toward them.

How the mechanism of "set to recall" works is uncertain. It may cause more frequent awakenings during the
course of the night; it may cause us to awaken specifically
from REM periods; or it may operate directly on the dream
itself, making the content more vivid and intense, and so
more memorable. One thing is certain—suggestions put to
the mind before one goes to sleep are often carried out in
some mysterious way. For example, I can almost always
wake up at a certain hour without the aid of an alarm clock
once I have given myself instructions to do so. And in a
broader setting, anyone who has undergone psychotherapy
knows that dream recall increases markedly if it becomes
apparent that the analyst welcomes dreams in his work
with a patient. Such experiences as psychotherapy, partici-

pation in dream experiments (many of my subjects reported increased dream recall at home after taking part in experiments), and even listening to lectures or reading books on the subject, all stimulate dream recall by combating the natural physiological processes which seem inevitably to lead to dream forgetting.

This is not to imply, however, that the psychological process of repression plays no part in dream forgetting, although this has not yet received much experimental support. Psychotherapists are only too well aware of the incompatibility of conscious and unconscious desires, the patient's consciously wishing to rid himself of the neurotic tendencies which are spoiling his life, at the same time unconsciously striving to maintain the status quo within the personality. The experiences mentioned above which sensitize one to awareness—psychotherapy, dream experiments and so on—probably assist in combating not only the physiological processes which cause dream forgetting, but also the unconscious psychological forces responsible for repression.

9. Nightmares

Margaret O. Hyde

"I HAD A nightmare last night. It was the worst dream I ever had. Something was chasing me, but I'm not sure what it was. Then I dreamed I ran into a burning building and saw a crowd of people whose clothes were on fire. Some were lying on the floor, writhing in pain. They were too heavy for me to lift, so I had to leave them there. Even the people who could walk could not come with me. They just moaned and groaned until everyone was burned to death. I can't stop thinking about them. At the time, I never wondered why I didn't burn. I guess that's a typical, crazy nightmare."

Was this really a nightmare? Some sleep researchers would call it an anxiety dream or a special kind of nightmare, partly because it was remembered in such detail. Night terrors, or nightmares that occur during nondreaming, or NREM, sleep, may be even more terrifying.

Nightmares have plagued people as far back as anyone knows. As with ordinary dreams, they were commonly thought to be caused by external forces. Even as late as the eighteenth century a popular explanation was that devils and demons were the cause. The latter part of the word nightmare comes from the Teutonic word for devil.

Freud's theory that dreams are unfulfilled wishes explained the nightmare as a dream in which unconscious thoughts break free of the ''censor'' and the mind and body of the sleeper are thrown into a very disturbed state. In nightmares, neurotic people may be carried back to childhood situations that originally made them neurotic. Or the nightmare might be related to a traumatic experience in adult life. Freud's theory is far more complex, but in it a nightmare is basically a very bad dream.

Although one would certainly expect nightmares to occur during REM sleep when dreaming is most common, Dr. Roger J. Broughton, at the University of Ottawa, made the startling discovery that what he called nightmares can occur during NREM sleep. The original triggering mechanism actually appears in stage III or stage IV sleep, and the nightmare, according to Broughton, takes place in an aroused, but not fully alert, state. Dr. Ernest Hartmann, professor of psychiatry at Tufts University School of Medicine and an outstanding authority on sleep and dreams, prefers to call this kind of nightmare a night terror. It is also referred to as an NREM nightmare.

Even more than a decade after the discovery that separated NREM nightmares from REM nightmares into their different sleep periods, confusion continues in defining the differences between these two unpleasant experiences. The experts differ. Some say that only children have night terrors *(pavor nocturnus)*. Others say that children awaken during night terrors but not during nightmares. Many people have the idea that children have night terrors and adults have nightmares and that both are forms of anxiety dreams. Since even the experts disagree about definitions, it is not surprising to find so much confusion.

Dr. Milton Kramer, in an article in the July 1979 issue of *Psychiatric Annals,* suggests that night terrors and nightmares be considered in one group and anxiety dreams in another, since the first two occur in NREM sleep and the last in REM sleep. Night terrors and nightmares, according to Dr. Kramer, are defined by the age of the person to whom they occur; that is, night terrors are experiences of children and nightmares are experiences of adults, but other authorities say night terrors can occur at any age.

When one experiences a night terror, three characteristics are always present. One is the feeling of impaired breathing. Another is a sense of overwhelming anxiety, and the third is the feeling of inability to move. Sometimes there is a sense of pressure in the chest. This last sensation may have inspired the famous painting by Henry Fuseli called "The Nightmare," in which a woman is lying sprawled across a bed on her back and a monster is pressing on her abdomen.

In small children, the ability to distinguish between what is real and what is imaginary is not fully developed. No wonder a boy, whose night terrors came from a tiger he believed was under his bed, was freed from the terrors when his mother pretended to toss the tiger out of the room.

In most cases, the causes and cures of night terrors and nightmares are complicated. Picture a five-year-old boy lying peacefully asleep in bed. He has been asleep for about an hour when, suddenly, his mother hears a blood-curdling scream. She rushes to the boy's bedside and finds him apparently awake, sitting upright with his eyes wide open. She talks to him, assuring him that everything is fine. She is with him and will see that no one harms him. But the boy does not respond to her comforting words. The only word that the mother can understand is "bugs." Certainly, the boy is hallucinating. He is in a cold sweat, his heart is pounding, and his eyes are staring. The mother realizes that, in his mind, the boy is confronted by powerful forces that produce terror of overwhelming intensity. But, as she watches, the night terror is suddenly over. It has run its course and the boy goes back to sleep. In the morning, when the mother asks about the "dream," the boy does not recall having one.

At one time, it was believed that the night terror type of

nightmare was seldom remembered, but careful studies indicate that there is some recall the following morning in about sixty-six percent of the cases. When people are aroused immediately after the experience, about seventy-eight percent are able to recall something about the experience. By contrast, the recall of REM nightmares appears to be one hundred percent, and the remembered content is more detailed than in the case of a night terror.

The content of night terrors is always overwhelmingly fearful, and fear of attack appears in about fifty percent of the cases. The following fears make up some of the other fifty percent of terrors and of other nightmares: fear of dying, fear of wires, fear of falling, fear of being chased, and fear of entrapment.

The nightmare experience is credited with influencing the creativity of many authors. Scientifically, it is not clear whether a story was developed from a nightmare experienced during NREM sleep or one experienced during dreaming sleep, since many authors inspired by sleep disturbances wrote at a time when there was no distinction between the two. Today, a knowledgeable person might recognize the dramatic symptoms of night terror: a scream, profuse perspiring, agonizing dread, and an increased rate of breathing and heartbeat. The night terror usually happens during the first half of the night.

The REM nightmare, on the other hand, usually occurs in the second half of the night. One lies in terror, unable to move or breathe easily, helpless in the face of great danger. This kind of nightmare is less intense than the night terror, but it is remembered in greater detail than a night terror or NREM nightmare. This leads one to suspect that many of the stories, poems, and other creative works arising from nightmares may have been inspired by REM nightmares.

Whatever type of dream experience was the source of material, many creative works begin with an account of the dream. Henry James's story "The Jolly Corner" is based on a sleep disturbance he had when he was thirteen, which he describes as "the most appalling, yet most admirable nightmare of my life." In the nightmare, and in the story, there is a terrible struggle between a man and a ghost that haunts him.

In his famous ghost story, "Turn of the Screw," Henry James has communicated the feeling of uncertain reality that follows a nightmare. The reader of the story is kept in a state of uncertainty as to whether the governess is hallucinating or not. Are the people she perceives real or ghosts? This borderline state, where it is difficult to distinguish whether the experiences of the nightmare are real or not, is characteristic of nightmares.

The ideas for many of his poems came to Samuel Taylor Coleridge at night. He claimed that he actually composed "Kubla Khan" during a dream. Medication containing opium caused him to fall asleep while reading a book that mentioned that Kubla Khan commanded a palace to be built. Just after reading the statement, Coleridge slept for more than an hour and dreamed the poem. When he awakened, Coleridge reported that he instantly wrote down several hundred lines of "Kubla Khan" just as he had dreamed it.

It is considered to be one of the most remarkable poems in the English language, but sleep authorities have difficulty believing that the poem was actually composed during the dream. It is more likely that the images, feelings, and memories of the dream inspired the poem.

Robert Louis Stevenson took many plots from his dreams and nightmares to write many of his stories, including the famous work *The Strange Case of Dr. Jekyll and Mr. Hyde*. From boyhood on, Stevenson suffered many nightmares and he noted that sooner or later the night-hag would have him by the throat, and pluck him, strangling and screaming, from his sleep.

Nightmares have played a part in other forms of creative expression, too. For example, the famous painter Francisco Goya suffered many nightmares after two periods of illness, one at age forty-five and one at age seventy-three. Some of his paintings depict the monstrous creatures and subject matter that confronted him at night.

No one knows how many sculptures, paintings, writings, and other creative works have been influenced by the "demons of the night," but the number is likely to be very, very large.

Estimates of the number of people who suffer from night terrors and nightmares may not be accurate, but it has been suggested that at least three percent of children under the age of fourteen have experienced at least one night terror. Severe cases tend to begin at an early age. Although they are frightening to both the child and the parent, they are not usually an indication of a serious problem. Most children have fewer and fewer attacks as they grow older and as their nervous systems mature.

Two-thirds of all adults have probably had a nightmare at some time in their lives, and many adults suffer from one or more nightmares each week. A large percentage of people who sleepwalk are beset by nightmares. During the nightmare attack some sleepwalkers are violent or prone to injury. Often they endanger themselves by opening windows from which they could fall.

Another sleep disorder that is sometimes found in combination with nightmares is bed-wetting, or enuresis. Nocturnal bed-wetting has been found to be as high as ten to fifteen percent among groups of children classed as "nervous" by medical personnel. Among Navy recruits who were discharged for psychiatric reasons, enuresis was reported to be as high as one in four. It is the most common form of sleep disorder among children. Since sleepwalking, enuresis, and nightmares most commonly occur in the same sleep periods, scientists are interested in trying to find how they are related.

Since nightmares have been described as the most terrifying psychic experience known to humans, it is not surprising that many chronic sufferers seek medical or other professional help. Self-treatment with certain kinds of sleeping pills may make things worse by depressing REM sleep, but there are medications in the benzodiazepine group that appear to be helpful when prescribed as treatment.

Psychiatrists and psychologists use varied approaches in treating nightmare sufferers. One is a technique known as behavior modification. The story of Dr. Leonard Handler's treatment of his eleven-year-old patient, Johnny, and the monster has often been repeated. A monster had been terrifying Johnny as often as two or three times a week over a period of eighteen months. Night after night, Johnny would awaken convinced that the monster was pursuing him. Sometimes it seemed to catch him and hurt him. Johnny was terrified each time the monster pursued him, and he continued to be afraid of it even in the daytime.

When therapy began, Johnny knew Dr. Handler and trusted him. He had faith that Dr. Handler would protect him. Nevertheless, when he sat on the doctor's lap and closed his eyes trying to follow the instructions to visualize the monster, he trembled. When Johnny succeeded and told Dr. Handler that the monster was in the room with them, the doctor pounded loudly on his desk and told the monster to go away and never come back. He threatened the monster in a very loud voice. With practice, Johnny was able to join Dr. Handler in shouting the monster away in the office.

Dr. Handler told Johnny to use the pounding and shouting to chase the monster away the next time it came to him in the night. At his next session with Dr. Handler, Johnny reported that he had yelled at the monster and it had vanished. This technique enabled Johnny to sleep without night terrors for the following six months, with the exception of two nightmares that were not about the monster.

Consider the case of Karen, who had recurrent nightmares. After each attack this young woman remembers dreaming of a rat nibbling at an orange. One time she dreamed that she was starving but the only food available was the nibbled orange, and that was repulsive because the rat had nibbled at it. Thus the recurring nightmare had an added conflict between starvation and repulsive available food.

Some of Karen's problem was traced to a hospital experience where she shared a room with a girl who had suffered many rat bites and had contracted a disease they carried. The doctors had passed around photographs of the rat-infested room in which the girl had lived, and had shown the photos to Karen. After Karen's hospitalization, the recurrent nightmares began two or three times a week.

Karen's therapist suggested that she visit a zoo where mice and rats were kept in attractive cages. The white rats there had little resemblance to the ugly rat in the nightmares. Through a series of sessions in which Karen was gradually able to tolerate a caged rat in the room with her, the nightmares decreased.

Many people succeed in chasing their dream monsters away through forms of behavior therapy. For example, a twenty-two-year-old man had a recurrent nightmare of being chased by a shadowy figure. This nightmare had occurred for a period of fifteen years between three and five times a week. Psychologists found he had no serious emotional problems other than this. The young man was treated by a behavior-modification technique in which he was taught to relax while visualizing various stages of the nightmare. Whenever the anxiety arose in therapy and at night, he told himself that it was only a dream. After seven sessions, the nightmares stopped. He was reported to be having only normal dreams even after eighteen months had elapsed.

In that young man's case, there appeared to be no anxiety about the dream content other than the specific situation in which the nightmare occurred. In another case, a young girl experienced a series of nightmares in which she feared falling from bridges. She was found to have a genuine fear of crossing bridges, so her treatment involved getting rid of the real fear rather than dealing with the nightmares. After the behavior therapy, she was able to cross bridges fearlessly in waking life and she no longer had nightmares about falling from them.

How does an anxiety dream or REM nightmare compare with a typical dream? The former contains more feelings of apprehension, misfortune, and physical activity, and certainly there is more unhappiness. Falling, a physical attack, and death of a loved one are common themes of anxiety dreams.

While the following interpretations are not true in all cases, falling is often thought to be connected with a fear of loss of love and an inability to show defiance to a mother who is very independent of her child. The dreamer might be dealing with a separation from parents by dreaming one symbol—falling—that stands for both loss and rage.

In the REM nightmares (anxiety dreams) in which a person is attacked, the dreamer might be dealing with separation from an overly protective mother, and the dreamer deals with separation by defending himself against the attack, which is interpreted as attachment.

In the case of nightmares that involve the threat of death to a loved one, that loved one is often a parent or sometimes a peer. This type of dream is more common in women than in men and less alarming than the other two types.

Surely, much remains to be learned about night terrors, nightmares, and anxiety dreams. The nightmare has been called a challenge to any dream theory. Fortunately, chronic sufferers can be helped by therapy and/or medication even though all the causes are not known.

10. ESP in Dreams

Louisa E. Rhine

EXTRASENSORY PERCEPTION (ESP) begins below the level of consciousness, in an area of the mind still so ill-defined that even the name of it is tentative. I refer to it as the unconscious, using the term to cover all of mind that is not conscious.

When ESP occurs, and a person gets information about some distant or hidden event, that information, or message as it can be called, was somehow *available* at this unconscious level.

An ESP experience—clairvoyant, telepathic, or precognitive—may occur as an intuition, realistic or unrealistic dream, or as a hallucination.

In dreams, the translation of the meaning into an appropriate message means the construction of imagery. And the process of making imagery differs depending on whether the end result will be realistic or unrealistic. The difference between the two seems slight at the start, but it can cause very different end products.

Realistic dreams tell their stories by imagery that pictures the event in some detail. They are therefore very good message carriers and tend to bring perfect messages. However, occasionally a realistic dream may be imperfect too. And those that are are important here, for they show

hat the process of making realistic and true imagery is not
quite what is seems. From the realistic dreams that bring
complete messages, it would look as if the imagery had
been made by something like photography, so that all the
details just had to be the same as the reality.

The imperfect cases show that the dream maker has
more freedom. He has a choice. He does not simply have
to copy; he can select the imagery and modify it upon
occasion. Actually he selects the entire scene as well as the
viewpoint for his imagery.

In this selecting and constructing of imagery to portray
the news item, and in playing freely with it, the actual
facts to be portrayed may be changed around, embellished,
or obscured in various ways. Often the identity of the
person the dream is about, the target person, is changed,
omitted, or another person substituted for the proper one.
Again, identity may be faithfully portrayed, but the event
in which the target person is involved may be unclear or its
main meaning missing. Sometimes it is easy, sometimes
not, to guess at the personal motivation that caused the
defect in the imagery. For instance in this case from
Minnesota, one can easily suppose a reason.

"It was five years ago; I was eighteen years old. I
woke one morning after a restless night with a very
vivid dream imprinted on my mind. I often wake
remembering my dreams, but this one bothered me
particularly. My mother at that time slept on a Hide-a-
bed in the living room, I in a bedroom adjoining. My
dream started with Mother and me standing in a
certain spot in the living room, looking down at the
body of one of our best lady friends lying dead on the
Hide-a-bed. Everything was exact. I was standing a
certain way, my mother the same. She sobbed five
words, 'She was my *best* friend.' The dream ended
and I woke up. I simply couldn't get this dream out of
my mind, but I shrugged it off more or less because it

seemed very unlikely that this friend would be dying anywhere, but particularly unlikely that it would be on *our* Hide-a-bed. She was in perfect health at that time and still is today.

"Exactly one month from the day of the dream it happened, but the situation was reversed. My mother died in her sleep of a heart attack. I awoke to hear her gasping, called the doctor and this friend immediately. The doctor arrived first and pronounced my mother dead. My friend came in, and we both assumed the exact positions as in my dream—and she said the very words in the same tone of voice."

It seems likely that in this situation, when the information was admitted and its unwelcome meaning grasped, the very construction of imagery was affected so as to *obscure the truth*. The dream maker preferred to dodge the fact, and the substitution was the way to do it with very little effort.

But though in that case the dreamer seemed to have a reason, an important motive for not dreaming true, it is not always thus. Take a case like this one:

"I was about sixteen years old and we were returning from a trip to Kansas to our home in Los Angeles. When we hit Holbrook, Arizona, we had car trouble and had to stay all night. That night I had a dream. I dreamed that I was back in Los Angeles and saw our neighbor standing in his front yard by an open grave. I walked over and asked him what had happened. He told me that Elaine (his little girl) had been hit and killed by a car. *Then he held his arm out—palm up—and brought his fingers up in a crushing motion and said, 'Her head was crushed just like an egg.'*

"I told this dream (with demonstration of the crushing motion) to my mother the next morning as we were walking a block to the post office. We had to stand in line at the post-office window. The Mexican just before us was telling the postmaster about an accident that had happened just outside where a Mexican had been hit by a train and killed. The Mexican apparently saw it—or arrived just after. He said to the postmaster (with the very same gesture I had seen in my dream), 'His head was crushed just like an egg.'

"Well, my mother looked at me with her mouth hanging open, and it gave me such a strange feeling that I have never forgotten it. My mother sometimes mentions it too."

Probably that dream was remembered mainly because it had no *real* reason. The only difference between the real and the substituted identity was the slight one that the dreamer knew the one person but not the other.

Just as an identity can be changed apparently for a very slight motive, so, too, sometimes other details are tampered with. An instance in which details were added to an otherwise perfect picture is given by a man in Wisconsin.

"For some time I have wanted to write of an experience I had twenty-three years ago. It is of quite a personal nature and so naturally I have hesitated to recount it, but after much deliberation have decided that you will evaluate it professionally and forgive me if I don't attempt to 'dress it up' and detract from its authenticity.

"In 1938 I lived in Rhode Island, and was married to a very sweet and lovely woman. During the winter months she had the opportunity to drive to Florida with married girl friends, and I encouraged her to go. While she was away, one of the husbands called me and we got together for a weekend and wound up in New York City. We had a fine time on Saturday night with much drinking but conducted ourselves honorably. Sunday afternoon, while at the bar at the Taft Hotel, two very

attractive girls came in and we became acquainted. I fell
rather hard for one of them, and we went to a nightclub
for drinks and dancing; and then since they were from
Bridgeport, we put them on the train at Grand Central
late Sunday night. We men drove back to Rhode Island
Monday, and I called Phyllis (this is not her name) at
her home in Bridgeport. She sounded quite pleased to
hear from me. I thought about her a lot in the succeed-
ing days. My wife came back from Florida, and things
returned to normal. I ran a filling station at the time. I
had introduced myself as Ed Tucker to Phyllis—not by
my real name.

"Soon after this a single friend and customer of mine
came into the gas station on a Friday night and told me
that he was driving to New York and asked me to go
with him. He was dating a New York model whom he
later married. I called Phyllis and told her I would be in
New York over the weekend, and she agreed to meet
me. I called home and told my wife that I was going to
New York for the weekend, and it was quite all right
with her. Bill and I stayed at the New Yorker, and I met
Phyllis at Penn Station on Saturday night. The four of us
had a nice evening with a lot of drinks, dancing, etc.
Phyllis and I spent the night together in her room and
early Sunday morning we awakened somewhat hungover.
She said, 'Good morning, Ed. I had the funniest dream!
I dreamed that I was at your home in Rhode Island and
you were married and lived on the waterfront. Your
house had a concrete wall in front of it with a dock and
boats tied to it, and you had three children. Your oldest
girl kept running after me saying, "Oh, you go out with
my father." Your wife was very slim, had dark hair that
she wore behind her ears, and a bun on her neck; she
was very young, and had a black tooth in the front of
her mouth.'

"The only thing that she missed on was the children.
I lived on the waterfront, there was a concrete retaining

wall with a dock and boats, my wife was ten years my junior (around twenty-two), she was tall and slim, had black hair that she wore behind her ears with a bun on her neck, and she had a front tooth that had darkened due to a dead nerve. I was aghast not knowing what to say, and in a few minutes she said, 'Ed, what's the matter? You're awfully quiet.' I certainly was.

"That afternoon Bill and I dropped her off on the way back to Rhode Island and stopped for lunch. I asked her to tell Bill about her funny dream, and she laughingly repeated it verbatim. Bill's eyes popped, as he knew my wife well.

"This girl didn't know my right name, and we had previously discussed Rhode Island, and she didn't know anyone there. This was truly authentic.

"I saw Phyllis a few times during the summer of 1939, spent a weekend at Cape Cod, another in New Hampshire, and a couple of times in Bridgeport. I was very, very fond of her but decided to bust it up before it went too far. When I saw her for the last time I told her I was married (which I had always suspected that she knew), and she shook uncontrollably. When she regained her composure, I reminded her of the dream, and she couldn't explain it, but said it was the truth, which I'm sure of."

Why should nonexistent children have been added? Had it not been for the telltale, "Oh, you go out with my father," it might have looked as if the reason probably was that in such a home children would be expected. But the phrase put into the mouth of a child tells more. It suggests that unconsciously this dreamer was not taking her association with this man quite as casually as it might seem. It tells also that the dream maker can embroider the imagery, if he cares to do so.

Sometimes the imagery seems simply not to cover sufficient perspective to transfer the complete meaning. It is almost as if a certain part of the situation caught the fancy of the dream maker, and he omitted part of the scene, thus leaving no key for its interpretation. A case like that comes from a woman in Virginia, and incidentally it is one of the rarer ones in which a happy, rather than a sad, occasion is the subject matter.

"One night back in 1953 I had a most unusual dream. Part of the reason it was unusual was that it was so very vivid and impressed me so much and seemed so real that I related it to my husband at breakfast. I had never made a practice of telling my dreams before because I think they are usually boring to the other person. After breakfast I still could not get it off my mind—it seemed like something beautiful that I did not want to fade from my mind as dreams usually do. I then did something that I have never done before or since—I wrote an account, or description, of the dream in my notebook. Here is what I wrote then, exactly as I wrote it—without change:

" 'March 7, 1953. Last night I dreamed that I came upon a clearing in a woods at night; and there was a house, all lit up, with glass doors all down the side toward me opening onto a terrace. I could see inside a long table spread with a white cloth and set as though for a wedding feast. There were many silver candlelabra holding as many as six candles each all down the table and between them small delicate-stemmed compotes of milk glass filled with small white chrysanthemums. The table was filled with all sorts of dainty food—tiny, white-iced coconut cakes and little sandwiches. The candles had not yet been lighted. It seemed that everybody must have gone to the wedding and left the house all ready for the return.'

"The thing that puzzled me so much when I was dreaming this dream was that there was nobody in the room—no servants or anyone to watch over it. My most distinct impression was that everything was ready and waiting for some special occasion, but there was no clue as to what the occasion was or who the people involved were.

"I went on about my business and naturally forgot all about the dream. The first part of April, 1953, my husband received a letter from his company saying that he had been with them for twenty-five years and that they wanted us to come to Richmond and have luncheon at a restaurant or hotel there on his anniversary the latter part of April. My husband thanked them and declined as I had recently come from the hospital after a serious illness. (I would like to add here that neither of us realized before they notified him that my husband had been with them twenty-five years.) Later in the month the manager called my husband and said that since we would not come to Richmond they had made reservations for the luncheon at an inn nearer to our home. So, somewhat against our will, we were forced to go.

"The inn was rather new at that time, and I had never been there. When we arrived, the men were all there (ten); and since I was the only woman, and they were all so nice, it was a wonderful occasion. I wore an orchid and kept having the feeling that it was my wedding day. (I was married during the Depression and did not have any frills, and that day seemed more like my wedding than my own wedding day had.) When we went in to lunch, I had the strangest feeling that I had been in the dining room before although this was the first time—and there was the long table running down the wall, all in white with white flowers. Down the other side of the room ran windows looking out upon green grass and trees. After my illness and everything, the day proved to be one of the most glorious of my whole life. And I kept feeling all the time that that was my real wedding day. And all the men seemed to enjoy it so much although they said that usually they rather dreaded these occasions—probably because they had to make up the work the next day and maybe because they were usually very dull and something that had to be done in the line of duty. But on that day they truly seemed to enjoy themselves.

"It was not until I got home later that night that it came to me suddenly that the dining room was the room of my dream—only in reverse—as in the dream I had been looking in from the outside.

"Dr. Rhine, this experience has always puzzled me, and I think about it from time to time. How could I have known ahead about all this when I didn't know it was an anniversary, didn't know the company was in the habit of giving these luncheons, had never entered the inn, and besides that we refused the invitation and were literally forced to go. This was an exceedingly pleasant experience."

Just why the dream maker chose to obscure the meaning in that instance would puzzle anyone looking for strong—if not sinister—motivations in the best of dreams.

Occasionally the meaning seems to be transferred, but like personal identity it may be transposed in some way so that the person is misled and fails to understand the dream correctly. An example of this kind, from a woman in New York, shows the details so transposed that probably a question could be raised whether this actually was a realistic dream.

"During the early part of November, 1962, I dreamt that my summer bungalow on Long Island was a veritable shambles from water coming down the ceiling and walls. Night after night for fourteen consecutive nights I had the same dream: ceiling plaster down, walls wet and bulging, furniture ruined, etc. I tried going to bed late in the hope that, being tired, I would not have the dream. One night I took a glass of wine. I never touch the stuff as it paralyzes me. I felt dizzy and numb, but that did not stop the dream.

"I mentioned the dream to my daughter, to my brother—a retired lawyer—to a friend living up on Nelson Avenue in the Bronx. I even called up my caretaker and, after telling her of my dream, asked her to have her husband check my place and see whether everything was all right. She reported that her husband found my place in perfect condition. She expressed amazement at my superstitious nature.

"I still felt uneasy and called my insurance man, related the dream to him, and made sure I was covered. He laughed, and said he could not believe I was so foolish as to give credence to a dream. Monday, December 31, 1962, I left the office at five and arrived home at six to find my dining room in New York a veritable wreck. Water was coming down my ceiling, down my walls; carpets, floors, and furniture were wet and ruined.

"Investigation disclosed that the tenant above me had installed a washing machine without the benefit of a plumber. The husband did the work himself and the pipes were not properly connected. Again on Friday, January 4, 1963, I returned from work to find my apartment a regular Turkish bath. A leak had developed in the steam pipe next to the radiator along the window in *the same dining room*, and the steam was splurting its hot water all over the place. The apartment was a wreck. The steam in the building was turned off and an emergency crew worked on the pipe which had to be cut. To install the new piece of pipe, threads had to be made above and below the cut part by a certain instrument on which they had to keep pouring oil or grease, and every time that thing went back and forth it spluttered oil, or grease, all over the wall, window, windowsill, floor, etc. As if this were not enough, two days later a fire from a defective wire broke out in the same apartment above me and more water came down. I almost had a heart attack and do not feel too well yet. I am planning to move out in the spring.''

The dream was realistic only in what happened, not in the objective details, for the scene of the event was transposed, and the details with it.

The transposition was of locality, rather than identity, but here it did not afford protection from unwelcome news. Whatever the cause, to transpose like that was neither practical nor realistic. But then, perhaps along with its other idiosyncracies, the unconscious is also sometimes impractical. At least from cases as jumbled up as that one, it is clear that the dream maker is not confined to reality in making his imagery, although it seems likely that concern for property, worry and anxiety about it, figured somehow in that particular mix-up.

In some instances in which the imagery appears to be reproduced exactly, the viewpoint, if not the entire scene, may be such that an important point in the information is not transmitted. In a case reported by a man in California the scene itself was one from which he could not tell which of two individuals was involved. (The intuitionlike "voice" in this case is atypical in a realistic dream.)

"I had a dream that revealed in clear-cut imagery a scene in which my oldest son was killed just before he was to graduate from an advanced course of training in the Air Force, in August, 1943.

"I had this dream about June 20, 1943. A younger son, in the Army, had just been shipped out from San Francisco—destination unknown. In this dream I was standing on the edge of a shallow, dry irrigation channel and looking toward a high ridge of mountains which seemed to be not more than a mile distant, and approximately 6,000 feet high. Above the level of the field to my right were the mountains. The field seemed to be dark on the surface, as if it had just recently been plowed and harrowed preparatory to planting. Scattered over the field at widely spaced intervals were a few large round-topped trees with dark green foliage. The entire area was remote from any place that I had ever seen before. Almost immediately after I was aware, in the dream, of my surroundings, four men in uniform came off the field carrying a stretcher bearing a body, and crossed over the irrigation channel just a few feet in front of me. They did not seem to notice me standing there, nor did I want to speak to them. However, I did hear a distant voice say to me that they were carrying the broken body of my son, but no indication of which one it might be. At this point I awoke and quickly tried to shake off the impression of the dream, but it persisted clear-cut in detail. However, I did not tell my wife or anyone else about the dream.

"About two weeks later we received a letter from our younger son in the Army saying that he was in the Aleutian Islands and that no activity was expected in that area in the near future. This quieted my fears, but the imagery of the dream remained clear-cut in my mind.

"Around two months later, on August 23, 1943, a call came from the wife of my oldest son. She told me that George had been killed in a plane crash late that afternoon. I told her we would come as quickly as possible, and we arrived there shortly after midnight. The next day we went out to the Air Force Base and made arrangements for having the body returned home, and for the services of the chaplain stationed at the base.

"After the funeral I again pondered the dream and its possible association with George's accident. I decided that I would revisit the base and see if I could get permission and an escort to go to the scene of the accident. I found that the topography of the area was exactly as I had seen it in the dream over two months before. I went and stood on the bank of the dry irrigation channel as I had seen myself do in the dream. To my right was the blackened field, with the dark-green live oaks scattered at wide intervals over the area. The

blackened surface of the field had been caused by fire
spreading from the wrecked plane and not from plowing
and harrowing as it had seemed to be in the dream. I
asked the lieutenant who had driven me out from the
base and who had been there with the rescue crew at the
time of the accident—and to whom I had not told anything about the dream—where the stretcher-bearers had
brought out the body and where the ambulance had
waited. He indicated that they had brought the body
from the field and crossed over the dry irrigation channel just a few feet in front of where we were standing.
This was again just as I had seen it in the dream.''

Certainly the idea that imperfect imagery, substitutions of
identity, place, etc., are used by the dream maker as
protection against too unwelcome news, falls down in
cases like this one. The person's anxiety was not decreased
by uncertainty as to which son was involved. As in several
other cases, the dream only imperfectly carried its message, presumably because an unfavorable viewpoint was
chosen. The reason why, one can only say, must lie
hidden in the puzzle of individual psychology.

A noticeable feature of many of the dreams that bring
imperfect messages is that the defect of scene or imagery
leads the person either to fail to get the complete meaning
or to misinterpret it in some way. The misinterpretations
are sometimes overinterpretations of the situation, sometimes underinterpretations. In the case of a man in Texas it
was overinterpretation.

"I was born and reared on a farm in Minnesota. I
left there at the age of twenty and was married in
Lawton, Oklahoma, in 1922. Shortly after we were
married, I woke up crying. My wife of course wanted
to know what in the world was the matter with me.

"I told her that I had a very terrible dream that my
father had been killed in a runaway. She assured me,

of course, that it was only a bad dream and that we would have heard from home if anything had happened. However, I was pretty badly shaken up and was for several days; but, on not hearing anything from home, the incident was forgotten.

"I had told her of my entire dream, that Dad was driving a team, spreading manure on the north forty of our farm, and that he had dropped one line and the team started running. The only thing he could do was to hold the one line and let them run in a circle until they tired out. In my dream that is what he was doing, but he fell off the heavy spreader and it ran over him, killing him instantly.

"The following year on a visit to Minnesota and the farm home, we were just sitting down to dinner, when Mother told me that Dad was nearly killed last year in a runaway. She said, 'Well, he was over on the north forty spreading manure and the team ran away when he dropped one line. He kept them running in a circle until they finally tired and stopped.' He was not hurt in the least, but was in danger of being killed at any moment. A runaway team is a very dangerous thing.

"Mother's story of the incident was exactly the same as my dream as to location and other details. We were unable to figure out, however, whether my dream was before or after the runaway, that is, to the exact date. We were able to figure that it was in the same month. At that time we were living at least 1,000 miles apart."

Does the dream maker sometimes allow his anxieties to run away with him, and instead of protecting himself from an unwelcome circumstance, overinterpret it instead, and see it as worse than in reality? It looks that way. It looks as if some people tend to face calamities one way, some another. In constructing dream imagery, innate characteristics affect the result just as they do all the other expressions of the personality.

Failure to interpret the imagery correctly sometimes stands out as in itself the imperfect feature of an essentially correct dream scene, although of course the question can be raised whether the scene was the correct one if it did not really disclose the message. Such a case is reported by a woman in Nebraska.

"In 1931, a few days before my second son was born, I was resting on the bed. I wasn't sleeping, yet 'like a dream' a scene or incident was lived by me. I saw a beautiful green parkway with a striped tent a hundred feet or so away; there was a carpet, and I was walking down it seemingly to my wedding on the arm of someone close (although not my father), and people were gathered on either side. I heard them saying, 'How brave, how brave.' I came to and thought to myself, how strange a dream or vision. Why should I be brave at my wedding?

"My son was born October 27, 1931. On December 7, 1931, my husband died suddenly. I returned to Omaha and sorrowfully stepped out of the funeral limousine at the cemetery which I had never before seen. And, I *beheld* the exact picture of *my dream!* It was cold and snowy; there were the carpet, the people, and the striped tent, and people saying, 'How brave!' And I leaned on the arm of my brother-in-law. This time I *felt* like I was in a dream."

In such cases, one must suppose that either the scene itself was mischosen to hide an unwelcome fact, or else the failure to interpret it, to know it was a funeral and not a wedding, was evidence of the same motive. Whichever it was, it worked. The reality the scene represented was touched upon, but not faced, as one can say, and probably was the result of a personality characteristic like the one that substitutes identities. Cases like it have often been interpreted to mean a hidden unconscious wish for the death of the person involved, just as a slip of the tongue may be taken as a giveaway of a hidden motivation. Sometimes this kind of interpretation may be correct. But when made without any more evidence than in a case like the one above, such interpreting goes beyond the facts, particularly in view of the many indications one gets that a message from the unconscious can be diverted, deflected, or misinterpreted for the slightest of causes.

From such examples we see that the making of realistic imagery is not mechanical, even though the large majority of reported instances offer practically perfect reproductions. The dream maker does have a choice, and he can elect to translate the reality into imagery that reveals the entire situation just the way it occurs, or he can modify and even obscure it.

The reasons for making other than perfect selections of scene or imagery are obviously personal ones. They seem to vary from the very important, like reluctance to face disaster, and its reverse, the overanxiety that reaches for the worst; from such slight ones as unimportant inferences about something that might be expected to a suggestion as casual as that made by some small element of similarity.

This is the situation then, when realistic dreams are featured. What is different, when they are unrealistic?

Unrealistic or symbolic dreams show no need to reflect objective events just the way they occur. In these the dream maker plays free and selects imagery as he pleases. As a result, the meaning may not at once be self-evident, as it is in realistic imagery. The degree to which it brings a complete idea depends on how far removed from the news item itself the fantasy may be.

In most of the cases it looks as if first of all the item of information *suggested* something else to the dream maker, and that influenced the imagery he constructed. It looks as if more than a mere association of ideas occurred, for the imagery is apparently fashioned according to the suggested idea, rather than according to reality itself. This makes it possible for the imagery to depart from the actuality, to almost any length. It is this freedom that makes it possible for fantasies to develop that give no surface indication at all of their actual basis.

These suggestions, arrived at in the unconscious, can arise apparently for causes as endlessly different as are the specific situations and personalities involved. Take for instance, one reported by a man at sea.

"During the Second World War, I was in the U.S. Navy assigned to a ship in the Third Fleet in Okinawa. I had received letters from my wife, who was in Norfolk, Virginia, at that time. There was nothing in her letters to indicate that anything was wrong at home, nothing to indicate she had not been well.

"One day I had a depressed feeling—a feeling that something was wrong at home or that all was not well. I even remarked to the Pharmacist's Mate on board my ship that I had a strong feeling that something was wrong at home. He asked me if my wife had indicated anything in any of her letters. I told him that was the strange part, that her letters were cheerful and gave all the latest information at home, but not even a hint that anything was wrong.

"That night after I had gone to sleep I had a dream that I was back in Norfolk, that my wife, several friends, and I were in a rowboat and we were pulling into the boat landing after a fishing trip. There were a number of boats tied up at this landing, and just as we were going in between two of these boats a sudden swell appeared and my wife (who was standing up in our boat) fell over the side. Her head was mashed flat. I managed to grab her arm and pull her back into the boat. I saw some people on the pier and asked if

there was a doctor present, at the same time they
helped to pull her body up onto the pier.

"One of the men knelt down and examined her and
said, 'She is all right, but her tonsils will have to be
removed.' I awoke immediately at this point. I noticed the time by my wristwatch. Sometime later I
received a letter from my wife in which she said she
had had her tonsils removed. She even gave the date
and time she was on the operating table. I compared
this time with our time in the Pacific (the time I was
awakened from my dream), and at the very moment I
was dreaming of her, she was on the operating table."

To a Navy man, what more natural than that an unspecified calamity would suggest imagery having to do with
water, drowning, etc.

In a similar vein, though different in detail, an earlier
worry or anxiety might well affect the making of imagery,
even when the actual anxiety was a thing of the past.

"My story is as follows: I grew up with one of the
toughest, meanest, most unpredictable horses that any
youngster ever tried to handle. He could be as gentle
as a lamb. Also, he would kick, bite, or run away at
the drop of a hat. It was impossible to work him
down and no one could anticipate his next move. We
called him 'Brown.'

"In December, 1918, I was returning home from
the Army. No one was expecting me. At about 4:15
A.M. the train I was riding derailed and there was a
terrible wreck. I was unhurt. I reached home after
dark some fifteen hours later. The first greeting from
my mother was, 'Where were you at 4:15 this morning?' I tried to keep a straight face and asked why
such a question. She then told me that in a dream
Brown and I had been in one of our acts which had
been unusually violent. Brown had come out of it

clear—not a piece of leather left on him—but nothing
was clear as to what had become of me. Then she
awoke and the clock stood at 4:15; she had been
worrying about me all day. Then, of course, I told her
about the wreck. This thing has puzzled me through
the years.''

As already mentioned, the imagery may tend to be symbolic
rather than real, and the symbolism may or may not be self-
evident. In the case below its origin is not difficult to see.

''A dream I'd like to tell you took place about eighteen years ago. In the dream, I was walking along the
street. No one was around, but at a distance I saw a
black-draped figure approaching who I finally recognized as a favorite aunt of mine. She had on long
flowing black robes and a black hat with a brim and the
hat had a heavy black veil over it which covered her face.

''I laughed when I saw her because she is such a neat,
well-dressed person that I couldn't imagine her being
dressed in such unbecoming attire. I remember I continued to laugh as she came nearer and nearer. I could see
her face; and she didn't smile. She just looked at me and
then passed me without saying a word. This too was
shocking because she and I were quite close, more like
mother and daughter. Then, as she passed, in reality
someone began knocking on the door. I answered, and it
was my landlady telling me someone wanted me on the
telephone. It was this same aunt calling to tell me my
grandmother (her mother) had passed away.''

Sometimes the reason for the suggestion seems to be a
memory, a connection that probably only in a dream could
be revived and made into an almost living thing. A woman
in Tennessee had such a dream.

''My mother died on December 4, 1959. She had

lived in my home here for fifteen years. She was sixty-nine, and in perfect health until cancer struck and took her from us suddenly.

"We had set out some shrubbery together the spring before she died. It has grown particularly well this summer, and I have often thought how pleased she would have been to see it.

"Then, last week, on Monday morning, August 28, just before I woke up, I had one of the most vivid dreams of my life. I thought I came home from the office in the late afternoon and found that a very dignified lady—a friend of my mother's from her hometown—had dropped by for a visit and decided to mow the lawn. That sounds silly enough. But the horrible thing was that she had also cut to the ground the beautiful holly bushes in our front lawn.

"I was in a perfect fury over it. I stood in the front yard and called to my mother to come to see what had happened (in the dream she was very much alive). But she did not come. So I ran into the house and back to her bedroom where she stood in the center of the room. I saw her so distinctly that I could see the pores of her skin. I kept thinking, as I saw her, how thin and tired and weak she looked, I felt ashamed of myself for bothering her with any problems at all (an attitude I had, of course, constantly during her last illness).

"But I was furious about those shrubs being cut down. I kept saying to my mother, 'Do you know what she did? Have you seen it?' She simply shook her head slowly from side to side as if to say, 'It doesn't matter. It's not worth getting worked up over. It's not worth losing your temper. Never lose your temper over trivial matters.' What she meant was perfectly clear, although she was only shaking her head.

"I was furious. And then I woke up—with the dream so real that, for a moment, I was rigid with anger.

"Then I realized it was all a dream, but my mother had been so real that I turned to tell her about the dream. Then it hit me—that she was gone, that she no longer lived.

"I was so shaken by her nearness in the dream, in the very bedroom where I was sleeping, that I began to realize that—real as her skin had seemed, and sure as her meaning had been in every gesture—there had been a certain unearthly grayness about her. She had a weariness about her that was unspeakable—almost as if she had been summoned from the grave by the calls of my dream.

"The dream was so vivid that I wrote my sister (in San Antonio) about it that day. I also told another friend about it. I told them that at least the dream had one great value: it had taught me to control my temper—not to become angry over trivial matters, things that could not be changed like a cut-down shrub.

"The following Sunday morning, September 3, a neighbor of mine called me to the door to tell me that at last he had found a man who could do some yard work for me (remove some topsoil). I gave them exact instructions about what to do with the topsoil (all in the backyard), and returned to my bath. While I was in the tub, I heard much chopping going on in the backyard. As soon as I could get out of the tub and into a robe, I looked out the window. Sure enough, they had done it—they had cut down the beautiful forsythia bushes that my mother and I had set out in the backyard two years ago.

"They had grown beautifully this summer, and I had been much pleased at the way they exactly filled the space we had wanted them to fill. I was furious. Nobody had ever said one word to the neighbor or the man about trimming any shrubbery. I started to go out and say something to the neighbor about it, and then the dream of my mother suddenly came to me. I held my tongue. I kept seeing her shake her head, indicating that I must control my temper. I said nothing to the neighbor.

"This is greatly detailed, I know. But the two situations were so similar that one seemed to forecast the other almost exactly. They were only seven days apart."

In unrealistic dreams too, the dream maker sometimes plays free with the matter of identity. One characteristic that recurs in either kind of imagery, realistic or unrealistic, is the dreamer's tendency to cast himself in the major role—sometimes probably just because he likes to be "in things." Such could explain that feature of the dream in this letter from a woman in California.

"ESP has been much a part of my life to the extent that my husband and I take it as normal for me. I am an ordinary housewife, but have creative talents and am versatile in many fields; life to me is most exciting.

"I dream every night and entertain my husband each morning by telling the dreams to him. We lived in Hawaii before, during, and after the last war. He worked at Pearl Harbor, and we got up at 4:25 each morning so he could drive the long way to work in the blackout. I told him my dream at breakfast so he can verify this tale. He said, 'You have the weirdest dreams, but this is the craziest one I ever heard.' Here it is: My husband, our ten-year-old son, and I were on a picnic on bicycles. (We had no bikes, but that is OK in dreams.) We had stopped to rest and put our bikes on the ground. A busload of sailors stopped and asked us the way to Waemea Caves. We told them there was a Waemea Falls, but no caves. They were disappointed, as they were going to the caves on a picnic. So they dumped all their picnic food into our laps. There were uncooked wieners, buns, pickles, boiled eggs. *And* a gallon jar of mustard—enough to feed a regiment. The dream ended there.

"That same afternoon this is what happened: My

neighbor, who lived down our road about a half-mile, came driving like mad into our driveway and was shouting with laughter as she climbed out and handed me a gallon jar of mustard! Then she gave me cartons of buns, uncooked wienies, boiled eggs, and the food I had dreamed of. I could hardly wait for her explanation of this windfall. She said, 'I was driving along in my Ford and was stopped at the Waemea junction road (where we had rested in my dream). It was a huge busload of sailors on a picnic. They asked, ''Lady, can you show us the road to Waemea Caves?'' She answered that there were no caves, but they were at the junction to take them to Waemea Falls. They did not want to go to any falls. She invited them to come to her beach house, where they could have their picnic and cook their stuff on her outdoor grill.

"They did that and had a fine time, and on leaving gave her heaps of food left over as they had planned for about fifty men and only twenty had come on the bus. She shared the food with me, her nearest neighbor. She gave me the mustard as her family never used mustard.

"If I had not told this dream *hours* before it came to pass, no one could be expected to believe it."

Many dreams that classify as unrealistic include a deceased person in their imagery, as in the earlier case about the shrubbery. In that example it seemed natural enough that the mother be a dream character. She contributed no new information, but she fitted in because of the associations and memories called up by the situation.

Sometimes the possibility seems stronger that the dead person did in some way play a part. This often appears to be the case if the deceased brings new information to the dreamer, as in an experience like the following from Arkansas:

"On September 11, 1929, my father died. He was a

prominent attorney here from before the turn of the century until his death. During our association after the death of my oldest brother, we were inseparable. It seemed that I took brother's place in Dad's heart. At sixty-nine now I still miss Dad and think of him often. My mother, his widow, still lives with me and is ninety-three.

"Thirty days more or less after Dad's death, while still in the stage of shock, but partially recovered—I was notified by the bank of a note Dad had signed in favor of a guardian of a First World War veteran (the mother of the veteran). Dad was her lawyer. The bank was the administrator or trustee of the funds.

"I knew there was a contract between Dad and the guardian which protected Dad for the $500 note he had signed. This contract provided that the guardian was to make monthly payments out of her allotments until the note was paid. The note Dad gave her was to replace funds she had taken in excess of that allowed her as her son's guardian, and to ward off prosecution for embezzlement.

"The court knew of it and commended Dad for his part in the solution to protect the guardian whose boy was her ward.

"The trustee, while he knew of it, demanded the contract for his files to clear himself. I searched Dad's files, but to no avail. Naturally, I was worried. When I went home that particular night I had not been able to shake it off my mind. I mechanically ate my supper and drifted into the living room, still haunted by that contract, as time was running short. I picked up the evening paper to get my mind settled. I don't think I read a word. I had a rear-back chair. I pressed the button and gradually fell back into a horizontal position. I must have been at the point of exhaustion or something.

"When I sat in that chair, I was fully clothed. Presently a carriage drove up with two white horses pulling it. Dad was in the front seat beside my oldest brother who had passed away ten years previous. My little sister, who died early in life, was in the backseat with a lifelong friend of the family—a noted, outstanding lawyer and close friend of Dad's during their lives.

"Dad got out laughing—showing his pretty teeth. He had all of them when he died. Only one he broke off, but had it put back on. Dad was seventy-four when he died and was very active. He had gone dove shooting with me the day before he died. I marveled at this sight. I asked myself—Am I dreaming?

"Dad walked over—just as plainly—reached out and shook my hand saying, 'How are you, Son? I thought I'd come and pay you a visit. I've been watching you and am pleased the way you have been taking care of Nellie (my mother). I wanted to find out if you wanted to unravel anything I could help you with.' I said, 'Dad, how did you get out of that concrete vault I put you in?' He answered, 'You are not talking to me; it's my spirit.'

" 'Well,' I said, 'there's just one thing I want to know—that is, where did you put that contract you had with Mrs.——?' (She was the guardian referred to above.) Dad said, 'I can tell you exactly where it is. I was afraid she would steal it. In the righthand top drawer of my desk you'll find it full of envelopes turned up edgeways and a piece of newspaper folded under them. Raise the newspaper, and you'll find the contract in a large manila envelope. It's got my name and her name on the underside of it.' As he said this, he looked up and said, 'It's beginning to get daylight. I've got to go, but I'll be back.' When he said this, my wife began to shake me, saying, 'Wake up, Honey; you've been mumbling incoherently for I don't know how long.' I was sitting on the side of her bed half-undressed. It was breaking day as Dad had said. I had gotten up out of the chair and taken my shoes off, and how I got into the bedroom, I don't know.

"I didn't lose any time. I put my clothes on and got into my car. I drove straight to the office. I was nervous, but felt relieved as I was entering the office. My mind was in a doubtful daze. Something was telling me to have courage.

"In the past when I got faint messages in dreams, they slipped out of my mind when I woke up. On my way to the office that morning—what Dad had said on his visit was as clear as if it were before he died. I didn't have to stop to think. I unlocked the desk and pulled that right-hand drawer out nearly too far. There before me were the envelopes turned up edgeways. Under them was the newspaper folded smoothly so it would lie flat to keep them even. Under the newspaper was that contract just as his spirit said it was."

This could be interpreted that the experiencing person could have discovered the location of the contract, and could have woven it into the dream imagery just as a playwright puts words into the mouths of his characters. The other interpretation, that the "spirit" was actually there, is naturally the one preferred by many. Whether it is the correct one, however, must remain undecided until the question of survival of death is answered. Until then, the complete explanation of occurrences that suggest survival, but which as here can be otherwise accounted for, must be deferred. At least the presence of dream fantasy in all such cases is undeniable.

The main difference between the imagery of realistic and unrealistic dreams is thus shown to be the fact that in the latter it is based on an idea suggested by the news, rather than on direct meaning of the news. The tendency to depart from the exact fact rather than simply to copy it suggests a personality difference—that the unrealistic dreamers are the fanciful, creative ones, the realistic-minded the more pedestrian. Of course, a fault may sometimes be a virtue, and vice versa. For carrying messages, originality and fantasy are likely to be less efficient than good old faithful copying.

11. Lucid Dreaming, Night Flying and Astral Travel

Gayle Delaney

HAVE YOU EVER had the feeling that a dream is like a movie you filmed while away on a trip? When you see the movie upon your return, you realize how much of the trip you have forgotten and how little of it could be captured on film?

Many dreamers, having sensed that their dreams are but recalled highlights of richer, more complex experiences in the sleep state, have experimented with various ways of increasing their conscious awareness of those experiences. Some have discovered that it is possible to become conscious while sleeping or dreaming as well as to actually fall asleep without losing consciousness. By increasing their conscious awareness of different sleep and dream states, they have been able to consciously participate in both the production and action of their dreams. Some have had experiences of participating in the events "behind" or "before" the dream-making process. Some feel they have been able to travel out of their bodies and "visit," or at least perceive, different realms of reality. Almost everyone who has achieved a moderate degree of consciousness within sleep and dream states has been able to recall dreams far more vividly than before and direct them in ways which are both beneficial and exciting.

DEVELOPING CONSCIOUS AWARENESS
WITHIN THE DREAMSTATE

The degree to which you can be conscious of your sleeping
activities can range from recalling nothing at all about
them to recalling vividly many dreams each night, to
becoming aware of the fact that you are dreaming during
the dream itself and participating in its creation. You can
go further; you can become aware of your experiences in
levels of consciousness which may form the raw material
from which dreams are made.

Watching the workings of your mind while your body
sleeps is a fascinating endeavor which will lead you to a
much fuller understanding of your dreams. It will also
increase your appreciation for the depth and variety of
experiences available to you when your consciousness is
free to focus its attention on your inner world.

In *lucid* dreaming, the dreamer is aware of the fact that
he or she is dreaming while the dream is happening.
You have probably experienced some degree of lucidity
if you have been recalling your dreams at all. How many
times have you said to yourself, "This is only a dream,"
while some dream enemy was chasing you? This is a form
of *prelucid* dreaming in which the dreamer, while sleeping, half realizes that some segment of the dream is only a
dream. A fully lucid dream is one in which you definitely
recognize that you are dreaming. In a lucid dream you can
use your awareness to change the dream you are having in
almost any way you choose. What would you like most to
do in a dream? Fly and soar like an eagle? Meet with a
wise old friend or relative? Ask each figure in a dream
what it represents? Or perhaps you would like simply to
watch the progress of a dream, knowing all the while that
you cannot be hurt by the most fearsome of its images.

There is a joyous quality to many lucid dreams that is
almost irresistible. Colors are filled with sunlight and moon-
light, and one often has the impression that everything in
the dream is more "real" and vivid than in waking reality.

If you hear music in a lucid dream, it will probably be sweeter than any earthly sound you know. Tastes and smells will delight you by their intensity, and the degree to which you can direct the progress of events will amaze you.

In her book *Lucid Dreams,* Celia Green, Director of the Institute of Psychophysical Research in Oxford, England, reviews the phenomenon of conscious dreaming. Patricia Garfield, in *Creative Dreaming,* has made an important contribution to the literature on lucid dreaming by analyzing her own lucid experiences in relation to those of the lucid dreamers reviewed by Green, and by suggesting certain techniques for inducing such dreams. I have drawn largely from these accounts and from the experiences my students and I have had with prelucid and lucid dreams.

You may have already noticed that with dream incubation, where conscious attention is lavished upon the dream process while the dreamer is in the waking state, is rewarded by an increased awareness in the dream state. The psychologist Kilton Stewart took advantage of this phenomenon in developing a theory of dream education which he called "creative psychology." Stewart evolved a set of directives which instructs dreamers *to "confront and conquer"* all harmful, useless, wasteful, rigid, obsolete, infantile, uncooperative, sick, or troublesome images in a dream. The dreamer is to kill, burn, melt, or somehow eliminate or change these images while he is dreaming them. At the same time, the dreamer is encouraged to help and to cooperate with all helpful dream images as well as to ask them for assistance and information. Stewart stated that, by studying and reviewing such directives in the waking state, one would eventually remember them in the dream state. The purpose of such directives and the dream action they encourage is to educate the dreamer to attain a greater awareness in the dream state so that he can outface and conquer dream representations of conflicting, fearful, and negative aspects of himself and thus unify his personality.

The Stewart technique is different from dream incubation in several significant respects. When you incubate a dream, you consciously choose the issue the dream is to treat, but your autonomous, usually unconscious, dream process is free to deal with the matter in its own fashion. Stewart's directives constitute a form of dream guidance in which one is to guide or influence the action of the dream once it is in progress. The directives are suggested to the waking mind, but they are meant for use by the dreaming mind, which is to guide rather than control the spontaneous dream action. Although dream incubation may precipitate lucid dreams, it does not require lucidity in the dream state. Dream guidance, on the other hand, does require at least a minimal degree of awareness while the dream is happening.

Because the degree of consciousness dream guidance requires is not very difficult to attain, it is often a stepping stone to lucid dreaming. Dream guidance can greatly benefit the dreamer if it is used wisely. My students and I have used a modified form of the Stewart technique to increase our conscious awareness of dreaming and to simplify and accelerate the problem-solving process in both our spontaneous and our incubated dreams.

Confronting the Monsters. I agree with Ernest Rossi and many psychotherapists that, until we can feel loving acceptance of negative (frightening, threatening, or frustrating) dream figures, we will not be free of their negative psychological influence. In the Stewart technique, the dreamer is told to take forceful aggressive action against any negative dream figure. She is to turn and confront pursuers rather than run from them. The dreamer is to create weapons or call forth friendly dream figures to help conquer aggressors, and, if all else fails, the dreamer must stand her ground and fight to the death in the consciousness that she is dreaming and cannot be physically harmed. Although it is certainly better to turn and fight one's negative dream images than to run from them, I believe that the directive to "always advance and attack in the teeth of danger" is unwise. The theory behind it is that "the spirit or essence of this dream character will always emerge as a servant or ally." However, it is not at all clear that the essence of a slain dream enemy is or will be helpful to the dreamer's psyche. In fact, it seems that slain dream enemies keep popping up in future dreams in various guises until the dreamer finally understands and accepts them as a part of herself. In reviewing dream accounts in the literature and in my research files, I find that very much more is to be gained by confronting threatening dream images with a desire to understand rather than to demolish them. I have found that asking a negative dream figure "What do you want?" or "What do you represent?" results not only in the transformation of the figure into a friendly one, but also in valuable insights into the parts of the personality represented by the originally threatening figure. For example, Mary Ellen dreamed:

I am in my apartment when a gang of young thugs walks in and says they are going to do something terrible to me. I manage somehow to trick them out of the apartment and lock all the windows and doors. I hope I am safe. I am still frightened. They get back in, and now they are in a new and terrifying form. They look like huge monsters with tentacles, bulging eyes, and sea-monster skin. I remember that I was not going to let fear get the better of me in my dreams from now on. So I swallow my fear and concentrate on saying, "Well you got back in. Now what do you want?" Immediately the monsters transform into friendly people who explain that they want to be my allies and help me understand myself. They proceed to demonstrate (in ways I've forgotten) why I've been so jealous of my best friend.

Their explanations are "right on" and I awake feeling more self-confident and far less jealous of her.

If you persist in suggesting to yourself while awake that you will turn and confront your negative dream images, and that you will then ask them why they threaten you, you will succeed. This may happen for you right away or it might take a couple of months, but you will be able to do it and, when you do, you will feel a great sense of accomplishment. This feeling will carry over into your day and give you a new sense of courage and prowess. If you succeed in asking your negative dream image what it wants, you will also bring into your waking consciousness surprisingly helpful insights.

Joe, before he came to his first dream meeting, had the following dream:

> I'm keeping order in some kind of institution. A BIG fellow, huge, keeps slithering backward across the hall floor. This is against institution policy. The first couple of times, I don't stop him. I'm afraid of him because he is so big, and he knows it. Finally, I go over to him and poke stiff fingers at his eyes. "What's that for?" he asks. I answer, "I'm gonna make you (obey? the rules?) one way or the other, even if I die in the attempt."

Joe sees himself as a nice, kind guy—which he is. He is also an assertive, aggressive human being. This was the part of himself he thought crazy and locked up. He saw this aspect of himself as very threatening, and had considered himself to be sliding backward on the path to maturity and spiritual enlightenment whenever he expressed even quite natural and appropriate assertiveness. Had Joe asked the threatening figure what he wanted, or what he was up to (instead of vice versa), Joe would probably have gotten a clearer insight into his "nice-guy" complex. As it was, Joe had confronted and outfaced his dream enemy. Though he felt glad to have stood up to him, he did not get very much out of the encounter except a hint (which he missed) that he was risking the well-being of his psychological life by keeping this big fellow in line with the rules of his nice-guy role. We encouraged Joe to suggest to himself that his frightening dream figures were really friendly ones distorted by his fear, and that he should try loving them. Then he had a dream about a tiger. In this dream he was seeking his lost pet tiger, who was hiding from him. When he found it, the tiger was dressed in women's clothing. Joe was gentler with the rule breaker this time, and the tiger's response gave him an important clue to the dynamics of the conflicts which led him to dress his aggressive and assertive tendencies in nice-guy behaviors (women's clothes). When Joe had experimented with a more accepting attitude toward his assertiveness and with the enhanced sense of self-esteem that required, Joe had the dream about his playful, energetic, pet lion. He was learning to love the lion inside him, and in so doing discovered its natural nature was not hostile but helpful to him. I believe he came to this realization sooner by practicing a more loving, non-attack-oriented form of dream guidance.

Virginia dreamt of a "big, black screeching blob." In the dream, she recognized it to be an acquaintance of hers. She then authoritatively told it to stop playing the victim role. Virginia added that it was responsible for its own actions and could not blame its misfortune on outside forces. Virginia's dream action was undoubtedly a healthier response than fright or agreement.

Another dreamer, Rick, had a dream almost every three weeks or so of being attacked by hateful, spiteful men. The men would appear as soldiers, tyrants, bullies, and landlords. Each time Rick had these dreams, he would manage to defend himself, and sometimes kill his attackers. Yet the dreams kept recurring in various forms until Rick was encouraged to reconsider what he felt was his justified hatred of his father. We thought that, if Rick could forgive his father and love him as a struggling human being, he (Rick) would be freed of the hatred and resentment that pursued him in his adult life. Although Rick's father had been dead for several years, he had strongly influenced Rick, who was still carrying his image of his father and a hatred toward him inside himself. Rick experimented with the idea of "hating the sin but loving the sinner" and began to see how he could forgive his father for his real or imagined wrongs. Rick even began to forgive the part of himself that was like his father. Although his hatred was still alive and strong, at least he could now consider that his attitude was not the only one available to him. During one of our meetings, Rick resolved to confront and try to understand his dream pursuers.

Before the next dream meeting, Rick dreamt that an armed soldier barged into his house. As Rick grabbed a gun to shoot him, he remembered his resolve and vaguely realized that he was dreaming. He put down his gun and mentally communicated to the soldier that he wanted to understand him. Rick said, "What do you want?" The soldier turned into a friendly contemporary of Rick's and said, "I want you to stop hating." Then the former soldier explained to Rick things he could not remember but which he felt brought him a profound understanding of something. Rick was feeling loving and grateful toward his unknown friend when the scene changed. Next, Rick was with his father, whom he saw as a man suffering with his own conflicts and who was far from malicious. For the first time, Rick felt a deep compassion and forgiveness for his father. Here the dream ended.

Rick told us that the dream had given him a taste of how it would be if he could give up his hatred for his father. He was encouraged to do so by the memory of the dream. Old hates rarely die overnight. Yet it is interesting to note that, since this experience, Rick has had only four dreams of attacking hateful, spiteful males in the last eighteen months. In each, he has been able to come to a compassionate understanding with his pursuer. Dream experiences like these have a wonderfully integrative effect upon the dreamer's personality.

To confront and understand threatening or perplexing dream images is, in my opinion, the best way to approach dream guidance, because the rewards of loving and understanding your enemies seem far greater than those of demolishing them. Most often, the conquering of a negative image ends the dream: The dreamer is left with a sense of achievement and courage. This is certainly preferable to having fled and not confronted the image at all. However, by not making the effort to understand the attacker, the dreamer has missed an opportunity to increase his understanding of that part of himself which the negative image represents.

In dreams where you are frightened by certain images, first try to tell yourself that you are dreaming and need not fear being harmed. Tell yourself that you are in another kind of reality in which time and space, cause and effect, operate according to dream, not waking, reality. Tell yourself that you are safe. Try to understand what is happening to you and ask your dream figures what they represent or what they want. If you can do this, you will surely learn much from the dream. You may also come to a clear realization that you are dreaming and become fully lucid. At this point, you will be free to experiment with your new state of awareness. It may take time and practice, not only to become fully lucid but to become conscious enough of the possibilities to take advantage of them.

Waking up in Your Dreams. Your first efforts to become conscious in the dream state may result in passing dream thoughts in which you reflect upon the dream process. They may not precipitate a full awareness that you are dreaming, but they are a beginning. One woman who dreamt she was on her way to a great council of all sorts of "people," understood that an elf would be present and wondered if her dream producer's representation of an elf would meet her high expectations of what elves should be like. After this thought, the dreamer lapsed back into a normal dreaming state. This is an example of a prelucid dream in which the dreamer had a glimmer of awareness of dreaming but did not quite grasp its implications. She did not become lucid, with a clear realization that she was dreaming.

Sometimes reflective thoughts about the dream process will lead the dreamer into a lucid awareness that he or she is dreaming. The next problem is for the dreamer to continue using critical faculties and not fall back into normal, nonreflective dreaming. The only remedy found for this is practice. Ten of us in the dream meetings have tried to focus on a given image in lucid and prelucid dreams, to examine it carefully, reminding ourselves to keep the image stable or to transform it through an act of will. The idea is not to forget that we are in a position to direct our dream imagery. So far, only three of us have had any success in doing this. Our success in calling forth the dream environment and experience of our desires has been limited to brief moments typical of novices.

Lucid dream direction, even when practiced by very skilled dreamers, has not been experienced as an ability to entirely control dream reality. Hervey de Saint-Denys, after extensive experiments with his lucid dream states, wrote, "I have never managed to follow and master all the phases of a dream, I have never even attempted it." The freedom to control even lucid dream environments is not limited but enhanced by the apparently autonomous or spontaneous characteristics of dream reality. It would seem that our deepest pleasures, joys, and comprehensions flow from the autonomous, often surprising and exquisitely creative elements of our dream experiences. The purpose in directing or guiding dreams is not to control dream reality completely or try to force it into the forms of waking experience but to taste dream reality as vividly and as fully as possible.

Lucid and prelucid dreamers sometimes find themselves deciding to practice manipulating their dream environment. Barbara, in her dreams of communing with trees and oceans and raindrops, often practices moving the clouds by her thoughts. I have had several dreams in which I have experimented with changing the size and quantity of objects around me. Once I dreamed I was in a nineteenth-century Bavarian bar. I looked at two beer steins on the table and decided to "think" them into three. It worked. Then I made one larger and one smaller, increased their number, and finally decided that there should be only one stein on the bar. This was great fun, and I had the distinct impression that I was perceiving and learning through play how to work with the true nature of reality. Since that dream, I have had others like it and have heard and read of similar stories from other lucid dreamers.

Perhaps lucid dreamers' fascination with altering dream images just to see if it is possible and what will be the results is a natural learning process. Some philosophical and spiritual texts propose the idea that our thoughts (beliefs, attitudes, hopes, desires, and fears) create reality—not only our response to reality but the events and objects of reality as we know it. Such texts explain that, if it were not for the time it takes for thoughts to manifest in physically perceivable form, we would not consider such an idea so unlikely. In dream states, where we are free of the constrictions of linear time, perhaps we recognize at some deep level that thoughts create reality not only in dreams but in three-dimensional, physical states as well. Even this form of manipulating lucid dream images is usually aimed not so much at controlling dream reality as at exploring the different ways it works.

The practice of dream guidance will lead you to thoughts in which you reflect upon the process and nature of dreaming. These thoughts can trigger lucid dreams if you fully realize that you are in fact dreaming. You might also choose a "trigger object." While awake, select an object you are likely to encounter in a dream, such as a tree, a familiar street or house, a part of your body, a friend, or any of your frequent dream images. Suggest to yourself during the day that seeing the trigger object will make you realize that you are dreaming. Another way to trigger lucidity is to suggest to yourself that in dreams you will become aware of incongruous and bizarre elements and that they will signal your dreaming state to you. This happened to me in the following dream about "The Quick-step," which is a dance in a series of national test dances which an ice skater must pass in order to get a gold medal (like karate's black belt) in ice dancing. In day life, this was the last dance I had to pass before receiving my medal in 1967.

I've just taken (danced) my test on the quickstep. It was pretty good and I think I've passed. But Lo! the judges fail me! All three of them! I think, "Oh well, I'll take it again as soon as the enforced two-month waiting period expires." I do want it to be a great test if it is my last before the medal. But I am disappointed, because I thought I had done well. I read the judges' comments on my score papers. "Lean back more here. Extend this edge there," etc. These comments are absurdly pica-yune and petty. They in no way justify my failing marks. I am angry but again think that it's OK, be-cause when I pass this test it should be so good that no one could give me anything but very high marks. . . . Then, wow! Wait! This is 1976 not 1967. I've already passed this test, and I don't have to worry about pleas-ing any judges. And because I'm dreaming, I can skate with wings on my blades. I then start to skate again, but this time I can do anything. When I jump, I am weight-less, and I fly as I turn in the air. When I spin, my balance is perfect. I feel a happiness that is one of the most profound I have ever known, and I am at one with the world. I feel all the forces of the harmony of the universe in my skating, and the intensity of my joy knows no bounds.

This dream deeply impressed me with the way I restrict my enjoyment of skating by being a picky, perfectionistic judge of it. The dream has brought about a significant, enduring change in my attitude toward skating. The morning after the dream, I skated with my partner and secretly decided not to work but to play at it. Bob is something of a perfectionist himself, and when he began to comment on how much better my skating was than usual, I knew that my dream had had a tangible effect. I think that our dream producers' most powerful agents of change are not threat and fear (which are powerful) but pleasure and peaceful, yet exhilarating, joy. A dream producer can show you what it is like to let go of an attitude or complex which limits you. Then, once you've seen Paris, it becomes awfully hard to keep yourself down on the farm tending old and comfortable, but limiting, attitudes. This is especially true in lucid dreams, where the intensity of perception can be so marvelously heightened.

After finding the incongruous elements in dreams, one is tempted to say, "This is not real, it is only a dream." Such a mental exclamation can be effective in precipitating a lucid dream. However, I prefer the response, "This is not waking reality; this is dream reality." This response better prepares the dreamer to operate within the dream state, which is, after all, real in its own way and follows its own laws.

Celia Green states that almost all the lucid dreamers she studied stressed "the importance of emotional detachment in prolonging the experience and maintaining a high degree of lucidity." Garfield also suggests that the lucid dreamer not allow himself to become too emotionally involved with the dream action because this might disrupt

the lucid state. However, both Garfield and I have experienced strong emotional involvement in some lucid dreams
without losing our lucidity. It may be that lucidity depends
not on avoiding the experience of strong emotion but on
maintaining a constant awareness or observation that you
are experiencing it. This would be similar to being both
the witness and the experiencer of your emotions and
thoughts, as is suggested in several forms of meditation. It
would seem that one of the greatest advantages of dream
lucidity is the clarity and intensity of perception and expression it makes possible. You can maintain lucidity while
experiencing this if you learn to observe your dream thoughts
and feelings as you experience them. This "witness principle" or critical faculty would seem to be at the base of
even the vaguest prelucid dream experiences, in which one
reflects upon the process or incongruity of the dream.

Before we go on to other ways of inducing consciousness in dreams, it might be good to consider one of the
major factors inhibiting many people's efforts in attaining
consciousness of the sleep state.

One clear night in 1970, I was in the French Alps at a
ski resort called Chamonix. I had skiied to the point of
"first day on the slopes" exhaustion. I dragged myself out
of the hot tub and tumbled into bed. I was so tired, I
wondered why I wasn't asleep after a few minutes. Then I
heard myself practicing my French. Then I noticed a short
dream that seemed to be happening while I was wide
awake. This was like a real dream, not the plotless, brief
hypnogogic images so common just before sleep. Then I
seemed to be reviewing the day and practicing both skiing
and French. After quite a while of this, I became very
impatient to fall asleep. I was tired and had a full day's
skiing ahead of me the next day. This was no time for
insomnia. Another dream intruded upon my more normal
thoughts. Finally I came to the conclusion that my body
had fallen asleep but "I" hadn't! I watched the next dream
with renewed interest. Then it occurred to me to replay it,

changing one dream event so that the dream would terminate with a resolution which would help me accept the inevitable fact that after this week I would never again see a certain Mr. X who had made a deep impression on me. It worked. The dream gave me a sense of peaceful acceptance that we would never be free to get to know each other, and I was grateful for that. This lucidity was very beautiful and helpful in the dream state, but it was irritating and boring in between dreams where I witnessed the endless chatter of another part of my mind that just wouldn't stop practicing French. I felt like a captive audience at a spelling bee. What a time to become lucid. I wanted to sleep, to go *un*conscious. I wanted to awake refreshed to a new world. I had seven days to enjoy in Chamonix. Why couldn't I experiment with my consciousness while I was back home in New Jersey? Try as I might, I couldn't go unconscious. Why it never occurred to me to move my body and so break the spell puzzles me. At any rate, several dreams and many mundane thoughts and pronunciation exercises later, the sun came up and I dressed for the ski slopes.

Although I expected to feel a great fatigue skiing, I seemed as rested as I usually do after a good night's sleep. During the following two nights, I had the same impression that I was wide awake and fully conscious. I seemed to be witnessing several other levels of consciousness operating simultaneously. While my daily review and "normal chatter" thoughts would occur, so would my French and ski practice sessions. On another level, dreams would periodically occur; on yet another level things were happening which I couldn't quite perceive. While all this was going on, I was also conscious of my reflections on this unusual state of consciousness and of my increasingly adamant desires to go unconscious. I really just wanted to be relieved of all this awareness. I kept wishing I could "pass out" of this witness role and not have to attend to it. I told myself that this was no time to be fooling around with my sleep; that no matter how much I had hoped for and tried to achieve consciousness of my sleep states, this was not the time for it. I kept telling myself to "fall asleep." On the fourth night, I finally had a normal night of mostly unconscious sleep. Years later, some of the dreams I had during those "lucid nights" are still amazingly vivid in my mind. I found that I could not willfully produce lucid nights upon my return to the United States. I have had such experiences only four times since Chamonix, and each time I was in a very high-altitude ski resort and had gone to bed physically exhausted.

Since my first experience with lucid nights, I have learned a little about meditation techniques of quieting the mind and have used these to reduce somewhat the seemingly endless "chatter thoughts" in my mind at such times. Although my experiences with lucid nights has consequently become more agreeable, and in spite of the fact that the lucid dream states of these nights are fascinating and sometimes very pleasurable, and in spite of the fact that I do not seem to lose any physical rest from them, I *still* resist staying conscious. I have become aware of attitudes I had not recognized I held about the desirability of not taking conscious responsibility for my sleeping activities. Although I lust after lucid dreams and expanded awareness of all of my experiences, I am willing to go only so far before I've had enough and seek escape in the refuge of unconsciousness.

The Tibetan yoga of dream control teaches that one can willfully and regularly allow the body to sleep while the mind remains fully conscious and free to manipulate in both dream and other sleep consciousness. You might ask yourself how much you really want to become conscious in your dream or sleep states. Of course, you needn't go as far as remaining conscious through most of the night. But if you become aware of your own desires not to attain consciousness in dream states, you will be better equipped to deal with them if and when they inhibit your progress toward lucid dreaming. Ambivalence toward new growth and awareness in both waking and sleeping states is natural and is best dealt with when it is confronted and understood.

LEARNING HOW TO WAKE UP AND HOW TO FLY

False Awakenings. A curious experience which you may have had is that of apparently awakening from sleep or from a dream, and then actually awakening and realizing that the first time you "awoke" you were still dreaming. These experiences are called *false awakenings*. If you can become aware that a false awakening is indeed that, you may become lucid. The next time you suspect that you are experiencing a false awakening, test your environment to see if you are truly awake or not. See if you can look at the bed you went to sleep in. If it is empty and you can touch it, and if all other things seem normal, then you are probably awake in waking reality. However, if you look back to your bed and your body is still in it, then you will know you are in a dream state having what is called an out-of-body experience (OBE). It is not always possible to think of or to find one's bed during a false awakening. In this case, the best way to explore the reality of your present environment is to see how it compares with waking reality. Is something out of place? Are basic laws of gravity and placement in space being violated? Do the lights go on when you flip the switch? Tests like these should tell you if you are awake in day or dream reality. If you realize that you are in a dream state, you may then either have a lucid dream experience or choose to conduct other experiments on your abilities in this state.

Several of us in the dream meetings have experienced two kinds of false awakenings. In the first, the dreamer, apparently awakening from a dream, then has another dream while under the impression that he is awake. This impression is then corrected by the actual awakening. In the other sort of false awakening, the dreamer, after having completed a dream, seems to awaken into the normal environment of his room. Sometimes the dreamer looks at the clock to see if there is enough time to go back to sleep before beginning the day's activities. Sometime later, the actual awakening occurs. When I have a false awakening of this nature, I seem quite able to read the clock, which in fact may be in another room or in my own room in extreme darkness. Sometimes I am vaguely aware that I am still asleep and am checking the time to see if I must awake my physical body or if I can go on sleeping. Usually this occurs within an hour of the time for which the alarm is set to go off. I have always had the impression that my sleep reading was accurate upon awakening.

Another sort of false awakening described by Celia Green is apparently awakening to the awareness that something is amiss. Usually the dreamer lies still in bed and is rather frightened. There is suspense in the air. The dreamer may hear voices talking about her or breathing. Then, if the dreamer does not awaken in fright, she might explore the situation by saying to herself, "What's going on here?" or by seeming to reach out to locate the source of the sounds.

Virginia had an experience like this. She seemed to awaken from a dream and was lying in her bed when she felt a threatening darkness or shadow come over her. She tried to open her eyes but couldn't. She tried to scream but couldn't. Then she wondered what was happening and heard two men talking about making some use of her body. She realized that she was dreaming and knew that she could not be harmed. Now she could open her eyes. The intruders became friendly. One was her brother, the other a friend of his. The three of them had a pleasant encounter dealing with their relationships, and the experience ended when Virginia started laughing so hard that she awoke. Whatever else this experience may suggest, it demonstrates once again how fear in sleep and dream states acts as a distorting lens. Whenever you can overcome fear in these states, you will almost always find that a frightening experience then becomes a nonthreatening one that may be enjoyable.

Dream Flying. An easier route to lucid dreaming seems to be flying. In these dreams, one can fly like Peter Pan or Superman without any mechanical assistance. If you have had flying dreams, you know how pleasurable they are. Many people consider them to be their most enjoyable dreams. It is possible to induce flying dreams through incubation and other techniques and thereby begin or increase your experiences with dream flying.

When you fly in a dream, you have a perfect opportunity to become aware of your dream state if you recognize that you are engaging in an activity that is impossible for you in waking reality. Sometimes you will notice that, while you are flying, your mind seems especially clear and you may be vaguely aware that this is one of your favorite dream activities. If you can push this awareness into the full realization that you are dreaming, you will become lucid and able to consciously direct your flight and other activities in this state.

Sometimes, after having become lucid in a dream, you may choose to fly simply because it's so much fun. Some lucid dreamers choose to see if they can visit friends, favorite places, or guides, or just practice their flying technique. Some dreamers report that they learn to improve their flying techniques with each new flying dream. The angle of an outstretched arm or leg or the rate of flapping the arms might be altered to improve the control of flight. I have had dreams in which I am instructed to remember the feeling of twisting my body, using my arms as helicopter-like propellers. The impression is that what I need to recapture in order to fly well is the *feeling,* not the specific body movements, which seem to be symbolic. As other lucid dreamers and I have found, the body movements we make to fly seem finally unnecessary once we have confidence that flying is directed by our thoughts and emotions.

Many dream flyers, lucid and prelucid, have practiced their flight to see how high or how far they could fly. Some have experimented with aerobatics as they develop their agility and confidence in flight. Judging from the accounts available to me, flying dreams tend most often to take place in outdoor environments. I have noticed that about half of my flying dreams (lucid or not) occur in a dance studio or an ice-skating rink. I am often practicing controlling my flight so that I can use it in my skating and dance. I may hit my head on the rafters, bump into a wall, or overshoot the ice surface in too long a jump. These experiences are always rather humorous and carry with them the knowledge that I am just a beginner and have much to learn. Over the past seven years of such dreams, I have clearly made progress in controlling and directing my flight, and this has brought with it enormous satisfaction. A number of dreamers have commented that, during a false awakening after a flying dream, until they actually awaken they are certain that they could fly in waking reality. I have had flying dreams (lucid and nonlucid) in which I was told by dream teachers or guides that I could learn to fly in my skating and dance in day life. I have said things like, "Do you mean that I can really learn to use this ability and actually use gravity for my own artistic purposes in the physical world, the world where I skate with steel blades on real ice?" The answer has always been *yes*. I awake to physical waking reality after such dreams with a sense that I could fly on earth if I could just master the skills and acquire the confidence. Rationally, I know that reports of levitation have never been scientifically verified and that what my dreams portray has never been done before in the three-dimensional world. Yet the dreams impress me so deeply that I will often follow them up by trying to recapture the flying states of mind and trying to fly or levitate in my dance or my skating. It hasn't worked yet, but insofar as the feeling of flying has inspired me to skate or dance better, it has had a welcome influence.

Surely the fact that flying dreams can seem so convincingly real as to encourage sane and rational people to think that flying is in fact possible suggests something of their intensity. Many dream fliers are entirely convinced that they do indeed have the ability to fly, at least in nonphysical dimensions of reality, which they consider every bit as "real" as waking reality.

There are several ways to induce flying dreams either for the sheer pleasure of them or to precipitate lucid dreams. The methods described will require practice and patience, but flying dreams are well worth the effort.

First, you can use dream incubation to request a flying dream. In your incubation discussion, describe how much and why you want to fly in your dreams. Recall and describe past flying or floating dreams and savor their delights. You might choose a location in which or to which you would like to fly. Describe it in your journal. Then formulate an incubation phrase such as, "I want to fly," or "Tonight I fly," or "Tonight I fly to the beach." Hold the phrase vividly in mind as you fall to sleep. Successful incubations for flying are more difficult to achieve than those for problem solving or inspiration. Perhaps this is because, in incubating a dream to solve a problem, you are already quite involved with the issue and your producer is freer to deal with it as he or she likes. Producing a specific dream action such as flying may require far greater conscious control of the dream process.

You can reinforce your dream incubation efforts by focusing upon the desired activity during the day. Tell yourself that tonight you will fly in your dreams. Look at birds, study their flight. Study photographs of birds, draw and paint them. If airplanes fascinate you, focus on their flight during the day. All your day thoughts about flying will increase the likelihood both of your flying in a dream and of your recognizing that you are dreaming while doing so. You may have dreams of flying freely in your own weightless body, or you may dream of flying in planes or floating in water. The sensation to look for is one of weightlessness. Dream friends may guide you in leaping higher and higher, or in floating in the air or water without fear. You may dream of showing others how to leap or fly or float. In demonstrating the art, you may recognize the wonderful, weightless, joyous sensation and realize that you are dreaming. You may also dream of falling. If you do, tell yourself not to be afraid and let yourself fall. Usually you will begin to float or fly and can continue the dream, perhaps becoming lucid in the process.

Exploring the Feeling of Freedom from Your Physical Body.
Alfred Adler's theory that we use flying dreams to express our will to dominate and be superior to others may apply to some flying dreams. Steckel's theory that flying dreams represent death because suspension in air suggests ghosts and angels seems useful when the dream includes images or feelings which connote death to the dreamer. Jung saw flying dreams as a symbolic representation of the dreamer's desire (or actual achievement) of breaking free of restrictions or a problem that he wishes to or has overcome. This interpretation makes sense in many cases where the dreamer's life situation corresponds to it. In such dreams, the flying may be used to escape from pursuers or overcome obstacles in one's path.

In interpreting flying dreams, it is important that you consider the feeling tones of the experience and your associations to it. Traditional psychological theories will help you to understand one level of many flying dreams; however, there may be a whole level of significance to these dreams which traditional approaches miss entirely. It may be that we really are flying, albeit in another dimension of reality and perhaps in another body. Many people throughout history and in the present have claimed to be able to leave their physical bodies in bed while a part of their conscious selves was free to travel to other places. These people further claim that, while their consciousness is away from the physical body, it seems often to be clothed in a lighter, more subtle "second body," which seems ghostlike to witnesses who have reportedly perceived it.

The second body, or double, is a well-documented phenomenon which has been studied by scientists since the 1920s. Hector Durville and other French experimenters used chemical screens and other devices to try to detect its presence. Durville used hypnosis both to "project" the double out of the physical body and to sensitize an observer who was to try to see the double. He claimed that the double not only caused physiological changes in the hypnotized subject but could consciously observe and feel and even move objects at a distance. More sophisticated research is being conducted at the Psychical Research Foundation in Durham, North Carolina; the Division of Parapsychology at the University of Virginia; The American Society for Psychical Research in New York; the Stanford Research Institute in Menlo Park, California; and in Russia. Although this research has not yet provided scientific "proof" that the double exists in physically detectable form, it has renewed scientific interest in the phenomenon. It is hoped that, as more sensitive devices to measure minute changes in the physical body and in the enviroment are developed, some tangible evidence for the existence of the double will be found.

One method of inducing an out-of-the-body experience (OBE) is becoming lucid in the dream state and choosing to fly. Another method involves the theory that flying dreams are metaphoric representations of actual traveling in the second body. Those who have practiced inducing OBEs say that, by becoming conscious while flying in a dream (either in a plane or in the body), one can become aware of the fact that her physical body is in bed and that she is in her second, lighter body. This double is also known as the *astral body*.

One model of OBEs suggests that in some sleep states the intuitive portions of consciousness leave the body while the "physically oriented portions of consciousness" remain in it. This event is apparently not perceivable by present technology such as EEG machines. At first, the absent consciousness is passive. It receives information from the "sources of its being" and from other "nonphysically oriented consciousnesses." Then this "absent consciousness" becomes active and participates in actions which serve as examples to clarify and reinforce concepts perceived in the passive state. Here the personality is rejuvenated. Guides, teachers, angels, or images of the higher self may instruct the absent consciousness. Often when this part of the personality returns to the body, other layers of the self, the body consciousness, and the subconscious interpret the information into dreams that will relate directly to, and in images of, the waking consciousness. It is at this point that the dream producer can translate general teachings into practical advice on a particular matter. This theory also states that the dream translations are not always necessary. The dream formation process is described as symptomatic of an unwillingness to accept the original experiences in their nonphysical form, so the dreamer translates the experiences, which seem too intense or simply unbelievable, into dream imagery which she can more easily relate to.

This theory seems very plausible in light of so many dream accounts that comment: "There was very much more to this dream, but I can't remember what" or "I understood things about myself on a very deep level, but I can't put it into words" or "Some wise people explained things to me which I can't remember exactly, although I *feel* that I remember them in my heart." Perhaps we have difficulty remembering not only things we want to repress but also information we perceive in nonphysically oriented images. Among those who have been conscious of out-of-body experiences, there is the "almost universal belief that [OBEs], particularly when they are on higher planes, bring sharper clarity of mind and more vigor to the physical body." Ernest Hemingway; Carl Jung; the poet Walter de la Mare; St. Ignatius of Loyola; J. H. M. Whiteman, a physicist and mathematician in South Africa; Camille Flammarion, the French astronomer; and literally thousands of others have had conscious awareness of out-of-body experiences.

The original accounts of OBEs and the studies conducted to explore them suggest many exciting possibilities for the out-of-body traveler. Perhaps it really is possible to visit friends while you and they sleep in your bodies. Perhaps it is possible to communicate with people who are dead and exist now in other dimensions of reality. Besides visiting alive and "dead" friends and relatives, what I have enjoyed most about becoming conscious while apparently out of my body has been the incredibly vivid and intense contact I have had with states of consciousness which seem extremely wise and intelligent and which give me much understanding and peace at very basic nonverbal levels of my being. Many lucid dreamers have reported the same attitude toward some of their out-of-body experiences. It may be that what feels like an OBE is instead an altered state of consciousness (perception and expression) that "takes place" within the physical body.

Virginia had this dream before her first conscious OBE:

> I see a little pale white transparent wisp come out of the center of my body. Then a larger one wells up from the perimeters of my body. It is as if I see them out of the corner of my eye. I question what they are. Then I realize the big one's me. I'm not sure of the small. Then it seems as if this lift out of the larger one is repeated over and over so that I can get the hang of it.

I had a similar experience in a prelucid dream (about which Virginia knew nothing):

I felt myself falling, slipping into my body, then rising out of it again and being filled with love. My friend Henry is present, sometimes watching or helping, or doing this himself and showing me how. I had a very strong feeling of increasing self-knowledge and self-understanding. I stopped. I was out of my body and enjoyed it so much I didn't want to go back into it again. Henry encouraged me to reenter, and at that I fall back into my body through the head. It feels like I'm slipping into an old, familiar, and very comfortable piece of clothing. Then, as I continue the practice of going in and out of my body, I begin to understand it better. I awoke very relaxed and happy in "the understanding of things."

Dreams which seem to portray learning how to get in and out of the body and operating outside of it may represent the dreamer's early encounters with the experience or may be a dream representation of his efforts to become conscious of an experience he has unconsciously and skillfully achieved many times before. The dreams themselves may be normal, prelucid, or lucid. The motifs of such dreams often include flying in an airplane or helicopter, floating in the air or water, rising upward in an elevator, or any number of activities that might simulate the feeling of flying. In some dreams, I seem to practice operating out of my body through learning how to water-ski. Typically, friends who are wiser and stronger and more skilled than I instruct me. In one dream, I failed to get up out of the water because the undercurrents were too strong, and my instructor said it was too late in the day for a good practice session. Had I gone to sleep too fatigued, or was I too close to morning-waking consciousness to maintain my focus in the dream state? In another dream's practice session, the water-ski instructors gave me a shorter cord to hold on to because I seemed to wobble and lose control with the longer one. Was this a dream representation of the silver cord referred to by many people skilled in the art of leaving their bodies? The silver cord has been described as the elasticlike cord which connects the two bodies. Sylvan Muldoon noted that it could stretch infinitely as the second body traveled away from the physical body. Two of the pioneer experimenters with OBEs, Muldoon and Oliver Fox, felt that dream action often parallels the movement of the second body as it leaves or enters the physical body and travels outside it. Each suggested that, by becoming conscious in such dreams, the dreamer would realize he was in his second body.

When you find yourself flying in a dream, or doing something that would give you the sensation of weightlessness, tell yourself that you are dreaming. Some astral travelers describe the double as leaving their physical bodies through the head, some through the center of the body, some through the feet; others describe it as welling up from all parts of the physical body at once. You may dream of trying to squeeze out of a skylight into the great outdoors as a symbolic representation of leaving the body through your head. Dreams of getting stuck halfway in or out of a room or box might represent the actual position of your double in relation to your physical body. One way to become conscious during such dreams is to suggest to yourself during the day that, when you meet similar conditions in your dreams, they will trigger in you the realization that you are dreaming. This is a form of dream guidance. Using dream guidance, neither my students nor I have ever had any unpleasant experiences in this apparently out-of-body state. There are a few techniques for inducing OBEs from the waking state, but they may result in rather frightening experiences and seem more complicated than the following OBEs experienced in a lucid dream state.

Sonia had a dream experience which involved a false awakening that may have been precipitated by the appearance of her father in his second body. Though she could not verify that her father had had an OBE the same night (because he had no dream recall that night), she did learn something important from this experience, which had the characteristics of a nonlucid encounter between two astral bodies. Here is her written account:

In waking life, my parents had just visited me and stayed overnight. I experienced a lot of old feelings and tensions having them in my house. I was nervous and could feel old habits and interactions happening again with them. I had a very restless night's sleep on the couch and missed my own bed, in which they were sleeping.

The next day I went to bed quite early, and sometime between 7:00 P.M. and 1:30 A.M. I dreamt:

> *My father was suddenly standing next to my bed as I was sleeping having the dream. His presence was so real it was startling (when I woke I looked for him to be there). I dreamt he was standing there. He touched my shoulder, saying "This is your father." Then as I sat up, I could see him, and my mother behind him. They had returned to my house again, and were again going to stay the night. I sort of groaned to myself, because I did not want to leave my nice bed and go sleep in the living room again. My father quickly said there was no problem and that he and my mother would make a place to sleep in the living room and that I did not have to move. They were quite cheerful about it. I saw them making up a place to sleep in the living room.*

I took this dream to mean that my father was "waking me up" to the fact that my parents *are* willing to accept my life and do not want me to feel pushed around by them.

They *are* willing to compromise. I think this is in fact the case. I had forgotten this the day before when I was so nervous and acted in old ways. The dream was so startling I was forced to remember the real situation of cooperation. I wonder if we were all out of our bodies by the end of the dream when I saw them in the living room.

I once had the distinct impression that, just after becoming lucid at the end of a dream, I found myself in the body of a good friend! It felt wonderful to experience what I thought was his state of mind, peaceful and very happy in a way that was peculiarly his:

> I am aware that John has just returned from an OBE and has invited me into his body to see what it would be like. Inside, I am fascinated to learn that the way he experiences happiness is typical only of his personality. I am glad to see this from the inside. I am also fascinated at the experience of having such big lungs. As I participate in his breathing, I seem to have a sense of what it is like to have his muscular body instead of mine. Very interesting. I then move out of his body and into mine via the top of my head. I am awake and feel that I have been since the moment when I entered John's body.

As I lay in my sleeping bag (we were on a camping trip with seven friends), I was dying to awaken John and ask him if he had just reentered his body and had some memory of my "visit." Before I could give in to my impulse, his daughter started to cry out for him. John seemed uncharacteristically irritated at this abrupt awakening. After he had tended to his daughter, I asked him why. He told me he had just returned to his body after an extremely pleasant OBE. I asked him if he had noticed my presence, but he had not. To my knowledge, this is an unusual OBE, and I present it here so that, if you find yourself apparently in someone else's body you will be less likely to panic and more likely to enjoy the experience.

After our first experiences of marveling at the awareness of being outside the body, my students and I chose to experiment with contacting other day-life friends who, themselves, might be in or out of the body. One student, Diana, incubated six dreams asking for a lucid OBE in which she would visit Sue, a friend thirty miles away. Each trial was on a different day over a period of one month. Sue had agreed to the "visits" but on only two occasions did she know what days Diana would try to visit her. On four of the six occasions, Sue had a distinct feeling of Diana's presence at the approximate time that Diana was sleeping after an OBE incubation. Three times Sue was awakened in the middle of the night by what seemed to be Diana's presence. On one of these nights, when she had been expecting Diana's visit, Sue was startled by a purple spiral she saw floating above her bed. She immediately thought it was a representation of Diana. Another time, Sue, who was wide awake and in a conversation, was suddenly vividly aware of Diana's presence. This was during a midday sleep period before which Diana had telephoned Sue to tell her she was about to attempt another visit. Curiously, Diana had no recall of any dream activity during two of the nap periods when Sue noticed her presence. Diana became lucid in only one dream about visiting her friend.

Another dream meeting member, Eileen, writes:

> Some dreams which I have fairly often are of myself floating toward the ceiling in a room. Usually I am teaching other people how to accomplish this themselves.

Most of Eileen's lucid dreams of being out of her body have been pleasant, but one was not. She writes that "the scariest dream I ever had was apparently shared by my husband Jony'':

> I was out of my body. A man dared me to get farther and farther from it. Finally he took it over. I was in a state of panic when Jony entered into my dream and helped me get back into my body. I woke up and had a feeling of terrible heaviness and evil in the house.

This was her commentary on the experience:

> Just then Jony woke up and said (without my offering anything) that he'd just had a terrible dream and asked if I were okay. At that moment Kim, my four-year-old daughter, started screaming. I went to her, and she said that something awful was in her room. She said, "A big monster is over my bed." She spent the rest of the night in bed with us. We all felt a very negative influence all night.

Robert Monroe and some others who have had conscious OBEs have recounted similar stories of frightening out-of-body experiences. It may be, as Yram and Fasher suggest, that in the out-of-body dream state the dreamer attracts experiences which correspond to his expectations, fears, and level of psychological development, as well as to his current emotional state. The fact that Eileen had been involved with frightening occult studies around the time this dream transpired might explain why she had such a frightful experience. Perhaps her daughter tuned into the same dream frequency as her parents and thus had a similar experience of fear. One of the few frightening experiences I have had in lucid dreams came at a time when I was quite fearful of what other realms of existence might be like. I had little confidence in my ability to handle the forces of the unconscious. Since I have adopted the belief that I can always awake into day consciousness and that I am capable of dealing with any frightening dream images, I have not had any frightening lucid or prelucid OBE dreams. A confident attitude toward dream experience tends to result in pleasant lucid dreams. One source suggests that, if you find yourself in a dream or OBE confronted with unfriendly figures or images, you need only say "Go in peace" to be freed of their influence. The idea is not to deal with a negative force on its level, fear. It seems that, if you can overcome fear, unpleasant OBEs as well as normal frightening dreams will lose their fearful quality.

To wind up our discussion of lucid experiences of being out of the body, here is an example of a romantic OBE. A year ago, during a three-week vacation in Switzerland, I missed my fiancé, Steve, very much. On four different nights, I incubated a dream, asking for a lucid OBE in which I would visit Steve in California. I hoped to assuage the longing in my heart and bring him cheer as well. After two of the nights I tried this, I had no dream recall at all. On a third night, Steve came to visit me in a happy dream. On the fourth try, I had what felt like success. I had a prelucid dream in which I was hugging Steve and feeling very happy to see him. I suspected that I might be out of my body, but I did not pursue the thought. Steve told me that he was glad to see me, and we talked about how we had missed each other. I awoke refreshed, as though we had just been together. Steve wrote me that, on that evening at the same time I had been sleeping for two hours in Switzerland, he had a "visitation" from me: "[I was] standing in the kitchen. Then without any precursor, I suddenly felt as if you were really there with me. I talked to you, felt warmed by you, and thanked you for coming." The only time Steve had this experience of my presence was the same night that I felt I had actually succeeded in visiting him. We were both less lonely after this experience.

As we have seen, you can increase your conscious awareness by using dream incubation and dream guidance. For those who would like to experiment specifically with out-of-body experiences, I have one more suggestion to add. If you choose as your goal in having an OBE not only exploring the experience but also bringing cheer to someone you would like to visit, I think you will find your first experiments less difficult. In our experiments, the use of this suggestion in an incubation request for an out-of-body visit has never been followed by an unpleasant dream. In fact, the nights on which we have used incubation phrases like "I'd like to visit my sister and bring her cheer" have generally been filled with exceptionally pleasant dreams and lucid and prelucid experiences of wonderful and warm visits.

12. Dreaming, Death, and Transcendence

Stephen LaBerge, Ph.D.

WHILE ASCENDING A mountain path, I began to find it more and more difficult to climb. My legs took on the familiar leaden feeling they sometimes have in dreams, and a dull heaviness spread through my rapidly weakening body. My feelings of weariness deepened relentlessly until I could only continue by crawling—but finally even this was too much for me and I was overcome with the feeling of certainty that I was about to die of exhaustion. This realization of imminent death focused my attention with remarkable clarity upon what I wanted to express with the one act of my life I had left: perfect acceptance. Thus, gladly embracing death, I let go completely of my last breath, when to my amazement and delight a rainbow flowed out of my heart and I awoke from the dream.

Years after this experience, the profound impact of this dream of death and transcendence continues to influence my beliefs concerning what may happen to us when we die. Because of this dream, I am inclined to share Walt Whitman's view that to die is "different from what anyone supposed and luckier." Yet I know that it was just a dream, and I wonder whether I, or others who have had similar experiences, have sufficient grounds for trusting the belief that they have seen the truth.

Whatever relation this dream of death may bear to reality, it illustrates an important truth about dreams. There is a common fear that if you die in a dream, you will not awaken at all. Consequently, people dreaming of death tend to fear and resist the experience. But my dream illustrates what could happen when the dreamer fully accepts a dream encounter with death. In cultures that consider death as transformation rather than annihilation, such dreams are easier to accept.

According to Greek mythology, sleep is the brother of death, an indication that the two concepts have long been closely associated in the human mind. The reason is easy to see: both states are characterized by an inactivity sharply contrasting with the animate movement of waking life. And since the soul was regarded as leaving the body temporarily during sleep and permanently at death, sleep seemed a short death and death a long sleep. The straightforward association of death and dreaming naturally follows from dreaming's connection with sleep. And the associations of sleep, dreaming, and death with the darkness of the underworld are all quite obvious.

Less obvious is that these symbolic associations have another side: dreams, the children of sleep, also represent the creative impulse to life, as expressed by the seed germinating in the dark womb of the earth. Moreover, sleep itself resembles the state of incipient life *in utero*. As Freud observed, "Somatically, sleep is an act which reproduces intrauterine existence fulfilling the conditions of repose, warmth and the absence of stimulus; indeed in sleep many people resume fetal position." This brings us to the paradox that death, for the dreamer, most often signifies rebirth. As Ann Faraday suggests, "The most interesting dream death is our own, for this indicates the death of some obsolete self-image, from which comes rebirth into a higher state of consciousness and authentic self-being."

The association between death and transformation has

long been recognized in literature. In Thomas Mann's great alchemical novel, *The Magic Mountain*, Hans Castorp's initiation into the mysteries of life takes the form of a dream, and a lucid one at that, which answers and resolves all of his questions about the seeming contradictions of life and death. Mann describes his hero as "searching for the Grail—that is to say, the Highest: knowledge, wisdom, consecration, the philosopher's stone . . . the elixir of life." Lost in the perilous mountains, battered and blinded by a blizzard that very nearly costs him his life, Hans loses consciousness of his surroundings and falls into the snow. During the same storm, he has seen in the "too perfect symmetry" of the flakes of falling snow the coldness of "the very marrow of death." But as he lies thoroughly immersed in the frozen ocean of death, he dreams himself another, wholly different world—this one as delightful a vision of sunshine, comfort, and harmony as the other one was a blinding vision of violence, elemental chaos, and harshness. Hans walks through this idyllic scene, joyously viewing the friendly and courteous behavior displayed everywhere by the happy, yet serious and in every way noble, people of his dream. But then he discovers, to his horror, a temple of human sacrifice in which he witnesses two hideously ugly hags tearing apart a child over a witches' cauldron. The shock brings him to his senses.

Upon half awakening to find himself lying nearly frozen in the snow, Hans Castorp says to himself, "I felt it was a dream, all along . . . lovely and horrible dream. I knew all the time that I was making it up myself. . . ." Without moving, he continues to reflect for some time on his "dream poem of humanity," which he discovers possesses "both rhyme and reason. . . . It is love, not reason, that is stronger than death." His lucid dream, he declares, has brought him to this profound insight: "My dream has given it to me, in utter clearness, that I may know it forever." Of this, Hans Castorp's creator wrote that "if he does not find the Grail, yet he divines it, in his deathly dream." Having done so, Hans awakens himself fully from his reverie, struggles to his feet, shakes off his frozen coat of snow, and returns to live another several hundred pages.

The reader may object that the experiences of fictional characters are, well, *fictional,* and therefore unrelated to actuality. But the fact is that—in life as well as in literature— people who have survived actual or imagined encounters with death frequently report them to have been accompanied by powerfully significant experiences. These life-changing visions currently are referred to most commonly as "near-death experiences" (NDEs). The particular contents of NDEs vary widely, as much as the contents of "out-of-body experiences" (OBEs), visions, lucid and non-lucid dreams. A useful picture of a thing sometimes can be constructed by combining features from a variety of different examples. Raymond Moody has provided the public with such a picture of the NDE in his best-seller, *Life After Life:*

> A man is dying and, as he reaches the point of greatest physical distress, he hears himself pronounced dead by the doctor. He begins to hear an uncomfortable noise, a loud ringing or buzzing, and at the same time feels himself moving very rapidly outside his own physical body, but still in the same immediate physical environment, and sees his own body from a distance as though he is a spectator. He watches the resuscitation attempt from this vantage point and is in a state of emotional upheaval.
>
> After awhile, he collects himself and becomes more accustomed to his odd condition. He notices that he still has a "body," but one of a very different nature and with very different powers from the physical body he has left behind. Some other things begin to happen. Others come to meet him and help him. He glimpses the spirits of relatives and friends who have

already died, and a loving warm spirit of a kind he
has never encountered before—a being of light—appears
before him. This being asks him a question, nonverbally,
to make him evaluate his life and helps him along by
showing him a panoramic, instantaneous playback of
the major events in his life. At some point, he finds
himself approaching some sort of barrier or border,
apparently representing the limit between earthly life
and the next life. Yet, he finds that he must go back
to earth, that the time for his death has not yet come.
At this point, he resists, for by now he is taken up
with his experiences in the afterlife and does not
want to return. He is overwhelmed by intense feelings
of joy, love, and peace. Despite his attitude, though,
he is somehow united with his physical body and
lives.

It is important to remember that this account is a compos-
ite put together by Dr. Moody from a variety of diverse
anecdotal accounts, no one of which possesses all of its
features. It is really therefore closer to fiction than description, and may only provide us with an idealized picture of
the NDE.

NDEs seem to exhibit varying degrees of completeness.
Kenneth Ring, a psychologist specializing in the study of
NDEs, describes the experience as unfolding in a five-
stage continuum. "The first stage involves a feeling of
extraordinary peace and contentment; the second stage is
characterized by a sense of detachment from one's physical body, i.e., an OBE; the third stage is described as
entering a transitional world of darkness; the hallmark of
the fourth stage is a brilliant light of exceptional beauty;
and the last stage is one in which the subject experiences
himself as 'entering the light.' " Dr. Ring found that each
of the five stages was reported by decreasing numbers of
NDE subjects.

The resemblance of the NDE to certain aspects of dreams

is quite obvious. For example, there are the *images* of relatives and friends who have already died and would therefore be significantly associated with the person's idea of death, which itself has been brought up by his fear or expectation of his own impending death. There is also the obvious element of wish-fulfillment involved in seeming to be in a different body than one's own.

The popular press has treated the NDE in a credulous and sensationalistic manner, interpreting it as providing positive "proof" for life after death. Considering the fact that no one who ever had an NDE was *really* dead, the experience provides no more evidence for survival after death than OBEs provide for the existence of any kind of "astral" body independent of the physical body. A neurophysiologist would be quick to point out that when the NDE occurs, the person's brain is still sufficiently intact to produce the experience. In this regard, it is of interest to note that a deceased person's brain shows considerable activity thirty minutes or more after clinical "death"—that is, heart failure.

Like waking life, OBEs, and dreams, the near-death experience is still an *experience*. The question is, does it occur during death or during a more reversible sleep? Since our current sources of information concerning what is supposed to happen at and after death are limited to what we gain in seances and "phone calls from the dead," we are not in a very favorable position to determine the validity of NDE reports! I am not at all certain this is the most important question to answer, anyway. A dream need not be literally true to be significant and meaningful—for example, my rainbow dream, which began this chapter—and the same applies to NDEs, which often possess the profoundest significance for people who have had them.

People who have undergone near-death experiences frequently show fundamental and remarkably positive transformations in their approaches to life. Noyes summarized the changes as follows:

A pattern of favorable attitude change resulting from near-death experiences was described that included the following: (1) a reduced fear of death; (2) a sense of relative invulnerability; (3) a feeling of special importance or destiny; (4) a belief in having received the special favor of God or fate; (5) a strengthened belief in continued existence. In addition to these elements that seemed directly related to the experience itself, several more appeared to be associated with a heightened awareness of death that resulted from it. These included: (1) a sense of the preciousness of life; (2) a feeling of urgency and reevaluation of priorities; (3) a less cautious approach to life; (4) a more passive attitude toward uncontrollable events. This pattern of change seemed to contribute to the emotional health and well-being of persons reporting it.

Dr. Noyes added that "an opposite pattern was described by a few and appeared to be associated with psychopathology . . ." However, for most people, the NDE has a profound and vivifying effect that those of us who haven't experienced it might well envy.

But is it possible to have an NDE or its equivalent without nearly dying? Kenneth Ring has suggested that the NDE experience can take many forms; he quotes a line from Plutarch that says, "At the moment of death the soul experiences the same impressions as those who are initiated into the great Mysteries." Ring notes that "the modern world is witnessing the emergence of a new mystery school where resuscitation techniques administered by physicians have replaced hypnotic procedures practiced by high priests. The initiates of course are those who have suffered clinical death and the initiation itself is the NDE."

Ring regards the greatest benefit to be gained from the NDE (at least in its highest form) as the possibility of realizing "who and what we truly are," a self far more expansive and all-encompassing than the one we show in our daily lives.

According to Dr. Ring, a person who has found this out, whether by fasting and prayer, drugs, accident, or as it were, "by itself," is no longer concerned about personal survival after death, because he or she has experienced "eternal" existence. They could say, with Richard M. Bucke, the author of *Cosmic Consciousness,* " . . . I became conscious in myself of eternal life. It was not a conviction that I would have eternal life, but a consciousness that I possessed eternal life then. . . ." In my view, and I believe Kenneth Ring would probably agree, the NDE is one path to a mystical experience. It is an experience open to others so inclined, including perhaps lucid dreamers, as we shall see at the end of this chapter. It may not be clear why I am calling some NDEs mystical experiences. In that case, the following account from a woman who nearly died during the delivery of her baby may clarify this point:

> The next thing I knew, I was in—I was standing in a mist and I knew *immediately* that I had died and I was *so* happy that I died but I was still alive. And I cannot tell you how I *felt*. I was, "oh, God I'm dead, but I'm here. I'm me!" And I started pouring out these enormous feelings of gratitude because I still existed and yet I knew perfectly well that I had died. . . .
>
> While I was pouring out these feelings . . . the mist started being infiltrated with enormous light and the light just got brighter and brighter and, as everybody says, it was so bright but it doesn't hurt your eyes, but it's brighter than anything you've ever experienced in your whole life. At that point, I had no consciousness anymore of having a body. It was just pure consciousness. And this enormously bright light seemed almost to cradle me. I just seemed to exist in

it and be part of it and be nurtured by it and the feeling just became more and more and more ecstatic and glorious and perfect. And everything about it was—it just didn't bear any relationship to anything! The feeling—if you took the one thousand best things that ever happened to you in your life and multiplied by a million, maybe you could get close to this feeling, I don't know. But you're just engulfed by it and you begin to know a lot of things. I remember I knew that everything, everywhere in the universe was OK, that the plan was perfect. . . . And the whole time I was in this state, it seemed infinite. It was timeless. I was just as infinite being in perfection.

One element of the NDE, as described in Western accounts, finds independent support in the traditional teachings of the visionary culture of Tibet: "the Clear Light of Reality," according to the Tibetan Buddhists, is briefly experienced by everyone at the moment of death. Moreover, "unless the dying person possesses, as a result of having successfully practiced *yoga* while incarnate, the *yogic* power to hold fast to the after-death condition in which the Clear Light dawns, he mentally sinks downward, stage by stage, and the Clear Light of Reality fades from his consciousness."

Adepts who recognize the Light of the after-death state as being of the same nature as dreams are supposed to transcend the dream of life and death. The means by which one attains this transcendence is the yoga of the dream state. Through the practice of lucid dreaming during his lifetime, the yogi is able to experience the "dream of death" lucidly as well.

Dream yoga is not merely intended as a rehearsal for the final sleep of death. The serious follower of dream yoga is attempting to awaken before death: "The whole purpose of the Doctrine of Dreams is to stimulate the *yogin* to arise from the Sleep of Delusion, from the Nightmare of Existence, to break the shackles in which *maya* (illusion) thus has held him prisoner throughout the aeons, and so attain spiritual peace and joy of Freedom, even as did the Fully Awakened One, Gautama the Buddha.''

The first steps toward the dream yogi's goal of awakening involve becoming proficient in ''comprehending the nature of the dream state.'' Once the yogi has become an accomplished lucid dreamer, he proceeds to the next stage, ''transmuting the dream-content,'' in which the initial exercise is the following: ''If, for example, the dream be about fire, think, 'what fear can there be of fire which occurreth in a dream!' Holding to this thought, trample upon the fire. In like manner, tread underfoot whatever be dreamt.'' After gaining sufficient skill in controlling his reactions to the contents of his lucid dreams, the yogi goes on to more advanced exercises, and by means of these he masters the ability to visit—in his lucid dreams—any realm of existence desired.

The next stage of practice is called ''realizing the dream-state, or dream-content to be *maya* [illusion].'' According to Buddhist doctrine, the entire universe of forms, or separate existence, is an illusory appearance or ''dream.''

At the third stage, the dream yogi is advised to practice the transformation of dream content into its opposite. For example, the lucid dreamer should transform the dream, if it be of fire, into water; if it be of small things, into large; if it be of one thing, into many; and so on. Thus, the text explains, the lucid dreamer comprehends the nature of dimensions and of plurality and unity.

After becoming ''thoroughly proficient'' in the art of transforming dream content, the yogi turns his attention to his own dream body: this, he now sees, is just as illusory as any other element of his lucid dream. The fact that the fully lucid dreamer knows he is not his dream body plays a crucial role in self-transformation, as we shall see below.

The fourth and final stage of dream yoga is enigmatically termed ''meditating upon the thatness of the dream-state.'' The text tells us that by means of this meditation, ''the dream propensities whence arise whatever is seen in dreams as appearances of deities, are purified.'' It is, ironically, by means of these ''appearances'' that the ultimate goal is reached. The yogi is, of course, aware that these ''deities'' are his own mental images. Bearing this in mind, he is instructed to concentrate in the lucid dream state, focusing on the forms of these deities, and to keep his mind free of thoughts. In the undisturbed quiet of this mental state, the divine forms are said to be ''attuned to the non-thought condition of mind; and thereby dawneth the Clear Light, of which the essence is of the voidness.''

Thus, one realizes that the appearance of form ''is entirely subject to one's will when the mental powers have been efficiently developed,'' through the practice of the yoga of lucid dreaming. Having learned '' . . . that the character of any dream can be changed or transformed by willing that it shall be,'' the lucid dreamer takes ''a step further . . . he learns that form, in the dream state, and all the multitudinous content of dreams, are merely playthings of mind, and, therefore, as unstable as a mirage.'' A process of generalization ''leads him to the knowledge that the essential nature of form and of all things perceived by the senses in the waking state are equally as unreal as their reflexes in the dream-state,'' since both waking and dreaming are states of mind. A final step brings the yogi to ''the Great Realization'' that nothing within the experience of his mind ''can be other than unreal like dreams.'' In this light, ''the Universal Creation . . . and every phenomenal thing therein'' are seen to be ''but the content of the Supreme Dream.'' And for the one upon whom ''this Divine Wisdom'' has dawned, ''the microcosmic aspect of the Macrocosm becomes fully awakened; the dew-drop slips back into the Shining Sea, in *Nirvanic* Blissfulness and At-one-ment, possessed of All Possessions, Knower of the All-Knowledge, Creator of All Creations—the One Mind, Reality Itself.''

Having described the realization reached by the successful seeker, let us consider some of the possible pitfalls on the path of inner growth through lucid dreaming. Primary among them is the tendency for the less than fully lucid dream ego to misunderstand and misuse the new access to power and control over dreams that lucidity brings. The semi-lucid dream ego is inclined to use "magical powers" to seek its own ends, which may be at odds with the person's real goals. Moreover, the semi-lucid dream ego's sense of greatly expanded power leads to a grandiose expansion of self-esteem, the condition Jung referred to as "inflation."

Although the inflated dream ego, like a power-intoxicated Roman emperor, bestows divinity upon itself, it proves to be filled with nothing but hot air. The hottest of the airs it puts on is the delusion that it *is* the self. The truth is that the dream ego is only a self-representation that tends to forget its nature.

The ego's tendency (whether awake or dreaming) to mistake itself for the true self is natural. The ego is a model of the self, designed to serve adaptive action; it is based upon disparate sources of information, ranging from how the self has actually behaved in the past to parental and social notions of how the self should behave in the future. From this collection of expectations, predictions of the self's future behavior can be made.

Since pretending to have a socially desirable feature is more frequently rewarded than truthfully admitting *not* to have it, much of our mental map of the self becomes pretense. The pattern of social pretense, of playing a role intended to deceive others, is later applied to oneself after society's standards have become internalized. If we are to pretend successfully to ourselves, we must also pretend that we are not pretending. Thus the person behind the mask forgets he has another face. The actor becomes his role, mistaking the part he plays for the whole he is; appearance usurps reality; the original plan is forgotten; and clothes mock the man.

All this has been said regarding the undeveloped or semi-lucid dream ego. Lucid dreams are experienced and interpreted, by such an ego, as "*my* dream." But the dream ego is not the dreamer; rather than dreaming, it is being dreamed. The unenlightened but semi-lucid dream ego falsely believes itself to be the only reality, of which all other dream figures are the mere projections.

The case of Ram Narayana vividly illustrates how far delusions of grandeur can be taken by the semi-lucid dreamer. Narayana, an Indian physician and editor, had been perplexed by the problem of how to convince "the creatures of his dream, during the dream state, that it really is a dream." He finally gave up trying, having decided that even if he succeeded, convincing them could serve no useful purpose. Therefore, Narayana resolved to enjoy himself instead and to pass his time while dreaming "as comfortably as possible." Consequently, next time he went to sleep, he addressed "the assembly of his dream characters" as follows: "Friends, why don't you try to attain the state of ecstatic and immortal bliss, entirely free from pain of every description? This state of bliss can be obtained only by entering into the celestial region, the abode of the Supreme Creator. To this region I go daily and enjoy its pleasures for twelve hours out of every twenty-four. I am the only incarnation and representative of the Supreme One."

Narayana indicated that "the majority of dream creatures believed in the above speech." A minority were skeptical of his claim of being the "only manifestation of the Supreme Diety." What about Krishna, Christ, Buddha, or Mohammed, demanded the doubters? They received the reply that "all those great men had come from lower regions and were only theoretical in their teachings and nobody ever attained salvation through them, that the dreamer alone came from the highest spiritual plane, and that he would teach them the only sure and practical method of reaching that region."

Having been made the usual promises, they were charged the usual price, being then told the chief condition of initiation was "to have implicit faith in their preceptor, the dreamer." Narayana went on to explain, in terms well known by the leaders of cults everywhere, that "the most effective means to hypnotize them all in a body was then employed, which consisted of looking intently into the eyes of the *guru,* the dreamer, while sacred hymns and songs of love and devotion were being recited in a chorus. They were further impressed with the idea that ultimately every one of them would reach the highest region, after one, two or more rebirths, but one having complete faith in the dreamer would reach there the soonest."

Narayana claimed that "the method proved so satisfactory that the dreamer was actually worshipped by every one of the dream creatures and was pronounced to be the only true spiritual guide. He now considered himself in no way less fortunate than so many leaders of the various faiths, in the waking world, who enjoy the pleasure of being devotedly worshipped by their disciples."

This comical parody of spiritual cults would have its tragic aspect as well, were it not for the fact that Narayana was eventually able to progress beyond this state of inflation. He dreamed that he fell among a group of yogis who managed to enlighten him in the following dream:

> . . . another elderly figure from amongst the dream creatures rose from his seat and overawed the assembly with his long grey beard and his *yogi's* staff. He began his oration in a curious and amusing manner, though with an authoritative tone, his voice quivering with anger and his gaunt index finger pointing towards the dreamer. "What reason have you to call us your dream creatures and yourself the creator of us all? If you are our creator we say equally emphatically that so are we the creator of yourself. We are all in the same boat, and you can claim no sort of higher existence than ours. If,

however, you want to be convinced of my statement, I can show you the Creator of us all, i.e., of yourself as well as ours.'' With these words, he struck the dreamer on the head with his heavy staff, who, in consequence, woke up and found himself lying in his bed with his mind extremely puzzled.

The yogi's point is that the dream ego (mistaken for "the dreamer" by Narayana) is just another dream figure. The actual creator of the dream is not a part of the dream at all—being, in fact, the sleeping self.

This is an insight fully lucid dreamers realize through direct experience. They know that the persons they appeared to be in the dream are not who they really are. No longer identifying with their egos, they are free to change them, correcting their delusions. As an immediate consequence of this, the self-representation of the ego becomes a more accurate map of the true territory of the self. The ego now encompasses the fact that "the map is not the territory," which makes it more difficult to mistake one's self-image for one's true self.

The fully lucid dreamer does not need to struggle to overcome his or her ego. He or she has become objective enough to no longer identify with it. In consequence, the ego now stands in proper relation to the self as its representative and servant. The lucid dreamer's ego now realizes its limitations: it knows it is only the limited part of the self that the person believes him or herself to be. Or perhaps even less— only what we can *explicitly* spell out about ourselves. This knowledge puts the ego's importance in modest proportion to the true, and perhaps as yet undiscovered, Self.

The fully lucid dreams we have been discussing are instances of transcendental experiences, experiences in which you go beyond your current level of consciousness. Lucid dreamers (at least during the dream) have gone beyond their former views of themselves and have entered a higher state of consciousness. They have left behind their former way of being in dreams, no longer identifying with the dream characters they play or thinking that the dream world is reality. In this way, fully lucid dreams are transcendental experiences.

Transcendental experiences are advantageous, in my view, in that they help us detach from fixed ideas about ourselves. The less we identify with who we think we are (the ego), the more likely it is that we may one day discover who we really are. In this regard, the Sufi master Tariqavi has written,

> The study of the Way requires self-encounter along the way. You have not met yourself yet. The only advantage of meeting others in the meantime is that one of them may present you to yourself.
>
> Before you do that, you will possibly imagine that you have met yourself many times. But the truth is that when you do meet yourself, you come into a permanent endowment and bequest of knowledge that is like no other experience on earth.

Before they meet themselves, lucid dreamers are at first inclined to seek the dream fulfillment of what they believe they have always wanted. This is natural enough. Yet after too many "wish-fulfilling" dreams, where the action is motivated by the ego-associated drives, passions, desires, expectations, and goals with which we are so familiar, a point of satiation may be reached. Lucid dreamers may then tire of seeking their habitual satisfactions, which may have become less satisfying due to effortless gratification. They grow weary of dreaming the same dreams, and equally of being the same self, night after night. It is at this point that the need for self-transcendence may arise. Such lucid dreamers no longer know what they want, only that it is not what they used to want. So they give up deciding what to do, and resign from deliberate dream control.

Having recognized the limitations of goals determined by the ego, the lucid dreamer has surrendered control to something beyond what he or she knows him or herself to be. The form taken by this ''something beyond'' will vary in accordance with the individual's way of thinking. For those comfortable with traditional religions, the surrender might naturally be phrased in such terms as ''submission to the will of God.'' On the other hand, those who find themselves uncomfortable with theistic terminology will probably prefer to express themselves differently.

If you follow the reasoning argued above for the self-representational nature of the ego, a very natural way to frame this surrender is available: giving control to your true self. Whatever you assume about the nature of your true self, surrendering control from who you *think* you are, to who you truly are, is likely to be an improvement. Including, as it does, everything that you know, your true or total self ought to be capable of making wiser decisions than your ego. Moreover, it knows what your ego may not—your highest goals.

Another formulation is surrender to ''The Highest,'' whatever this may ultimately prove to mean. Such questions as whether this is a part of yourself or something beyond yourself need not be resolved at this point. It is with this term that I personally find myself most comfortable. Besides, it is, by definition, with ''The Highest'' that the ultimate decisions rightfully rest.

Though lucid dreamers give up control of the course of their dreams, they still require lucidity. But now they need it to respond creatively to whatever the dream presents and to intuitively follow the intentions of the higher will. The following lucid dream illustrates the process of self-transcendence we have been discussing. Although it is one of my own lucid dreams in the sense that *I* awoke from it, it felt more like *it* had me:

Late one summer morning several years ago, I was lying quietly in bed, reviewing the dream I had just awakened from. A vivid image of a road appeared, and by focusing my attention on it, I was able to enter the scene. At this point, I was no longer able to feel my body, from which I concluded I was, in fact, asleep. I found myself driving in my sports car down the dream road, perfectly aware that I was dreaming. I was delighted by the vibrantly beautiful scenery my lucid dream was presenting. After driving a short distance farther, I was confronted with a very attractive, I might say a *dream* of a hitchhiker on the road just ahead. I need hardly say that I felt strongly inclined to stop and pick her up. But I said to myself, "I've had *that* dream before. How about something new?" So I passed her by, resolving to seek "The Highest" instead. As soon as I opened myself to guidance, my car took off into the air, flying rapidly upward, until it fell behind me like the first stage of a rocket. I continued to fly higher into the clouds, where I passed a cross on a steeple, a star of David, and other religious symbols. As I rose still higher, beyond the clouds, I entered a space that seemed a vast mystical realm: a vast emptiness that was yet full of love; an unbounded space that somehow felt like home. My mood had lifted to corresponding heights, and I began to sing with ecstatic inspiration. The quality of my voice was truly amazing—it spanned the entire range from deepest bass to highest soprano—and I felt as if I were embracing the entire cosmos in the resonance of my voice. As I improvised a melody that seemed more sublime than any I had heard before, the meaning of my song revealed itself and I sang the words, "I praise Thee, O Lord!"

Upon awakening from this remarkable lucid dream, I reflected that it had been one of the most satisfying experiences of my life. It *felt* as if it were of profound significance. However, I was unable to say in exactly what way it was profound, nor was I able to evaluate its significance. When I tried to understand the words that had somehow contained the full significance of the experience—"I praise Thee, O Lord!"— I realized that, in contrast to my understanding while in the dream, I only now understood the phrase in the sense it would have in our realm. It seemed the esoteric sense that I comprehended while I dreamed was beyond my cloudy understanding while awake. About what the praise did not mean, I can say this: in that transcendent state of unity, there was no "I" and "Thee." It was a place that had no room for "I" and "Thee," but for one only. So which of us, then, was there? My personal "I," my dream-ego sense of individuality, was absent. Thus, what was present was "Thee." But in that realm, "I" *was* "Thee." So I might just as well have sung "I praise Me . . ." except that there was really no "me" either! In any case, it should be clear why I have called this lucid dream a transpersonal experience.

This brings us back to the question of whether it is possible to have the equivalent of a near-death experience without nearly dying. That the answer is "yes" should now be evident. I say this because the experience provided by transpersonal dreams (whether lucid or not) is symbolically synonymous with the process of dying to our old ways and being reborn to new lives. Whether this new attitude carries over into waking life is another matter, but from the point of view of dreaming, death and transcendence are the same thing.

In reply to the question, "what will we be after death?" as far as we are individuals, death appears to be the end of us. Were we to leave it at that, this would be nothing more than the "modern" view of death as annihilation. Yet the preceding pages suggest that our individuality is not our truest being, but only a representation of it. What you take to be your individuality is a mental image of yourself. "Who you think you are" is only a thought, a transient process occurring in time and space, and doomed to pass like everything else that exists in time.

However, according to the point of view we have been

considering, your essential being transcends space and time: your transpersonal identity transcends your personal identity. This, your transpersonal individuality, may in the end prove identical with the nature of ultimate reality—"the Shining Sea" referred to above: "Possessed of all possessions, Knower of the All-Knowledge, Creator of All Creations—the One Mind, Reality Itself." At death, "the dewdrop slips back into the Shining Sea." Thus it may be that when death comes, although you are annihilated as an individual and the dewdrop is lost in the sea, you at the same time return to the realization of what you have always essentially been: the drop recognizes itself to be not merely the drop it thought it was, but the *Sea*. So to the question "What will we be after death?", the answer may be given, "everything and nothing."

13. Dreams and Visions in the Bible

Rev. John A. Sanford

THE BIBLE REGARDS dreams, visions, certain trances, appearances of angels, and experiences of the spirit as similar in source, construction, and significance. Here, the Bible is on solid scientific ground.

All of us know from our firsthand experience what a dream is. Psychologically we call a dream an experience a person might have during sleep, i.e., during a naturally unconscious state. A dream is in fact a "story" which "happens" to us during sleep, of which we are a part, or at least a spectator. A vision can be understood as a "dream" we have while semiconscious or awake. If the unconscious breaks through into our consciousness during our waking state with a dreamlike image or action then we are experiencing a vision. It is sometimes supposed today that to have a dream is permissible enough, but to have a vision is a sign of insanity or mental derangement of some kind. This, however, is not the case. It is not the vision which is a sign of mental derangement, but the point of view from which the ego regards the vision. In insanity the vision is accepted as literal, external reality, and consciousness does not distinguish between the external and the internal world. In the normal ego, however, the vision is recognized for its subjective, internal nature. It is not the vision that is a sign of sickness, nor the unconscious that is "insane," but the ego which is sick or has lost its bearings, and the fact that the insane are more prone to visions than the more stable individual is simply due to the vulnerability of their weakened and shattered ego-structure to invasions from the unconscious.

When, therefore, the Book of Numbers says: "And he said, 'Hear my words: If there is a prophet among you, I the Lord make myself known to him in a vision, I speak with him in a dream,' " thus equating clearly the common origin and significance of dreams and visions, it is resting upon very good psychological foundations. But the Bible likewise often equates the appearance of an angel with a dream or a vision. Take, for instance, the following passages from the Gospel of Matthew: As Joseph considers putting Mary away quietly after discovering her pregnancy we read that "the angel of the Lord appeared to him in a dream," bidding him to retain Mary as his wife and telling him her child is of the Holy Spirit. Later, the Wise Men having found and worshiped the child Jesus are "warned in a dream not to return to Herod." Immediately after, Joseph again is visited by an angel of the Lord in a dream, bidding him flee to Egypt for safety. And after a sojourn in Egypt he is bidden once more by an angel in a dream to return to the land of Israel. In still another dream the angel bids him to return not to Judea, but to Galilee. We thus find in the first two chapters of Matthew no less than five dreams, and we further establish that every decision in this action-packed section is based upon a revelation made by God through a dream. Further, four of these specifically cite the appearance of an angel, so that the Bible clearly equates the revelations given by angels and the revelations by dreams and visions.

Matthew is not the only one who equates angels and dreams. We find, for instance, in Luke that Zechariah's experience with the angel Gabriel is a vision, and that the angels who appeared to the women after the Resurrection were regarded as a vision. To cite only one example from the abundant material in Acts: the Centurion Cornelius has an experience in which an angel comes to him in a vision. And from the Book of Revelation we learn that the entire revelation given to John by an angel is a vision, a fact borne out by the visionary quality of the book as a whole.

Even experiences "of the spirit" are frequently regarded by the Biblical writers as similar in kind to experiences of visions and dreams. The similarity between having a vision or dream and being "in the spirit" is abundantly shown, for instance, in the Book of Ezekiel. Again and again in Ezekiel we read verses such as these: "He put forth the form of a hand, and took me by a lock of my head; and the Spirit lifted me up between earth and heaven, and brought me in visions of God to Jerusalem. . . ." Ezekiel, however, is by no means the only book where experiences of the Spirit are equated with visionary experiences. St. Paul himself goes on to describe "visions and revelations of the Lord," and the Book of Joel is quoted in the Book of Acts in this significant verse: "And in the last days it shall be, God declares, that I will pour out my Spirit upon all flesh, and your sons and your daughters shall prophesy, and your young men shall see visions, and your old men shall dream dreams. . . ." We have then a very fine line indeed between visions, dreams, the appearance of angels, and an outpouring of the Spirit of God.

In the Book of Samuel, when Saul is not able to find God any longer, we read, "And when Saul inquired of the Lord, the Lord did not answer him, either by dreams, or by Urim, or by prophets." Here we see dreams regarded along with revelations from the prophets (who themselves probably gained their knowledge through dreams), and with the sacred lots (Urim), as one of the three means by which a man might know the mind of God. In the story of the boy Samuel we read, "And the word of the Lord was rare in those days; there was no frequent vision." The story then goes on to describe Samuel's visionary experi-

ence with God whereby he ascertains the divine authority
for his coming career.

In I Chronicles the prophet Nathan receives the "word
of the Lord" bidding him to speak to David regarding the
house of the Lord. Later we read: "In accordance with all
these words, and in accordance with all this vision, Nathan
spoke to David." Thus the source of the word of the Lord
which came to Nathan was a vision.

Since dreams and visions were regarded as revelations
from God we would expect that abuses would enter into
their interpretation. This condition we find to have been
the case, when it is hinted at in Numbers, where dreams
are referred to as the "dark speech" of God. The prophet
Jeremiah speaks quite clearly about the divine authorship
of dreams, and he warns against false interpreters and
those who pretend they have had dreams when they have
not. For instance: "Do not listen to the words of the
prophets who prophesy to you, filling you with vain hopes;
they speak visions of their own minds, not from the mouth of
the Lord."

Is this reverence for dreams to be found everywhere in
the Bible? Was it something peculiar to the Old Testament
or the New? Was it late in the development of Israel or
early? The divine authorship of the dream is found from
first to last in the Bible! The Book of Genesis is filled with
dream material, and the Bible closes with the Book of
Revelation, which is itself entirely a vision. Turning to the
Book of Genesis for a moment, we can summarize some
astonishing and most beautiful dream material, beginning
with an important manifestation of God to Abraham.

"As the sun was going down, a deep sleep fell on
Abram; and lo, a dread and great darkness fell upon him.
Then the Lord said to Abram, 'Know of a surety that your
descendants will be sojourners in a land that is not theirs,
and will be slaves there, and they will be oppressed for
four hundred years. . . .' " Then after continuing with this
prediction of things to come we read, "When the sun had

gone down and it was dark, behold, a smoking fire pot and a flaming torch passed between these pieces. On that day the Lord made a covenant with Abram. . . ." The Book of Genesis only hints at the epic dream experience which came to Abraham when he beheld God as a fiery furnace. We certainly have a precursor here of those experiences which have led men to picture the Holy Spirit as fire.

To appreciate the abundance of dream material in Genesis, consider only the following further examples: "But God came to Abimelech in a dream by night. . . ." In this dream Abimelech is warned by God that Sarah is Abraham's wife.

> And Jacob went out from Beersheba, and went toward Haran. And he lighted upon a certain place, and tarried there all night, because the sun was set; and he took of the stones of that place, and put them for his pillows, and lay down in that place to sleep. And he dreamed, and behold a ladder set up on the earth, and the top of it reached to heaven: and behold the angels of God ascending and descending on it. . . .

Joseph dreams of his sheaf standing upright in the field and those of his brothers bowing down, and then again, of the sun, moon and eleven stars bowing down to him. The seriousness with which this dream was regarded may be surmised by the hatred which it enkindled in his brethren, and the fact that "his father kept the saying in mind. . . ." The chief baker and chief butler dream their dreams and take them so seriously that Joseph is called upon as an interpreter. Joseph says: "Do not interpretations belong to God? Tell them to me, I pray you. . . ." Pharaoh dreams of the seven fat cows being devoured by the seven lean cows, and then again of the seven good ears of corn being swallowed up by seven withered ears of corn. When he asks Joseph to interpret them, Joseph says, "It is not in me; God will give Pharaoh a favorable answer." And later adds, "The dream of Pharaoh is one; God has revealed to Pharaoh what he is about to do. . . ."

It is clear from these examples that in the Book of Genesis dreams were regarded as manifestations of divine intention, as one of God's ways of communicating with men. A person inspired by God might interpret dreams with great benefit to the dreamer, for through understanding his dreams and acting in accordance with them, Pharaoh was able to avert a great catastrophe.

There are entire books in the Bible which are asserted to be dreams or visions. The authors of the books of Obadiah, Nahum and Habakuk, claim that their books contain visions. Now how much of these books actually is visionary and how much is of more conscious origin is hard to say. Certainly the authors felt it important to claim them as visions in order to strengthen their authority. Two other books in the Bible are of considerable interest with regard to dreams and visions: the Books of Job and Ezekiel. In the Book of Job we find that the one thing which Job, his three "friends" Eliphaz, Bildad, and Zophar, and his later antagonist Elihu, can agree upon is the significance of dreams. Eliphaz cites a vision as the source of his knowledge:

"Now a word was brought to me stealthily,
    my ear received the whisper of it.
Amid thoughts from visions of the night,
    when deep sleep falls on men,
dread came upon me, and trembling,
    which made all my bones shake.
A spirit glided past my face;
    the hair of my flesh stood up.
It stood still,
    but I could not discern its appearance.
A form was before my eyes
    there was silence, then I heard a voice:
'Can mortal man be righteous before God?
    Can a man be pure before his Maker?' "

We might note that the message Eliphaz received from this experience is a good and sound message. Eliphaz's error in argument was his conclusion that Job's misfortune was the result of great deliberate sin and that the remedy would be repentance, thereby missing the point of Job's human demand for justice.

Not only Eliphaz but Elihu as well regard dreams as revelations from God, intended to sway us from our one-sided path in life, avert approaching catastrophe, and preserve our soul. He says:

> "Behold, in this you are not right. I will answer you.
>   God is greater than man.
> Why do you contend against him,
>   saying, 'He will answer none of my words'?
> For God speaks in one way,
>   and in two, though man does not perceive it.
> In a dream, in a vision of the night,
>   when deep sleep falls upon men,
>   while they slumber on their beds,
> then he opens the ears of men,
>   and terrifies them with warnings,
> that he may turn man aside from his deed,
>   and cut off pride from man;
> he keeps back his soul from the Pit,
>   his life from perishing by the sword."

And finally Job himself says:

> "Therefore I will not restrain my mouth;
>   I will speak in the anguish of my spirit;
>   I will complain in the bitterness of my soul.
> Am I the sea, or a sea monster,
>   that thou settest a guard over me?
> When I say, 'My bed will comfort me,
>   my couch will ease my complaint,'
> then thou dost scare me with dreams
>   and terrify me with visions. . . ."

The book of Ezekiel begins without any preparation (except the date) with these words, " . . . as I was among the exiles by the river Chebar, the heavens were opened, and I saw visions of God." The prophet then goes on to a mighty vision which sets the tone of the entire book and completely dominates the next seven chapters. In fact, so mighty is this vision that there is frequently a reference back to this primary experience, even though other visions also haunt the prophet.

This basic vision of Ezekiel is especially interesting from a contemporary point of view because of its clear mandala symbolism. A mandala is a design usually found in Eastern religions. It depicts the idea of wholeness by a symmetrical shape or by a circular form. However, the Christian religion also knows mandalas, as for instance the so-called "rose windows" in many Gothic churches. These symbols well up from the depths of the psyche and express themselves autonomously in our dreams, visions, art, and religion.

In the case of Ezekiel's vision the mandala is contained in the image of the cherubim and of the whirling wheels. Notice in the description of the cherubim an emphasis upon the number four: there are four living creatures, each with four faces, one facing in each of the four directions. These are terribly and wonderfully made creatures who seem to express by their quaternity something very important. We find that four in religious symbolism throughout the world has always stood for the number which embraces everything essential. There are four rivers that form the Garden of Eden, there are four corners that embrace all the earth, the heavenly Jerusalem will be laid out with four equidistant sides. Carl Jung has shown that there are four functions of the psyche, which if they are all proportionately developed will lead a man to his own completeness. The four is a number which stands for the All.

We might also note, in passing, that the movement of the cherubim is described by Ezekiel in a manner which brings to mind the supposed movements of flying saucers. "And each went straight forward; wherever the spirit would go, they went, without turning as they went. . . . And the living creatures darted to and fro, like a flash of lightning." This gives some credence to Jung's thesis that the visions of flying saucers could be spontaneous projections from the unconscious with religious meaning.

Turning now to the fiery wheels, so well known from the Negro spiritual, "Ezekiel Saw the Wheels," we see again the compelling way in which the unconscious has seized the prophet. This time the image is in circular form. Like the cherubim, the wheels move in a strange way. The vision concludes with the sight of the remarkable God-man of fire, whom the Christian must take to be the preexistent Christ and Jung would describe as the image of the self, that is, the wholeness of God as it has been realized in man.

The most complete treatment of dreams in the Old Testament, however, is found in the Book of Daniel, which consists largely of a series of dreams or visions. This is one of the latest books of the Old Testament, written probably in the second century B.C. Scholars theorize that the author of the book was trying to get a message across to his people, currently struggling against the detestable oppressor Antiochus Epiphanes, who was profaning the Jewish religion. Not being able to write his message directly, the author writes a book about a Jew called Daniel who had also lived under foreign oppression during the exile in Babylonia, and beneath the dreams, visions and events of Daniel's life, there is a message for the people of the author's own time. The Book divides into two halves, each with six chapters, the first part being narrative, the second a series of visions of worldwide scope. The historicity of Daniel as a person is debated by the scholars. For our purposes, however, the point is not essential, for the fact remains that the book is a clear demonstration of the regard in which dreams were held.

Daniel is an Israelite youth of great ability. Along with three friends (Shadrach, Meshach, and Abednego) he is regarded highly for his learning, skill, and wisdom. Daniel especially had "understanding in all visions and dreams."

In chapter 2 there occurs the story of Nebuchadnezzar's dream, a remarkable account in its psychological acuity. The chapter begins: "In the second year of the reign of Nebuchadnezzar, Nebuchadnezzar had dreams; and his spirit was troubled, and his sleep left him." Here we have the familiar picture of a man afflicted with insomnia, which is frequently the result of conflict between the conscious and unconscious. However, during his restless sleep Nebuchadnezzar is aware of dreams. He knows he had dreams and that they were disturbing and important, but he is unable to recollect what they were. The Babylonian magicians are confronted by the King with the task of helping him, but while willing to venture an interpretation of a dream, they are unable to do so unless he can tell the dream to them. The King does not accept their ignorance of his dream as an excuse, and in his anger determines to slay all the wise men of Babylon. Daniel is included in this ultimatum, but he alone believes he might solve the King's problem and accordingly secures an appointment with Nebuchadnezzar. This done, Daniel returns to his dwelling and beseeches his comrades to "seek mercy of the God of heaven concerning this mystery. . . ." And accordingly, "the mystery was revealed to Daniel in a vision of the night."

Armed with this message from God, Daniel confronts the King and speaks these words:

No wise men, enchanters, magicians, or astrologers can show to the king the mystery which the king has asked, but there is a God in heaven who reveals mysteries, and he has made known to King Nebuchadnezzar what will be in the latter days. Your dream and the visions of your head as you lay in bed are these: To you, O king, as you lay in bed came

thoughts of what would be hereafter, and he who
reveals mysteries made known to you what is to be.
But as for me, not because of any wisdom that I have
more than all the living has this mystery been revealed to me, but in order that the interpretation may
be made known to the king, and that you may know
the thoughts of your mind.''

The last phrase is especially significant to us, for it is
exactly what the interpretation of a dream does for us: it
reveals to us the thoughts of our unconscious mind. The
word "mind" can literally stand for the word "heart." It
means the inmost man, the secret thoughts and deepest
emotions. It is part of the naïveté of modern man that he
thinks he knows his own thoughts, when nothing is farther
from the truth. We harbor thoughts in the unconscious
which are not known or recognized by us, but of which we
can become aware through the understanding of dreams,
even as Daniel says. This is strikingly in accordance with
modern psychology.

Daniel then proceeds to tell the King his dream, a dream
in which an image appeared wrought of many magnificent
metals, but which was broken by no human hand and
crumbled. Daniel gives an interpretation which clearly also
contains a message for the people resisting Antiochus
Epiphanes.

However, later Daniel interprets another dream of Nebuchadnezzar's which is of more psychological interest. This
time Nebuchabdnezzar remembers the dream and tells it
to Daniel.

" . . . I saw, and behold, a tree in the midst of the
earth; and its height was great. The tree grew and
became strong, and its top reached to heaven, and it
was visible to the end of the whole earth. Its leaves
were fair and its fruit abundant, and in it was food for
all. The beasts of the field found shade under it, and

the birds of the air dwelt in its branches, and all flesh was fed from it. I saw in the visions of my head as I lay in bed, and behold, a watcher and an holy one, came down from heaven. He cried aloud and said thus, 'Hew down the tree and cut off its branches, strip off its leaves and scatter its fruit; let the beasts flee from under it and the birds from its branches. But leave the stump of its roots in the earth, bound with a band of iron and bronze, amid the tender grass of the field. Let him be wet with the dew of heaven; let his lot be with the beasts in the grass of the earth; let his mind be changed from a man's, and let a beast's mind be given to him; and let seven times pass over him. The sentence is by the decree of the watchers, the decision by the word of the holy ones, to the end that the living may know that the Most High rules the kingdom of men, and gives it to whom he will, and sets over it the lowliest of men.' ''

Daniel sees at once the extraordinary meaning of this dream. He finds it so dreadful that Daniel ''was dismayed for a moment, and his thoughts alarmed him.'' What follows is a sound bit of dream interpretation. The dream, Daniel warns the king, says that King Nebuchadnezzar has become like the tree, great and spacious, flowing with life and beauty. But because Nebuchadnezzar has regarded himself as the author of his power, and has assumed divine prerogatives and a godlike role, the Almighty God will cut him down. The dream is an attempt to compensate for Nebuchadnezzar's *hubris*.

Because the king does not heed the warning he loses his mind. We can see this from the report about the return of his sanity. ''At the end of the days I, Nebuchadnezzar, lifted my eyes to heaven, and my reason returned to me, and I blessed the Most High, and praised and honored him who lives for ever and ever. . . .'' Notice that Nebuchadnezzar's fate could have been averted. Daniel himself says this when he urges Nebuchadnezzar to change his ways in order "that there may perhaps be a lengthening of your tranquillity." Because Nebuchadnezzar's inflexible conscious point of view about himself does not change, he has to be brought down to earth by his strange psychosis. Interestingly enough, his seven years of insanity during which he lives on the ground as a beast is directly compensating to his previous years as an exalted king. When the time has elapsed, he is restored to his reason, this time no longer afflicted by his megalomania but more truly himself. The whole story is an excellent example of the compensatory nature of the unconscious relative to the ego.

The story of Gideon centers around a dream. In the Book of Judges, Gideon is instructed by God to go against the camp of the Midianites, and there he would be reassured by what he heard. Gideon, as he arrives there, overhears a man telling his comrade a dream:

> " 'Behold, I dreamed a dream; and lo, a cake of barley bread tumbled into the camp of Midian, and came to the tent, and struck it so that it fell, and turned it upside down, so that the tent lay flat.' And his comrade answered, 'This is not other than the sword of Gideon the son of Joash, a man of Israel; into his hand God has given Midian and all the host.' "

And the story concludes: "When Gideon heard the telling of the dream and its interpretation, he worshiped; and he returned to the camp of Israel, and said, 'Arise, for the Lord has given the host of Midian into your hand.' " So began Gideon's mighty deeds, with a dream.

Most of us remember that Solomon was considered the wisest of men, but many of us have forgotten that this gift of wisdom came to Solomon through a dream. In recognition of Solomon's devotion, the Lord appeared to Solomon in a dream by night and said, "Ask what I shall give you." In the account which follows Solomon asks for understanding and God promises him the gift of a wise and discerning mind. The story concludes, "And Solomon awoke, and behold, it was a dream." There is some question about how wise Solomon really was as an historical person, but it is clear how significant a dream was to the ancient author.

Turning to the New Testament, we find that at least two of the greatest religious experiences related there were visions. First there is the experience of the Transfiguration, which is concluded in Matthew's Gospel with the words spoken by our Lord: "Tell no one the vision, until the Son of man is raised from the dead." Second, there is the experience of St. Paul on the road to Damascus. This was clearly of a subjective visionary nature, for only St. Paul saw it (though one source says others heard the voice). Further, in Acts, Paul before Agrippa describes his vital experience as a vision.

On the basis of this abundant material we must conclude the following:

1. Dreams and visions were regarded in both Old and New Testaments as revelations from God. Those skilled in their interpretation, such as Daniel or Joseph, were revered; those who understood the revelations God had given them, e.g., Abraham or Solomon, became great and wise; those who were overcome by their inner experience, such as St. Paul or Ezekiel, became great missionaries and prophets.

2. Viewed from this perspective the entire Bible is the story of God's breakthrough into man's conscious mind via the unconscious.

And finally two other conclusions can be drawn which have not yet been deliberately stated:

3. Many other religious experiences, e.g., Jacob's wrestling with the adversary, or Moses' encounter with the burning bush, were of a visionary kind.

4. The early Church regarded dreams the same way as the Bible: as revelations from God.

The men of the Bible did not first sit down to intellectualize about God. God broke through into them with a personal experience. He "convinced" them, as he did St. Paul, to use the word which literally in the Latin derivation means "to overcome." Only after their experience did the men of the Bible sit down and think about God, to give structure to and expand the meaning of their experience.

The presence of God is a disturbing presence, especially when His voice is as close to us as our nightly dreams. We cannot deny the closeness of His presence, for we also dream dreams as did the men of the Bible. But we must look at dreams not only from the point of view of inspired intuition, as did Daniel, for instance, but also from the objective viewpoint of modern science.